KV-012-105

THE CHOROGRAPHY OF SUFFOLK

THE CHOROGRAPHY

OF SUFFOLK

Edited by
DIARMAID MACCULLOCH

1976
SUFFOLK RECORDS SOCIETY
Distributed by The Boydell Press
VOLUME XIX

Introduction and editorial matter (c) 1976 Diarmaid MacCulloch

First published 1976 by The Suffolk Records Society
Distributed for the Society by The Boydell Press Ltd
PO Box 24 Ipswich IP1 1JJ

ISBN 0 85115 069 1

KING ALFRED'S COLLEGE
WINCHESTER

942.
64   0146326 8

SUF

Printed in Great Britain by Dramrite Printers Ltd
129 Long Lane London SE1

CONTENTS

Illustrations

ACKNOWLEDGEMENTS

My chief debt in this work must be to Dr John Blatchly of Ipswich School; without our frequent discussions this edition would not have materialised. I must also thank Dr A.Hassell Smith of the University of East Anglia, Professor G.R.Elton of Clare College, Cambridge and Norman Scarfe for their valuable comments and suggestions. I owe a more long-standing debt to Miss Joan Corder and Mr Leslie Dow for their encouragement in the work which led to the discovery of the Suffolk Chorography, and to the Master and Fellows of Churchill College, Cambridge for their generous financial help towards the fieldwork which has produced the commentary on the church notes in the MS. I am very appreciative of the helpfulness and courtesy that I received from the staff of the Manuscript Department in Cambridge University Library, the Bodleian Library, the two Record Offices at Bury and Ipswich in Suffolk and the Norfolk Record Office, also from the Earl of Iveagh and his staff at Elveden Hall. I have also used MSS in the collection of the College of Arms in London.

Diarmaid MacCulloch,
Churchill College,
Cambridge, 1976.

Abbreviations used in the notes

APC	*Acts of the Privy Council* (H.M.Stationery Office, 1907).
Aylsham	NNRO, Aylsham Collection, numbered by bundles (no individual items numbered).
Bacon, *Annalls*	Nathaniel Bacon, ed. W.H. Richardson, *Annalls of Ipswiche,* Ipswich (1884).
BL Add.	British Library Additional MSS.
BL Eger.	British Library Egerton MSS.
BL Lansd.	British Library Lansdowne MSS.
Bodley	Bodleian Library, Oxford.
CCN	Consistory Court of Norwich.
Copinger.	W.A.Copinger, *The Manors of Suffolk*, London, 7 vols. (1905-11).
Corder	Joan Corder, *A Dictionary of Suffolk Arms*, Suffolk Records Society VII (1965).
CPR Eliz.	*Calendar of Patent Rolls, Elizabeth I* (HMSO, in progress).
CRS	Catholic Record Society publications.
CUL	Cambridge University Library.
Darby	Church notes by Rev. John Wareyn Darby, 1791-1846, Rector of Shottisham, arranged by Hundred; MS now in Ipswich Central Library.
Davy	MS notes on Suffolk by David Elisha Davy (1796-1851), 33 vols. arranged by Hundred, now BL Add.19,080-19,113.
DNB	*Dictionary of National Biography.*
EANQ NS	*East Anglian Notes and Queries*, New Series, 13 vols. (1885-1910).
ESRO	Suffolk Record Office, Ipswich division.
Hassell Smith	A.Hassell Smith, *County and Court: Government and Politics in Norfolk 1558-1603*, Oxford (1974).
Hen.	Cambridge University Library Hengrave Collection (with volume number).
Hood	Christobel M.Hood (ed.), *The Chorography of Norfolk,* Norwich, 1938.
Howard	J.J.Howard, *The Visitation of Suffolke*, Lowestoft, 2 vols. (1867).
Iveagh/Phillipps	Phillipps Collection of MSS, *penes* the Earl of Iveagh, Elveden Hall, Thetford, Norfolk.
Muskett	J.J.Muskett and Frederic Johnson, *Suffolk Manorial Families*, Exeter, 2 vols. and 3 parts (1900-14).
NNRO	Norfolk and Norwich Record Office.
Papworth	John W.Papworth and Alfred W.Morant, *An Ordinary of British Armorials*, London, 1874.

PCC	Prerogative Court of Canterbury Wills (and Administrations), by book, now preserved in the Public Record Office.
PRO	Documents in the Public Record Office (with piece number).
PSIA	*Proceedings of the Suffolk Institute of Archaeology*, 33 vols, 1848-date.
Ryece	Lord Francis Hervey (ed.), *Suffolk in the XVIIth Century. The Breviary of Suffolk by Robert Ryece*, London, 1902.
Weever	John Weever, *Ancient Funerall Monuments*, 1st edn. London, 1631.
WSRO	Suffolk Record Office, Bury St.Edmunds division.

worlde it floweriheth. And wher some will affirme that
noe comtrye is so playnly manifestid by diseriprō
as England, they are derryued, for as euery Shire in England
by mr Saxton: So euery pedimrs in framre by mercator
as also of the Low Comtrees and disrreyted.

To conclude my desire is to acquaynt yow wth the order
wch I haue obsrued in the distinguishinge of the perternulies
in the mappes. for I thowght it necessarye to add a
difference to euerye of them, whereby may be knowne
Cyttyes from towres, towres from parishes, parishes
from Hamlettes, hamlettes from howses, howses from
Castlies, &r. which markes and carrectars, ye shall find
in some voyde parte of the mappes, and to the rude that
theis notes and distinctions, should be the more apparant
I haue not set downe the forme of a howse for a town
but a little circumfere nce, wth the perticuler distinction
that derlareth the thinge what it is. Thus haue I done
the rather for that the quantitie of the Mappes will
hardily beare the superfluous formes of howses

Thus wishinge yow profit of my trauryle & only
craue a fauorable contenstion of all thinges; and of yo
comtrsis to reforme any apparant fault wout reproche
ye selfes also may add many profitable thinges vnto this
my labors in youre own comtryes wher ye are resydent. fare
ye well & for Christ. Decembr 14. 1592.

Yo as fare as my trauryle may steede yow
Jo: Norden

And wher some will affirme that
framers and the low
comtrees as playnly
distribed as England

Seuerall distinction
in the mapps to show
theis diffrences of places

Chelsworth

30 . E. 1

Inter Thom
de S̄cō Phil.
Quer et Ben
manerio de
ac̄r trā 2 a
medietate
Jus Benedict
Hugoni et
Fines Suff

helsworth
Doms

est 12 mare carū 4
Rectoria valet 8 · 8 · 9 Dec 16 · 10 ½
A parsonage presentative the King patron no
-toms, all paid in Specie There is a portion of
by some esteemed of the third part of the towne
of old did belong to the Abbot of Bury to finde
horses oates these tithes now belong to Sr Henr
Rt some say they should go out of the deme
of the mannour — The Lord of the mannor
the Leet is Sr Antony Wingfield Kt unto whome
descend from his grandfather who amongst ot
things had it by mariage of the coheir of the
of Oxford who came to it by mariage of
of Howard who were long tine owners of he
the fines arbitrable. There be no demeans
Fince were all the demeanes parcelled out into
hold in which nature they rest now confirm
long prescription no mention where the man
house stood yet at the west end of the Chur
appeareth the seat of a most ancient house enui
with ditches or mootes according to the form
Antiquity ·

Dns Johes
Philberto

W:H pen S L pag 61

Cambridge University Library Hengrave MS 6 f.19: part of a folio from the
Hengrave scrapbooks. At the right is p.318 of the original Chorography text,
at the left, Thomas Allen's transcript of the earlier part of the Chelsworth

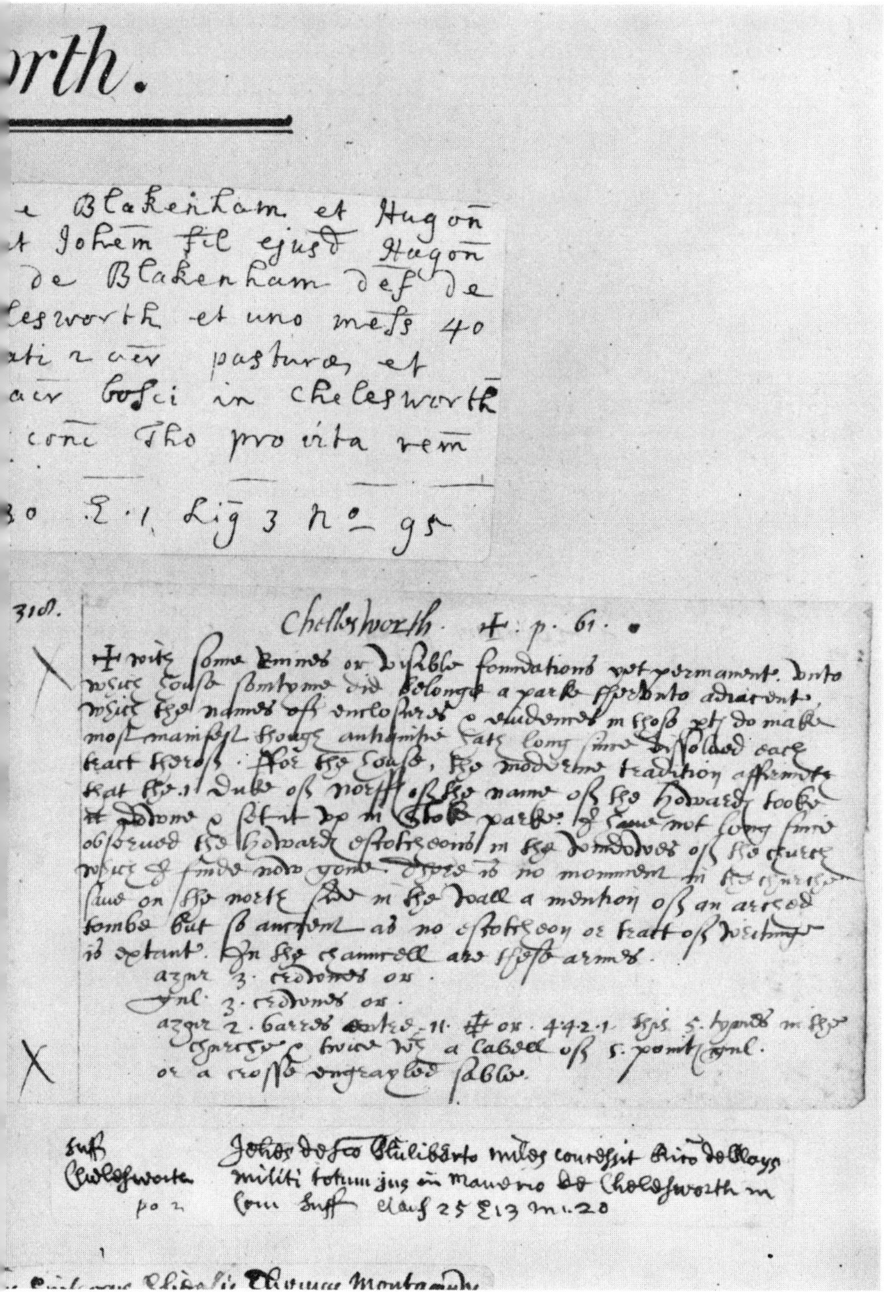

e Blakenham. et Hugon
t Johem fil ejus Hugon
de Blakenham def de
lesworth et uno mess 40
ati r acr pasturas et
acr bosci in chelesworth
cont Tho pro irta rem

0 E. 1. Lig 3 nᵒ 95

310.

Chellsworth. + : p. 61.

[several lines of secretary-hand text, largely illegible]

azur 3. redvvos or.
vnl. 3. redvvos or.
azur 2. barres ... 11. + or. 442.1 ... 5. ... in ...
... a label of 5. point vnl.
or a crosse ... sable.

suff   Johes de~ Guliberto miles ...
Cholesworth   militi totum jus in manerio de Cholesworth in
po 2   Com Suff clauf 25 E13 m. 20

entry. Allen's hand is also on the scrap above, and Peter Le Neve's on the small scrap at bottom right. Reproduced by permission of Cambridge University Library.

NNRO Aylsham 15, a letter from Thomas Browne of Poringland to Thomas Deye. Reproduced by permission of the Norfolk Record Office.

INTRODUCTION

The Manuscript and its history

THE MS HISTORY OF Suffolk here edited for the first time is the counterpart of *The Chorography of Norfolk* edited for publication by Mrs Christobel Hood in 1938 and by her ascribed to the great topographer John Norden the elder.[1] Reasons will be given below for doubting this ascription and for considering a more local authorship. However, unlike the Norfolk Chorography, the Suffolk volume is in several hundred fragments and no longer complete. Tom Martin noted of the Norfolk MS that 'there was another of the same hand and size with this, relating to the county of Suffolk, which the late Peter Le Neve Esqr. took to pieces and plac'd each town alphabetically amongst his collections for the county.'[2] The fragments of this Suffolk Chorography are now in at least six different MS collections.

Like the Norfolk Chorography the Suffolk volume can be traced back with reasonable certainty to the library of the great physician and author of *Religio Medici*, and *Urne Buriall*, Sir Thomas Browne. The MS catalogue of Browne's library is now in the Bodleian Library and was printed by Browne's 19th-century editor, Simon Wilkin, with annotations as to the whereabouts of the MSS as far as he could discover them; Wilkin's version includes the following entries among the quarto volumes:

> 'No.20 – An Historical and Chorographical Description of Suffolk.
> Not found.
> No.27 – An Historical and Chorographical Description of Norfolk.
> Probably with No.20.'

Since the Chorographies are entitled *An Historicall and Chorographicall Description* and are in quarto volumes, there can be little doubt as to the identification of Browne's MSS.[3]

Wilkin, then, noted that the Suffolk and Norfolk MSS no longer formed part of Browne's identifiable collection, and it is probable that soon after Browne's death in 1682 they passed to that indefatigable if somewhat misguided antiquary Peter Le Neve.[4] Le Neve certainly possessed them or had access to them by 1696, for in that year he wrote an abstract of the information in the Halesworth entry of the Suffolk Chorography.[5]

Le Neve at first kept the volumes intact, and used the Suffolk volume in particular for making notes of his own about the places that it described. In 1720, for instance, he copied into it various extracts from John Anstis's copy of Robert Ryece's *Breviary of Suffolk*; he also inserted many notes derived from the Register of Butley Priory then in his own possession.[6] However, soon after that he conceived the unfortunate notion of dismembering the volumes and incorporating them in his monumental collections for Norfolk and Suffolk, which were arranged alphabetically by Hundred and parish. This was Le Neve's usual habit; Thomas Hearne said that 'His whole collection, it seems, consists of thousands of little scraps of Paper, on which he used to write, w'ch was occasioned by his parsimony, a specimen of w'ch scraps I have by me, being sent to me since his death by Mr West.'[7]

Since the Chorography was written on both sides of the paper its dismemberment presented some problems. Le Neve's method was to keep all leaves that bore information and if there was information on the back of these, to copy this on to another scrap, ready to be placed under the appropriate parish. In fact Le Neve himself did little of the work, leaving most of it to his amanuensis Thomas Allen, whose characteristic large round hand soon becomes familiar to anyone who examines any part of the Le Neve collections.[8] When Allen had copied out any entry which had been condemned to be the reverse of a scrap, he crossed out the original text and marked it 'posted' or 'po.'. The pages of the original volume which bore only headings of a parish without any information about it were presumably thrown away; oddly enough, despite his reputation for 'parsimony' Le Neve did not reuse them for other purposes, and none of the Chorography's characteristic paper appears in the Le Neve collections unless it bears text from the dismembered volume.

Le Neve was still regarding the volumes as complete units in 1720, for Allen had to recopy many of the Ryece extracts that Le Neve added to the Suffolk Chorography in that year.[9] However by 1722 the Suffolk volume had all been 'posted' — there is a note to that effect by Allen on the blank page 272 of the text. It was taken to pieces as far as page 271, that is, to the end of the 'alphabet' of parishes; the Introduction, and the appendix of church notes and additional material, were left intact, presumably because cutting them up into useable fragments was too complex a task. The Norfolk volume was more fortunate, for it remained intact. Allen only copied out a few of its entries, duly marking the copied originals 'posted'; the copies are to be found in their respective places in Le Neve's Norfolk Collections.[10] In September 1729 Le Neve died, and presumably it was this that brought the work of antiquarian vandalism to a halt.

If the Le Neve Collections had survived to us intact and as a unit the dismemberment of the Suffolk Chorography would not have been too serious a crime; however, the collections were dispersed less than half a century after Le Neve's death. Le Neve naturally wished them to remain a unit, and did his best to provide for this, but the eccentricity that had marked his life affected the fate of his MSS on his death. The great antiquary Thomas Hearne noted that 'Mr Le Neve has left an imperfect Will. His MSS relating to Norfolk and Suffolk to be laid up in the Church of Norwich. The rest to be disposed of in such a manner as he should direct by a note for that purpose, which note for some time could not be found, 'till of late, when found upon his Desk, probably the last thing he wrote, unfinished ...'[11]

The bulk of the Le Neve collections of printed books and MSS were left to a distant relative of his who took no interest in them and had them auctioned off at Covent Garden on 22 February 1730; although Thomas Martin of Palgrave was among the major purchasers, great portions of the collections were dispersed for ever.[12] However, little Suffolk or Norfolk material appears in the Sale Catalogue; as Hearne said, it had been separated from the general collections and Martin secured it for his own use by a rather bizarrely premature courtship of Le Neve's widow.[13] Its subsequent fate is best described by Richard Gough.

'A more ample and exact history was long hoped for from the large materials collected by Peter Le Neve, Norroy, who spent about forty years in amassing at great expense and trouble the greatest fund of antiquities for his native county that ever was collected for any single one in the kingdom, which passed into the hands of that industrious antiquary Mr. Thomas Martin, of Palgrave, Suffolk, who married his widow, and spared no pains to continue and augment the collection.

'Dr. Smyth in his *Synopsis Bib. Cottoniae*, p.42, mentions Le Neve's work as preparing for the press, and calls it *Ampla & accurata comitatus Norfolciensis historia & descriptio*. Mr. Martin died March 7th 1771, and since his decease these and all his other collections for this and the neighbouring county of Suffolk, his books, papers, pictures, etc. came into the possession of Mr. Worth, Chemist, of Diss, F.S.A. who gave 600 l. for them. The library he immediately sold to Mess. Booth and Berry, booksellers in Norwich, who dispersed it by a markt Catalogue, after an undigested one had been taken and printed by way of offering the whole to some private purchaser. The pictures and lesser curiosities Mr Worth sold by auction at Diss, and some of the papers and more valuable curiosities at London, 1773 and 1774. Mr. Ives of Yarmouth, Suffolk herald, bought some of the most valuable MSS ...'

'It being expected that some society would have been desirous of possessing Le Neve's collections, they were reserved for some time; but no offer having been made, dampness and neglect would soon have destroyed them, and these authentic papers extracted from the original records of this kingdom at such an expense of money, time and incredible labour, would most probably have been no more heard of. To rescue them from destruction, they were purchased by Mr. Fenn, who sincerely wishes they were in the possession of those who would arrange them and preserve them as honourable monuments of the indefatigable industry of their original collector. What remained on the death of Mr. Worth in 1774, consisting chiefly of his own collection of books, and the papers relative to Thetford, Bury, and part of the county of Suffolk, were bought by Thomas Hunt, a bookseller at Harleston. The dispersion was completed by the sale of Mr. Ives's collections in London in March, 1777. Such has been the fate of this capital fund of materials for the history of this and the neighbouring county which had engaged the lives of five eminent antiquaries to form it, and contained the united labours of Le Neve, Tanner, Blomefield and Martin!'[14]

It was on the death of Tom Martin, then, that the Suffolk and Norfolk Chorographies parted company for the first time. The Norfolk Chorography was bought by Richard Gough himself at Mr Worth's sale in London in 1773, and was described in the Sale Catalogue as 'A Chorographical Description of Norfolk, by Dr Beckham, *fair*, 7s 6d.'[15] With the rest of Gough's MSS it found a safe home in the Bodleian, where it remains.[16] The history of the Suffolk Chorography is a good deal more complicated and obscure.

The bulk of the Le Neve collections for Suffolk were bought by the Gage family of Hengrave Hall near Bury St Edmunds; both Sir Thomas Gage, the seventh baronet, and John Gage Rokewode, his younger brother, were able and enthusiastic antiquaries. The actual purchase was probably made from Fenn's part of the current material, perhaps not directly purchased from Fenn. The current Catalogue of the Hengrave MS collections describes these particular volumes as collections formed by Sir Thomas, but neither he nor John Gage seem to have thought of the collections as primarily Le Neve's, as surely they would have done if they had purchased straight from Fenn; both referred to the collections as Bishop Tanner's, and Tanner never owned them or made substantial contributions to them.[17] The Gages were probably responsible for mounting the immense collection in the eighteen folio volumes which still house them; the volumes appear to be early 19th century, and the Thingo and Thedwastre sections in particular are designed to house the considerable accretions of John Gage's own material. When the Gage baronetcy became extinct Hengrave was sold, but the MSS remained there until the death of the last secular owner of the house, Sir John Wood, in 1952. Hengrave then became the home of a religious community and the MS collections were presented to Cambridge University Library, including the Le Neve volumes, now Hengrave MSS 2-19. The remainder, including a folder containing the Chorography Introduction, was given to Bury Record Office.

The Le Neve collections had already become fragmented before the Gages' purchase, however. The most substantial stray was the Appendix to the original volume, which had survived without dismemberment. Gough states that 'Dr.Thomas Beckham's collections for this county [Suffolk], 1602, quarto, were bought at Mr.Ives's sale by the earl of Surrey; as were also those of Mr.Blomefield, in two quarto and two folio volumes.'[18] The Earl later became the Duke of Norfolk, and his executors gave the four volumes and the fragment of the Chorography to the College of Arms in London in 1837. The fragment remains there, lightly tied into one volume of the Blomefield notes.[19]

The Hartismere volume in the Hengrave part of Le Neve's collection is clearly very incomplete. This is possibly because Mr Worth had chosen to separate out most of the Hartismere material from the main body of the collection since it related to the area round his home town of Diss, and this may have been the material on 'part of the county of Suffolk' which he had kept back and which was sold to Thomas Hunt in 1774. Alternatively it may have been the 'Suffolk collections relative to the Hundred of Hartsmere' which formed lot 4544 of Booth and Berry's auction on 5th June 1773 or 1774.[20] Whatever the explanation, much of the Hartismere section of the Le Neve collections together with other substantial portions of the Suffolk material came into the hands of the antiquary Craven Ord. Craven Ord had it bound up in nineteen volumes, and these passed with many of his other collections into the hands of Sir Thomas Phillipps. These Phillipps MSS were purchased by the first Lord Iveagh just before the First World War and are now preserved among the muniments at Elveden Hall in Suffolk.[21] 'Craven Ord Le Neve' contains a few more fragments of the main body of the Chorography text.

Together with two single fragments of the text, of uncertain history, preserved in the Suffolk Record Office at Ipswich and in the Bodleian Library, a fragment and some transcripts abstracted by Tom Martin now at Bury and a transcript by Bishop Tanner's amanuensis of the church notes in the Chorography now also in the Bodleian,[22] these are the sources of the Chorography text reconstructed in this edition. They probably represent about 95% of the original text. It is quite likely that further fragments exist in collections like that of the College of Arms which are less accessible to scholars than those already consulted.

4

The Original Format

THE NORFOLK AND Suffolk Chorographies appear to have been identical in arrangement, written on the same line-watermarked paper forming small quarto volumes rather less than 8 inches by 6 inches. They appear to have been working notebooks rather than finished volumes, but the hand employed was a neat and miniscule reformed secretary hand of the end of the 16th century or beginning of the 17th, with frequent use of a rather distinctive italic for personal names and place names. The neatness of the hand suggests that the volumes were intended to be circulated in MS among favoured gentlemen, in much the same way as Robert Ryece's *Breviary of Suffolk* was over the next two and a half decades.[22a] The Norfolk volume comprises 410 pages; the Suffolk volume had the peculiarity that it was foliated for a few leaves near the beginning.

The arrangement of the Chorographies is unlike that of Ryece's *Breviary* with its discussion of the county under various topic headings. They open with an Introduction of general remarks, seven pages long in the Suffolk Chorography and eight in the Norfolk volume; the Suffolk Chorography was thought of as the first of the two, for the Introduction for Norfolk refers back to the other volume for its discussion of the East Anglian kingdom, 'as in Suffolk appeareth'.

The main body of the text followed. This was intended to be a gazetteer of every place in the two counties, arranged more or less alphabetically; the place-names were taken from Christopher Saxton's maps of Suffolk and Norfolk of 1575 and 1574 respectively, and even followed his spelling remarkably closely. Where Saxton had omitted a township from his map the Chorographer noted this fact in his text, although since the Saxton Suffolk map was more accurate than that of Norfolk there is only one such entry in the Suffolk Chorography, under Tuddenham St Mary.

Each place listed was allotted one blank half-page in the original volumes, apart from market towns and a few other places which received a page. The place-name heading was allotted three symbols, a letter for the hundred in which it lay, 'Sf' or 'Sd' in the Suffolk Chorography according to whether it was in the Archdeaconry of Suffolk or Sudbury, and a number for its rural deanery (see below, p.22). Into this scheme the Chorographer first copied basic information like a note of markets and a number of literary references to individual places, mainly culled from Camden's *Britannia* (see Appendix III). After this he copied in information as he received it; various different colours of ink are traceable in the text.

Under the heading of Norwich in the Norfolk Chorography the Chorographer promises that 'you shall have at another tyme a large and playne description'[23] but it is likely that there were descriptions of Bury St Edmunds and Ipswich in the Suffolk volume, since it has gaps in its pagination where they would fit into the scheme (see Appendix II). The Bury entry was probably lurking among the 'very large collections for a history of Bury by Le Neve, T.Martin &c. late in the hands of Mr Worth, F.A.S.' which Richard Gough noted on p.245 of *British Topography* as 'now in my possession': however these Bury collections do not appear to be among Gough's Suffolk MSS now preserved in the Bodleian

Library; neither is there any clue as to the present whereabouts of 'one volume of collections for the history and antiquities of Ipswich' which Gough mentions on p.258 as among the MSS 'purchased at Mr Martin's sale' by Thomas Astle — this might well have contained the Ipswich entry. [23a] However, since neither Bury nor Ipswich are in areas covered by personal visits from the Chorographer it is possible that the entries relating to them were not very full.

After the main text, which occupied pp.7-271 in the Suffolk Chorography and pp.8-359 in the Norfolk, came an Appendix which took the Suffolk text to at least p.319. This consisted of information which was either too long to fit into the half-page format of the main text or had overflowed from it; the material was entirely first-hand information and consisted mainly of church notes. Two further fragments of text which do not fit into the text as it stands and Le Neve's note under Orford indicate that the Appendix of the Suffolk Chorography was longer than the existing text (see p.178 below and n.85).

Such was the original state of the Chorographies, but there is another copy of the Norfolk text which Mrs.Hood bought from Messrs.Dobell of London in 1924, with no indication of provenance. [24] It is a transcript by the 18th century Norfolk antiquary Anthony Norris of Barton, omitting place-name headings that have no further information against them and incorporating the material of the Appendix into the main text; it is otherwise a fairly faithful transcript for its period. It was this text which Mrs.Hood used as the basis for her edition. Norris had access to Le Neve's collections while compiling his notes on Norfolk in the 1730s. [25]

The Suffolk fragments and their settings

Cambridge University Library

AS HAS BEEN said, the volumes now styled Hengrave MSS 2-19 contain the bulk of the Le Neve collections, although they are not yet recognised as such in the Library's catalogue of the Hengrave Collection. The backbone of the collection consists of the transcripts of various original documents made by Le Neve and Thomas Allen, but there is also a great quantity of original material, including many hundred of medieval deeds, an early 17th century abstract of escheators' records, an autograph copy of Hawes's *History of Loes* and two copies of Candler's mid-17th century Survey of Suffolk. One of these latter is the extension of Candler made by Fairfax c.1690; of this Gough says that 'Dr Fairfax attempted an account of Suffolk; but Peter Le Neve, Esq., purchased his MS and cut it up into parcels, putting each description to the proper towns.' [26] Tom Martin added a good deal to the collections, including his own rough church notes and the original of the early parish registers of Burgate; finally John Gage Rokewood contributed to the collection with original deeds and transcripts. Amid all this are the fragments of the Suffolk Chorography, both original text and transcripts by Le Neve and Allen; what exists of the Appendix in Cambridge is all in the form of transcripts by Thomas Allen except for the original text of pp.318-319, which was detached from the rest of the Appendix since it gave a direct continuation of the main text describing Chelsworth and was therefore 'posted' to Chelsworth. Comparison between Allen's transcripts and the original text shows that his transcription is remarkably faithful except in minor details of spelling and punctuation.

One unfortunate feature of the Cambridge volumes is that practically all the slips were securely pasted into the volumes by the Gages. Transcribing the text on the reverse of original fragments has therefore been a difficult task.[27]

The Iveagh/Phillipps Collection

THIS CONSISTS OF much the same material as the Hengrave volumes; one interesting series of original documents is the complete return for the county to a Royal Commission of 1562 enquiring into the working of the Henrician and Marian Statutes against undue apparel and the keeping of horses and armour by appropriately qualified gentry. Considering that most of Le Neve's material for the Hundred of Hartismere is in this collection, it is disappointing to find that it includes only one insignificant fragment of the Chorography's text about Hartismere parishes — particularly disappointing in view of the fact that the Chorography Appendix shows that the Chorographer visited many villages in Hartismere himself and probably had a good deal to say about them. The Hartismere portions of the extant text are still, therefore, incomplete. Among the few fragments of the rest of the text in this collection, a transcript by Thomas Martin of the entire Le Neve scrap collection for Bildeston has preserved a most interesting entry about this town.

College of Arms fragment

THIS IS THE bulk of the text of the Appendix, pp.272-317, p.272 being originally blank, and is tied into a quarto volume of Francis Blomefield's church notes. The College of Arms pressmark is MS Suffolk 9, R.R. 38B Shelf E. Frederick A. Crisp, the genealogist and antiquary, had a copy of the whole volume made early this century, and this is now in Ipswich Central Library.

Isolated fragments

APART FROM THE Introduction preserved in the Hengrave collections at Bury, few further stray bundles from Le Neve slip collections have so far been discovered; one, tied into the back of the Bodleian copy of Borret's mid-17th century Suffolk church notes concerns Saxham, Saxstead and Stanton and provides pp.216-217 of the Chorography text.[28] Another is now in the Suffolk Record Office at Ipswich and deals with Dunwich and Eye; this provides pp.16-17. Tom Martin abstracted some scraps of the slip collections including one fragment of the original Chorography text, and these are to be found bound into his church notes now at the Record Office at Bury St.Edmunds.[29] In addition, Sir Thomas Gage's own collections for the Hundreds of Thingo and Thedwastre contain a transcript of a Chorography passage referring to Great Barton. There is apparently no trace of the original in the appropriate Le Neve Hengrave volume.

Date

QUITE APART FROM the hand in which they are written, the Chorographies can be dated with reasonable precision by their content. The MS was begun in the very last years of Queen Elizabeth's reign. The Introductions refer to the Sheriffs being nominated by 'the Queen hir Ma'tie', and one of the first pieces of information under Cawston says that the town 'appertayneth to the Queenes Ma'tie.' [30] The list of patrons given under Bergh Apton is dated 1600, [31] and in the Suffolk Chorography the Halesworth and Henstead entries are dated 1602. The work seems to be no earlier than 1600; the extracts from Camden's *Britannia* used in the text were among the first entries that the Chorographer made in his blank book, and they appear to have been taken from the Latin edition of Camden published by George Bishop in 1600. This included material not published in earlier editions which is used in the Chorography (see Appendix III). Thereafter at least the sequence of the Chorographer's visits can be deduced from the order of places described in his Appendix.

The Chorographer probably ceased to add material to his work about 1605. The last specific date in the text is 1604 (Suffolk *sub* Badingham), and the entries about property belonging to the Wingfield family in Suffolk refer to Sir Anthony Wingfield as a living person; his will was proved in February 1606 (New Style). [32] One of the two alterations in the Suffolk Chorography later than those made by the Chorographer himself before Le Neve began making his additions, under Milden, is dateable to before the death of Sir Isaac Appleton in 1609 [33] — it is notable that the hand is distinctively later in character than that of the Chorographer's.

Primary Sources in the Text

MUCH OF THE Chorographer's information was first-hand either gained from his own observation or perhaps in some instances from a set questionnaire that he had sent out to the leading gentleman of a particular place. That he occasionally employed the latter method may be suggested by an entry in the Norfolk Chorography under Shotesham St Botolph where he says that 'all these informations concerning the Shotshams I rec' of Mr Edmond Doyly 9 May 1603'. [34] There is little doubt, however, that most of his first-hand information, particularly the church notes, was the result of personal observation. At Chelsworth in Suffolk, for instance, we know that the Chorographer made more than one visit: 'I have not long since observed the Howardes escotcheons in the windowes of the church which I find now gone.'[35]

The Chorographer had first-hand information on a rather higher proportion of places in Suffolk than in Norfolk; although Norfolk has about 150 more parishes than Suffolk it has 111 entries which may reasonably be assumed to be first-hand, and Suffolk has about the same number (see Appendix IV). Moreover his visits were very unevenly distributed in both counties. In Suffolk, for instance, the hundred of Babergh was well covered, as were the hundreds of Hartismere, Blackbourne, Cosford, Loes, Plomesgate, Wangford and Wilford; the area round Halesworth was covered in 1602 and an area round Badingham in 1604 while other areas were not visited at all. In Norfolk the western hundreds boast only a few first-hand entries; and the main concentration is in the area bounded by Harleston, Wymondham, Norwich, Acle and the Suffolk border.

The Chorographer's interest in observation centred on three main topics: 'spiritualia', 'temporalia' and church monuments. 'Spiritualia' comprised details of the parson's house and glebe and descriptions of tithe customs, if any. 'Temporalia' dealt mainly with manors, their descent and tenurial custom, with occasional notes of the parish's 'taske' or assessment for the antiquated tax of fifteenths and tenths. Only occasionally did the Chorographer describe antiquities other than funeral monuments, but in this he was typical of his antiquarian contemporaries. However, unlike so many antiquaries of his period, such as Tillotson, he did not confine his interest in monuments to a bald list of the heraldry that they bore, and his descriptions of them are unusually careful, detailed and informative for his period.

Literary Sources in the Text

THE CHOROGRAPHER MADE a number of extracts from a number of older MS sources, using much the same sort of material for both counties. He seems to have had access to the Diocesan records kept in Norwich, for one of his chief literary sources was an early 14th century survey of ecclesiastical parishes which he calls 'Domsday Book', more usually abbreviated in his marginalia to 'Domsd'. This document, which lists the patron of the benefice, its estimated value in marks and the amount of its procurations and synodals, is preserved at Norwich Cathedral and is originally of c.1300, as its content shows. The present book, however, is a copy probably written by the cathedral sacrist Richard Middleton between 1420 and 1440. The content of its individual entries is much fuller than, although similar in style to, the Chorographer's Domesday extracts; however, in one or two cases the Chorographer's version has additional information, such as the amount of the synodals at Herringfleet, which may indicate that he was working from an abbreviated and variant text to the one which remains at Norwich.

The Chorographer also used Diocesan records in quoting from 15th century surveys of episcopal manors in Suffolk, from a few wills, from the Bishops' Registers and from the Diocesan Institution Books ('Lib Inst.' in the margin). It is difficult to trace any logical arrangement behind his use of these sources, and he may have been using someone else's transcripts of the originals.

Another of the Chorographer's chief literary sources was an updated abridgement of the original *Valor Ecclesiasticus* of 1535, a *Liber Valorum* recording values of benefices, tenths rendered and patrons, which he habitually refers to as 'Lib.val.' in his marginalia. The copy that he was using was probably middle to late Elizabethan in date, since under Norfolk it mentions the Earl of Leicester as still alive – he died in 1588 – and under Suffolk Sir Thomas Kitson, who was knighted in 1578 and died in 1603. The present copy of a *Liber Valorum* in the Public Record Office dates only from the 18th century.[35a] Again, only about a quarter of the parishes in both counties have an entry from the *Liber* with no apparent reason for this capriciousness.

A prominent source occurring in the text is the Royal Inquisition of 9 Edward II listing the lords of townships and now known as *Nomina Villarum*. Several MS copies of this were circulating at the end of the 16th century, and the extant copies relating to Suffolk are listed by Vincent Redstone in vol.XI of the *Proceedings of the Suffolk Institute of Archaelogy*, p.174. In particular he mentions 'a small quarto volume containing the returns for Norfolk and Suffolk ... in the handwriting of about 1610 ... This copy appears to have been made for private use.' The volume was then (1920) in the possession of Sir William Gowers, having been owned by Anthony Norris of Barton in Norfolk in 1780; Gowers gave it along with other papers to Ipswich Borough Library, as a pencilled note in their copy of the *Proceedings* reveals. It sounds temptingly like a product of the Chorographer himself, but, most unfortunately, none of Gowers' gifts to Ipswich Library can now be traced.

The use of the *Nomina Villarum* is the only substantial difference in the sources of the Norfolk and Suffolk Chorographies; the Suffolk volume has 92 extracts from it but the Norfolk one only sixteen. Various other later Inquisitions, probably Inquisitions Post Mortem, are also occasionally used in both volumes. One or two gentlemen also contributed their private deeds for the Chorographer to use.[36]

Various scraps of information taken from various printed sources were among the first entries in the Chorographies. Most of them were taken from Camden in an independent translation from the Latin, generally without acknowledgement (see Appendix III); however the chronicles of Stow and Holinshed are used and acknowledged on four occasions. One somewhat unusual reference, under Blythburgh, is to Hieronymus Henninges' *Theatrum Genealogicum*, published in Magdeburg in 1598. Evidently the Chorographer had access to the latest antiquarian material in print; not was he afraid to contradict Camden when he had access to a more reliable source.[37]

Authorship

THE CHOROGRAPHER WAS singularly reticent about his identity. The Norfolk Chorography does not even bear a dedication although this is understandable if the volumes were intended to be preliminary notebooks to be added to at the author's leisure. Nevertheless this means that we are left with only one direct clue as to the Chorographer's identity. On the flyleaf of the Bodleian Norfolk Chorography Tom Martin has inserted a note that 'The late Reverend Dr Tanner, Chancellor of Norwich and afterwards Bishop of St Asaph, said this book was the handwriting of Thomas Beckham, D.D., Rector of (*blank*) ... see the beginning of the Suffolk book for a fuller account of the author.'

Alas, the beginning of the Suffolk book has not survived to enlighten us as to Dr Beckham's identity. No Dr Thomas Beckham can be traced during the relevant period at either English University. Mrs Hood notes a Dr Edmund Beckham of King's College, Cambridge, who held the livings of Gaytonthorpe and South Pickenham in Norfolk, died in 1714 aged seventy-six and was buried at Gaytonthorpe. [38] This Dr Beckham might possibly have been the writer of the fair copy of the Norfolk Chorography of c.1700 published by Mrs Hood, but he could not possibly have written the two original volumes, and it was these that Tanner claimed were in the hand of Dr Beckham. The Beckhams were an established family of minor gentry in late 16th century Norfolk, and their pedigrees produce two Thomas's of the right date. BL Harl.1164 f 67 has Thomas Beckham of Fakenham, son of Robert of Creake; Harl.1363 f.44 concentrates on the Narford branch of the family and has Thomas, second son of Walter, of Knapton, son of Robert, of Westacre. Neither of these Thomas's appear to have taken orders, however; nor does their area of Norfolk receive much prominence among the personally observed entries in the Norfolk Chorography.

Peter Le Neve as well as Bishop Tanner regarded Dr Beckham as the author of the Chorography. After the Chorographer's mention of John Wentworth under Somerleyton in the Suffolk Chorography he noted that Wentworth was 'no relation to the old family but of different name as it should seem by this auter Dr Beckham who lived at the time.' [39] Apparently he did not communicate this knowledge to Thomas Allen who in his transcripts habitually referred to the MSS as the work of Robert Ryece, the author of the *Breviary of Suffolk*, or simply as 'MS 1602'. Later authors such as Martin were generally content to refer to the volumes as 'MS Le Neve Quarto'.

It is significant that Sir Thomas Browne's Library Catalogue did not attribute an author to the Chorographies, as surely it would have done if the authorship had then been known. It is also worth noting that Tanner's attribution of the MSS to Beckham was based solely on his knowledge of Beckham's hand. It may be that the name Beckham is a corruption of a similar surname, but in any case the attribution of the Chorographies to Dr Thomas Beckham must remain doubtful.

Mrs Hood in her introduction to the Norfolk Chorography goes to considerable lengths to credit the authorship of the Chorography to a far more famous Elizabethan topographer, John Norden the elder. The case that she argues is an attractive one, although it is based solely on stylistic comparison with Norden's known topographical works. The comparison is indeed very close. The very title *An Historicall and Chorographical Description of Norfolk* echoes the title of the first part of Norden's great unfinished enterprise of *Speculum Britanniae, An Historicall and Chorographicall Description of Middlesex*, published in 1593. Like Norden's Chorographies the Norfolk Chorography opens with a general Introduction, whose content is remarkably similar to that of Norden's Introductions. The main text, like Norden's, is an alphabetical gazetteer, and the Norfolk Chorographer uses the same device as Norden for giving each place described symbols for the hundred and the rural deanery in which it lies, although he adds a symbol for the appropriate archdeaconry as well. Norden at his most detailed has much the same interests as the East Anglian Chorographer – his style is particularly similar in describing church monuments, although none of his known works have the threefold division into Spiritualia, Temporalia and church notes characteristic of the Chorographer's first-hand observations.

It is very tempting to fit the Suffolk and Norfolk Chorographies into the sequence of Norden's known works – Middlesex, published in 1593, the Home Counties and Channel Islands descriptions ready in MS in 1595, Hertfordshire published in 1597, and a long gap until the publication of Cornwall and Northamptonshire in 1610. The dates established for the Suffolk and Norfolk Chorographies, 1600-05, lend particular attraction to this hypothesis since we know that Norden was working in East Anglia during 1600 and 1601, making an elaborate survey of Sir Michael Stanhope's estates round Orford; the area round Orford is quite thoroughly covered in the Suffolk Chorography.[40] One could also link the abandoning of work on the Suffolk and Norfolk notebooks around 1605 with Norden's grant on 30 January 1605 (New Style) of the Surveyorship of the Duchy of Cornwall[41] and the consequent shift in his interests to Cornish antiquities which produced his greatest work, *A Topographicall and Historicall description of Cornwall.*

However, the hand of the Chorographer of Norfolk and Suffolk is not the same as John Norden's, as comparison with his attested work will show.[42] Since the Norfolk and Suffolk Chorographies are apparently working notebooks they can hardly be the work of a copyist, so this is a very serious objection to Mrs Hood's hypothesis. Nor can Norris's fair copy of the Chorography be attributed to the shadowy figure of John Norden the younger, as Mrs. Hood suggests.[43]

Neither Dr Thomas Beckham nor John Norden the elder, therefore, are particularly satisfactory candidates for the authorship of the Chorographies of Norfolk and Suffolk. Who, then, did write the two volumes? From internal evidence in the volumes we can say a little about the author. He was evidently a sympathiser with the 'Commonwealth' notions which had gained a fashionable currency during the reign of Edward VI and which were to survive into the more radical atmosphere of the Interregnum. In his preliminary notes on Ranworth in Norfolk he notes of Mr Henry Holditch that his 'worthy father was a great p'tectour & defender of the commons in the contry about him against those Lords whose consciences are as large as any common whatsoever.'[44] Again, when retailing Camden's story of the miraculous growth of pease on the shore at Aldeburgh during the 1555 famine he adds that while a rational explanation of the occurence is likely, 'yet in it are we to consyder the great goodnes of God who in that scarcitie in this mannour p'vided for the poore, on whome hardhearted Richmen could not fynde in their hearts of their abundance to bestow some small portion.'

Like most of his contemporaries, the Chorographer was not averse to spicing his information with occasional pious remarks, as the last quotation also illustrates.[45] However he also betrays a sympathy with the difficult economic situation of the lower clergy which was far less usual. Under Stoke by Nayland in Suffolk he fulminates against the 'irreligious and unconscionable composition betwene the Bishop patron & incumbent' which deprived the vicar of his fine house; under Brent Eleigh he sarcastically notes 'there ought to be 10 or 12 acres and a pension of 8 marc. p' ann' paid to the Vicar but if the Vicar can keep himself honest they that detayne those gleabes and marks from him will take order he shall be an honest poor vicar.' The patron of Brent Eleigh, who was probably the culprit, happened to be a Catholic recusant,[46] but even godly gentlemen were not exempt from the Chorographer's critical scrutiny if they were usurping church revenues; under Cookley he tells us that 'Mr Attorny Generall S'r Edward Cooke detaynes 2 acres worth 40s yearly & others in the towne other p'ts of the gleabe.'

The Chorographer therefore reveals a certain clericalism in his writings perhaps suggestive of Dr Beckham, but one should not exaggerate the radicalism of his Commonwealth ideas. He rails against Kett's 'execrable rebells' in a conventional manner,[47] and far from showing any antagonism to the gentry class as such he seems to have a definite attachment to one particular group of gentry families in East Anglia, a group either partly Roman Catholic in belief or at least opposed in temper to the radically Protestant group of leading gentlemen who tended to dominate East Anglian life during the Elizabethan and Jacobean eras. This 'anti-Establishment' circle had as one of its leading figures that stormy petrel of East Anglian politics, Sir Arthur Heveningham of Ketteringham in Norfolk and Heveningham in Suffolk, whom the Chorographer describes as 'that worthy Knight ... the (*blank*) knight in order of his house.'[48] Both Ketteringham and Heveningham earned personal visits from the Chorographer. Moreover the Chorographer in the course of his notes on the church at Hethersett takes the opportunity to make sneering remarks about Edward Flowerdew, Baron of the Exchequer, who had gained Sir Arthur's bitter enmity; he speaks of Flowerdew's father's 'covetous desire of the leade' from the chancel roof which caused the removal of a tomb to the south aisle of the church, and finally says that the Baron himself 'for want of a gravestone of his friends costs is covered w'th one taken of another man's grave'[49] — the ultimate example of hitting a man when he is down. In the Suffolk Chorography occurs his only original mention of a road, 'that famous lane so much spoken of for myre & dirt', Christmas Lane near Metfield. Sir Arthur's efforts to collect money for the repair of Christmas Lane against the oppostion of most of East Anglia's ruling élite during the 1580s and 1590s had been one of the *causes célèbres* of his troubled career in East Anglian politics, and this must have been known to the Chorographer.[50]

The Heveninghams were closely related to the Rous's of Henham, Dennington and Badingham in Suffolk, and both Badingham and Dennington were among the places visited and described by the Chorographer. The Rous's included a number of religious conservatives in their family, but not as many as their relatives the Hobarts of Hales Hall near Loddon in Norfolk.[51] Hales Hall was the centre of one of the areas which the Chorographer visited himself, and he seems to have taken a particular interest in the family. Under Monks Eleigh in Suffolk he notes Attorney-General Sir James Hobart's origins in the village, and remarks

13

about the family also occur under Milden and Oulton in Suffolk and Loddon, Holt and Intwood in Norfolk.

The Pastons are another East Norfolk family with Roman Catholic leanings who frequently occur in the Norfolk Chorography, and they had close links with the Heveninghams; their properties, their history or their monuments are mentioned under nine different parishes, and information which must have been gleaned from a Paston source occurs in the Ellough entry of the Suffolk Chorography. Mr Edward Doyly of Shotesham, who, as we have seen, supplied the Chorographer with information, also came from a family of conservative religious sympathies and Mr Henry Holdich's 'worthy father' was conservative in religion. [52] It is unlikely, however, that the Chorographer was himself a Catholic sympathiser; under East Dereham he translates Camden's comment on St Withburga with a pejorative ring: 'bycause she was most farre from lasciviousness & levitie was accounted a goodesse.' [53] Neither had Sir Arthur Heveningham any traceable sympathy with Catholicism; his battles with his radical Protestant fellow-gentry seem to have been inspired by differences of political attitude and of personality. Political alignments in Elizabethan East Anglia tended to be influenced as much by family ties as by ideology, and if the Chorographer bore any allegiance to the Heveningham/Rous/Hobart alignment it would be for the former reason.

If one could say that the Chorographer had strong East Anglian connections it would militate against an attribution of the Chorography to Norden, for he appears to have been a native of either the West Country or Middlesex, and to have had a house at Fulham. However, the evidence is not strong enough, although, as we have seen, the Chorographer could become emotionally involved in East Anglian affairs – he also had access to snippets of local gossip stretching back over half a century, as his remark about Sir Ambrose Jermyn's acquisition of the manor of Nedging Hall in Suffolk illustrates. Nor is it possible to detect a greater degree of familiarity with either county in the Chorographer's work, although it may be significant that the Suffolk volume came first of the two, that its Introduction contains more original material than the Norfolk Introduction, and that Suffolk has proportionally more first-hand observations than Norfolk (see above, p.9[54]).

Having considered the internal evidence, Dr Hassell Smith has suggested a new solution to the problem of the Chorographies' authorship. He puts forward the candidature of Thomas Browne of Poringland near Norwich, a minor Norfolk gentleman heavily involved in the administration of Norwich diocese in the 1590s. Browne was the younger son of Edward Browne of Caistor next Norwich, later of Poringland, one of a family of substantial yeomen from Tacolneston, himself a lessee of the Dean and Chapter of Norwich and a deputy of Thomas Godsalve, at one stage Principal Register to the Diocese [55] Thomas's elder brother, John Browne of Poringland, was secretary first to Sir Roger Woodhouse of Kimberley, yet another anti-Puritan, and by 1589 to Sir Arthur Heveningham; Sir Arthur sufficiently esteemed John to propose a match between his son and John's daughter Elizabeth in 1612.[56]

Thomas was secretary successively to Bishop Edmund Scambler and Bishop William Redman; however when Bishop John Jegon succeeded Redman in 1602 Browne was replaced by Anthony Harison, compiler of the *Registrum Vagum*, an invaluable collection of diocesan administrative papers. [57] In addition Browne was briefly feodary of the diocese and steward of certain episcopal manors under Bishop Scambler, and continued to act as deputy Steward of diocesan manors to his friend, Scambler's son Adam. He lived at Poringland even after his elder brother inherited it from Edward, and gained considerable wealth. His career ended tragically when he drowned himself in 1612.[58]

Browne seems to fit the *internal* indications of the Chorographies very well; he would have had access to the diocesan records and had a professional interest in ecclesiastical affairs. He had strong links with Sir Arthur Heveningham and his circle; Poringland lies close to Ketteringham, well within the area of Norfolk which received most first-hand visits in the Chorography. Dr Hassell Smith suggests that if his hypothesis of Browne's authorship is acceptable, one might connect his beginning the Chorography with his losing his job as episcopal secretary in 1602 – an attempt to use his new leisure.

Since Norden has been rejected as an author of the Chorography on the evidence of handwriting, it is unfortunate that specimens of Thomas Browne's hand do not seem to correspond to the Chorographer's hand either; the mode of writing 'p' in particular is consistently different in the two hands, despite the general similarity of their secretary character.[59] Nevertheless one should not reject outright the links between the Brownes and the Chorographer. One of the Brownes even quoted entries from the Norwich Domesday when setting down details of the livings at Great and Little Poringland among his private papers, while Edmund Doyly, who provided the Chorographer with his information about Shotesham, was not only patron of Poringland but a friend of John Browne.[60] Another entry in *Bibliotheca Martiniana* may be relevant:

'4499. Antiquarian Collections relative to Norwich, by John Browne of Norwich; very fair, 5s.'

When we remember that the Chorographer promised his readers 'a larger and playne description' of the city, it is tempting to suggest that John Browne's collections represent this missing work, even if one objects that Tom Martin ought to have noticed the similarity in the hands of the two works both in his collections if such a similarity existed.[61]

Finally one might ask whether the earlier Brownes had any connection with Sir Thomas Browne, who had the Chorographies in his library later in the century. Traditionally Sir Thomas has been thought to have come from a Cheshire family and to have had no connection with Norfolk before he settled in Norwich on the suggestion of college acquaintances, but in 1906 Walter Rye raised the possibility that he might already have had relatives in the city. Sir Thomas's father, Thomas, the Cheapside merchant, had two brothers, Edward and William, of whom nothing else is known. An Alderman William Browne of Norwich was styled esquire in his will of 1639 and was a flourishing draper of St George Tombland – can he have been Sir Thomas's uncle? Also of St George's parish was a John Browne, father of Edward born in 1613 and buried in 1617, Edward born in 1629 and William born 1634 – was this the John Browne of the antiquarian collections for Norwich? The origins of the Brownes of Poringland in the Tacolneston family are beyond dispute, but John and Thomas Browne did have a 'cousin' Edward Browne of Norwich and a 'brother in law' Edward Browne who might be the same person. May this be the link between the two families of Browne?[62]

15

Whatever one makes of all this, Sir Thomas's ownership of the Chorographies only about half a century after they were written requires explanation. Authorship by one of the Browne family would provide an explanation, and would seem generally to have a slight edge of plausibility over either Bishop Tanner's or Mrs Hood's suggestions. One can at least say with certainty that whoever he was, the Chorographer knew the gazetteer scheme of the Norden Chorographies and imitated it very closely in his own work.

The Significance of the Chorographies

THE CHOROGRAPHIES CONTAIN much information of value on tithe and manor custom, ownership of land and the vicissitudes of markets and communities; the Suffolk volume provides a gazetteer of practically everyone of any importance in the Suffolk of 1600, and its contents are a valuable supplement to the monumental and also monumentally slipshod published work of W.A.Copinger on the descent of Suffolk manors. The descriptions of church monuments are more satisfactory than any known Suffolk church notes of before the Civil War.

All this information is particularly valuable as far as the Suffolk section goes because it has hardly been used since it was written. Most counties have a line, or more than one line, of antiquarian tradition and plagiarism stretching back to the first antiquaries of the area — Suffolk, for instance, has the tradition that starts with William Tillotson in the 1590s and carries on through Matthias Candler and Dr Fairfax to the great 19th century synthesiser of Suffolk history, D.E.Davy. The Suffolk Chorography does not lie within any such line, and Suffolk still awaits its definitive county history; unlike the Norfolk Chorography, which was extensively quarried by Francis Blomefield for material while it was in Tom Martin's possession,[63] nothing from the Suffolk volume has ever appeared in print with the exception of a single quotation used by John Gage in his *History and Antiquities of ... Thingoe Hundred*.[64]

The Chorography also has a special interest because it can lay claim to being the first attempt at a general topographical survey of Suffolk on the classical lines that William Lambarde had pioneered in Kent a quarter of a century before: a hitherto unsuspected appearance in the ranks of the English county histories which stretch from Lambarde's work to the Victoria County Histories of our own age. Its claim for priority is closely challenged by Robert Ryece's *Breviary of Suffolk*, thought to have been begun about 1602 though surviving copies were given their final form between 1618-19 and 1622-29; like the Chorographies the Breviary remained unfinished, with a gazetteer of no more than about 50 churches.[65] The Chorographer indeed has a first-hand description of Preston, Ryece's home village, and mentions him as patron and landlord there without saying anything of his antiquarian work or of the great display of Suffolk heraldry for which he was responsible in Preston church; nor do Ryece or any of the early 17th century East Anglian antiquaries say anything of their colleague and rival. Until the Chorographer's hand can be positively identified the identity of this remarkable pioneer of East Anglian studies must remain an open question.

NOTE ON TRANSCRIPTION

APART FROM MINOR rationalisation of punctuation the text is transcribed without alteration, and abbreviations have only been extended where they were represented by obsolete symbols. The original page numbering has been indicated in the margin where it is known; a new page of the original starts at the beginning of a line of the present text unless specifically indicated otherwise. All editorial additions are in italics; transcripts of the original text are printed when the original has not been found, within brackets and quotation marks. *'PLN transcripts'* are those made by Peter Le Neve; *'TA transcripts'* are those made by Le Neve's amanuensis Thomas Allen. Gaps in the text are indicated between the surviving text.

It is impossible to be certain whether some of Thomas Allen's and Le Neve's transcripts in the Hengrave Collection form part of the Chorography text or not. Such passages have been included in the text, with a cautionary note, where there is a reasonable chance that they are by the Chorographer.

1

An historicall & chorographicall description of Suffolcke[1]*

It is called Suffolck as it were Southfolcke of the Saxons *Sudfolc* in respect of Norffolcke.

It is a part of Eastanglia inhabited by the people called Iceni as appeareth by the names of many townes in this shire retayning the very sounde of Iceni as Ikensworth, Ikenthorp, Ickboro, Iken, Isken, Ichlingham, Eike &c.

When as the Saxons had in this lande erected their heptarchie or governement consisting of 7 kingdomes, this province inhabited by the Iceni was converted into the kingdome of the EastAngles, which by reason that it is seated in the east part of this Islande they called it in their language *Eastangleryc*, the kingdome of the EastAngles. Their first king was Uffa of whome all the successours in this kingdo'e were called Ufkines whose line ending in St.Edmonde, the Danes invaded this Region & wasted it lamentablye by the space of 50 yeers untill Edward the Elder having overcome them ioyned it unto his empire of the West Saxons. After which tyme it had governours or vicegerents, which office in the first arrivall of the Normans was committed to one Radulphus who for conspiring against Willia' the Conquerour was deprived of this honour & dignitie & banished whome succeeded Hugh Bigod &c.[2]*

The limits & principall boundes of Suff.

Suff. is situated in the east parts of this Islande borduring on the north upon Norff. divided from it by 2 rivers Ouse the lesser & Waveney. It hath on the west Cambridgshire separated from it by the Dike commonly called the Devills Dike &c. it hath on the east the german sea, on the south Essex parted from the same by the river Stour.[3]*

The Nature of the soyle.

The nature of it is divers as my selfe can testifye havinge travayled in most p'ts of the same. That p't of it which is called the Woodlande & High Suffolck is exceeding fruitfull comparable to any p't of Englande for pasture for oxen & kine, not so good for sheepe. In this p't of the contrye are made butter & cheese in exceeding great quantitie of wonderfull goodnes comparable to any in the Realme. The commoditie therof is unspeakable unto the inhabitants of the same amongst which are very many yeomen of good credit & great liberalitie, good housekeepers, but the wayes & common roades in this contrye are verye fowle & uncomfortable in the winter tyme to travayle in. The other p'ts westerlye of the contrye are very fruitfull

2

also, but the woodland carryeth (*page changes*) the chiefe creditt for goodnes of grounde. That p't of the contrye that is nere unto the sea is nothing so fruitfull neyther so commodious for cattell as the other, but more fitte for sheepe & corne. The soyle also about Burye to Newmarket warde, Mildenhall, Elden, Barton &c. is mostly heathy & barren fit only for sheepe & conyes although in some places of the same there be some spots of good and fertill groundes as their botomes & medowes.[4*]

Suffolck is a great shire the lenght of it which we account from east to west is above fiftye myles, the circuit about 150 myles.

A description of the Rivers in Suff.[5*]

Suffolke is divided from Norff. with two rivers both springing at Loppham forde, the one called Waveney which runneth to the easte, the other the lesser Ouse & runneth unto the west.

Waveney fl.

Out of the fenny places about Loppham springeth Waveney fl. & runneth by Dis in Norff., at Osmondeston commonly called Scole it rec. a litle river springing at Ockolde & Aye. from thence it runneth by Harleston Market & Homersfeld by Flixton to Bungay & Beckles. Drawing neerer the sea, it laboureth (but in vayne) with a double streame to enter into the sea, for the streame runing eastward (called

Mutford water
Fritton fl.

of Hollinshed Mutford Water) is at Kirtlow a mile from the sea stayed. But that streame that floweth northward runneth by St.Olavs where it rec. a litle river called Fritton and so into the Hyerus fl. about Burgh Castle. By his double streame it maketh the Peninsula called Lovingland anciently Luthinglande.

Ouse mi. fl.
Thet fl.

The lesser Ouse which is the other River that parteth Suff. from Norff. springeth also in the fennes about Loppham, it runneth westwarde. At Thetford it rec. the rill Thet which springeth at Tostock by Wulpet & runneth by Ikesworth & being augmented therwith in a fuller streame it runneth directly into the greater Ouse.

Burne fl.

Not farre from Burne Bradfeld above the greater Feltham[6*] springs another litle river that runneth to Nawton, Burye, Fernhams, Hengrave, Flempton, Lackforde, Ichlingha', Berton, & Mildenhall & betwene Islam in Cambridgshire & Worlington in Suff. it meteth

Dale water

with another litle river that springeth about Catlidge (called the Dale water) in Cambridgshire & Lidgate in Suff. which from that in a continuall streame dischargeth it selfe into the greater Ouse betwene Ely & Litleporte in Cambridgeshire.

Stour fl.

On the south side of Suff. is the river Stour the head wherof is about Bradley Ma. in Suff. it cometh downe by Haverill where it enlargeth it selfe like to a litle sea that is called (*page changes*) Stourmere, but gathering in it selfe by litle & litle a mile from Haverill it runneth in

Clare fl.

a meane streame to Clare, where it rec. a litle river or brooke springing at Poslingford called Clare from thence by Long Melford to Sudburye, but before it cometh to Sudburie it rec. a litle river springing at Wickham brooke & Debden, from Sudburie Stour runneth to Neyland & Stretford where it rec. 2 rivers more, the one springing at

Waldingfeld, the other having 3 springs, the most westerley of them is at Cockfeld, the midlemost at Ketlebasto', the third & most easterly at Bretenham, which three springs runne eyther severall unto Chelsworth where they frendly ioyne together & make the river

Breton fl. called Breton which runneth to Semer & Hadley Market & about Stretford dischargeth it selfe into the Stour, which from Stretford runneth to Catiwade, where it divideth it selfe into two streames (over w'ch are two goodly woden bridges) but it soone gathereth it selfe in againe & in a great & large streame it continually floweth even untill it cometh into the sea w'ch is at Harwich in Essex.

Orwell
fl.
At Ratlesden springeth the river Orwell & not farre fro' Stow market towardes Nedham Market it rec. another as large as it selfe springing at Bacton. From Stowe it floweth to Nedham Bramford & Ypswich, & about Freston it rec. a litle river springing at Chatsham. From Ypswiche it floweth in a great largenes & depth sufficient to rec. ships of many tunne & seven miles from thence dischargeth it selfe into the sea by Harw'ch in Essex, where it maketh the goodly haven called Orwell haven where Queene Isabell wife to K: Edward 2 of England landed with 2757 men & the Prince of Wales (after K.Ed.3) &c. determininge to make warre against the king the 25 Sept.1326.

Deben
fl.
About Wetheringset & Mendlesham springeth another river called of Mr.Camden, Deben which cometh downe to Debenham market unto which it giveth name, from thence to Wickham Market, Ufford & Woodbridge, betwene Woodbridg & Waldringfeld it rec. another litle river consisting of two litle brookes the one wherof springeth at Otley, the other at Akenham united together betwene litle Bealinges & Martlesha'. From Woodbridge it runneth in a large & contynuall streame to Bawdsey & entreth into the sea where it maketh the haven called Baudsey haven, betwene Baudsey & Alderton it rec. a

Brightwell
brooke
litle river that springeth at Foxall called Brightwell brooke. At Falkenham is a litle Cricke that runneth into the Deben hard by the haven.

4
About Wantisden are two springs which about Chillesford unite (*page changes*) themselves & runing together in one by Butley sodenly enlargeth it selfe into a great breadth & runneth by the west side of Orfford & soone dischargeth it selfe into the sea. I take the name of this river to be Chill.

Or fl.
About Framlyngham springeth the river Or cometh downe by Parham & Marlesforde & at Farnh'm it rec. a litle river that springeth at Cranesford called of Hollinshed the Gleme, it runneth downe by Dunningworth & Snape, hard by Snape bridge it rec. another litle river springing at Carleton by Saxmondham, from Snape it runneth to Iken & by the east side of Orford & so into the sea where it maketh the haven called Orford haven.

Ford fl.
Holinshed
At Yoxford springs a litle river that floweth to Fordley & to Theberton where is the bridge called Eastbridge & so directly into the sea where it maketh the haven called Mismere haven.

Blith fl.
At Wisset springeth the river Blith & runneth to Haleswrth where it

is augmented by the receyt of a litle river springing at Ubpeston. From Halesworth it runneth to Wenhawesto' & Blithborowe & dischargeth it selfe into the sea at Walderswick.

Willingham Water At Willingham springs a litle river that runing right east by Hensted disburdeneth it selfe into the sea at Keslande.

The temporall government & division of Suff. according to the Hundreds.

Suffolk hath yeerlye a sheriffe nominated & elected by the Queenes Ma'tie & fower Lieutenants [7*] in matters of warre whose office is to see trayned souldiers mustered &c.

Suffolck hath 21 hundredes v'c't.

A	Lovyngland		M	Bosmere & Claydon.
	Mutford	hundred.	N	Samforde.
B	Wangforde.		O	Cosforde.
C	Blithinge.		P	Stowe.
D	Plomesgate.		Q	Blackborne.
E	Wilforde.		R	Lakforde.
F	Colnes.		X.	Thyngowe.
G	Carleforde.		T	Thredewardestre.
H	Loes.		U	Baber.
I	Hoxon.		X	Rysbryge.[8*]
K	Hertesmere.			
L	Tredlynge.			

5

The ecclesiasticall governement

This shire in matters of the churche is under the iurisdiction of the Bishop of Norwiche.

It is divided into two ArchDeaconries v'c't:

ArchDeaconry of Suffolck hath under it the Deanryes of

1. Luthinglande.
2. Waynforth.
3. Donewich.
4. Wyleforth.
5. Carleforth.
6. Ypswich.
7. Claydone.
8. Bosmere.
9. Hoxon.
10. Lose.
11. Orforth.
12. Colneyse.
13. Samforth.

Archdeaconrye of Sudbury hath under it the deanryes of

1. Fordham.
2. Tynghowe.
3. Stowe.
4. Tedwardestre.
5. Sudburye.
6. Blakeburne.
7. Hertesmere.
8. Clare.

What townes are contayned in every Denrye.

	Luthinglande		Luthingland & Mutforde
	Donwich		Blithinge
	Southelma')		Wangforth
	Waynforth)		
	Wilforth		Wilforde
	Carleforth		Carleforde
ArchDeaconry	Ypswich	which con-	belongs to Bosmer & Claydo'
of Suffolc	Claydon	tayneth the	Tredlynge
hath under	Bosmere & p't	townes of	Bosmere & Claydone.
it the	of Claydon	the hundred	
Deaneryes of	Hoxon	of	Hoxon
	Loes & halfe		Loes.
	of Wilforthe		
	Orforth		Plomesgate
	Colneys.		Colneys
	Samforth.		Samforde.
6	Fordham		Lackforde
	Tynghowe		Thynghowe.
ArchDeaconry	Stowe	w'ch contay-	Stowe.
of Sud-	Tedwardestre	neth the	Thredwardestre.
burye hath	Sudburye	townes of	Cosford & Baber.
under it the	Blakeborne	the hundred	Blakeborne.
Deaneryes of	Hertesmere	of	Hertesmere.
	Clare		Risbryge.

In Suffolck are

	Dunwych.		Framlyngham.
	Eaye.		Hadley.
Townes	Ipswych.		Haveryll. Bildeston (*sic*)
incorporate.	Orforde.		Halesworth.
	Sowoulde.		Laneham.
	Sudburye.		Lestofft.
			Mildenhall.
	Aldeborough.		Newmarkett.
	Beckles.		Nedham.
	Bungaye.		Saxmundham.
Market	Burye.		Stowe.
townes	Boudesdale.		Wickham.
	Brandon.		Woodbrydge.
	Debenham.		Wulpit.
	Clare.		

Aldham.	Hoxon.	Redgrave.
Alpheton.	Huntingfelde.	Smalbridge.
Bliborough.	St.James.	Stoke.
Brome.	Kenton.	Stradishill three.
Brusyarde.	Laneham.	Waldyngfelde.
Candishe.	Letheryngham.	Waybred.
Chevington.	Melles.	Westhorp.
Framlyngha'.	Muncksoham.	Wetheringset.
Henham.	Nettlested.	
Hevenyngha'.	Parham.	

7

An Alphabet of the townes, villages
& houses of name in Suffolck.

The letter after the name of the towne or village betokeneth the hundred wherin the towne &c. is contayned, the figure sheweth the Deanrye, Sf the Archdeaconry of Suffolck, Sd the Archdeaconrye of Sudburye.

Acolt vide Ockold 180 pag.

Acton u Sd 5

A vicarage valued at £9.6.8d the tenth 18.8d. it is in the nomination of the Bishop of the diocesse. The Personage was hertofore appropriated to the Prior & Covent of Hatfeld Peverell, & was valued at 22 marks. The Impropriation belongeth to Mr.Frauncis Danyell 9* who also presenteth to the Vicarie which vicarie hath 20 acres of gleabe & halfe of all manner of tithes w'th the sheaf-corn & all which they part in the field.

Temp.

The mannour of Acton now belongeth to S'r Nicholas Bacon k't & Banneret [1] by reason of his wife coheire of Buttes somtyme owner of the same by mariage of the coheire of Buers who of long tyme were Lordes therof. The Leet belongeth to the hall called Acton Hall.

In the churche are some most ancient monumentes of the Buers which long since there dwelled & dyed but defaced by antiquitie. One only remayneth perfect w'h this epitaph.

Hic iacet Andreas de Buers et Robertus de Buers filius eiusdem, milites. dictus vero Andreas obijt 12 die mensis Aprilis a'o D'ni 1360 et dictus Robertus obijt 7 die mensis Octobris a'o d'ni 1361 quor' a'i'abus p'pitiet'r deus. Amen. [2]

vide p.317.

8.

Spirit.
Lib.val.
Domsd.

9 Ed.2

Akenham m Sf 7   Alkenham

a Personage, subs. 16s valued at 9.11.5½, the tenth 19.1¾.

Heres Joh'is de Lanffa est p'ronus eiusd. D'n's Edmundus le Bacun quondam erat ratione custodie dicti heredis aest. 10 marc. syn. 20d.

Joh'es Bacon d'n's 9 Ed.2.

Aldham o Sd 5

Spirit.
L.val.

a Personage p'sent. valued at 12.13.4d the tenth 25s 4d. Subs. 18s.

Domsd.

Aest. 16 mar. Carnag. 4d.
9 Ed.2 Comes Oxonie d'n's.
Taske 40s ob.
ded. 10s ob.
red. 38s.

(*TA transcript; the only entry which it seems plausible to place on the missing f.9:*
'South Elmham All S'ts b Sf 2   Allhallowes
calld Elmham o'i'u' S'cor. A parsonage   valued at 8 li the tenth 16s.'*)

10

Aldebrough d Sf 11   A market towne, the market kept upon the _____ (*blank*). A towne of good shippinge otherwise called Aldburgh — the old towne. In a dearth 1555 there sprang up pease in great abundance about this towne without any helpe of man, & was accounted for a miracle, but since they have still contynued in growing there, which hath caused some of the wiser sort to iudge that those pease were cast on the shore out of some shipwrack & tooke rooting and grew there to the benefitt of all the inhabitants,[3] which coniecture is very p'bable. But yet in it are we to consyder the great goodnes of God who in that scarcitie in this mannour p'vided for the poore, on whom hardhearted Richmen could not fynde in their hearts of their abundance to bestow some small portion.

Spirit.

A personage valued 33 6 8 the tenth 3.6.8.

(10v)

Aldertone e Sf 4

Spirit.

A Personage p'sent. valued 14.18.4 the tenth 29s 10d Subs. 26s.

Domsd.

D'n's Rex Anglie est patronus eiusdem. Proc. 7.6d Syn. 4.6d.

Joh'es
Sone fil.
Joh'is
ille Francisci Sone
juris consulti qui
acquisivit
maneriu'
de
Alderto'
Naunto' 4

This towne is in the libertie of St.Audrie. In it are 3 Mannours
1. Alderton hall alias Alderton Nanton, the L: therof Mr James Bacon of Friston in Suff. by purchase of Mr John Sone whose predecessours had it of Nanton. This mannour is holden of the king by Kn'ts service. To this mannour belongeth the patronage of the church, the Lord herof holdeth only court Baron & no leete hath wayfe & straye the fine arbitrable. The custome of this manour hath that the yongest sonne hath all the coppyelandes.
2. Alderton comitis commonly Earle Alderton.
3. Alderton Howes the proprietie of both these are in the Bishop of Norw'ch, the lease of them hath Mr James Bacon afores'd. The fines arbitrable the custome as before.

Inquis.9
E.2

In the tyme of K.Ed.2. Hugo de Naunton D'n's de Alderto'.

Taske 54
8d. Ded.
11s Red.

4. Mannour of Cowesley Lord Mr James Bacon, fine arbitrable.
5. Mannor of Raynes was Mr Mi'hil Hares of Brusyard.[5] Lesse S'r Francis Walsingham of Mr Thomas Denny of Baudsey gent. sonne of

Richard Denny a servant in Butley abbye which service was his making. To the rectorie belongs an house with 20 acres of gleabe, all tithes are p'd in kind save for lactage is p'd 3d a cowe, for wood an harthenne.

Aldringham c Sf 3

Domsd. D'n's de Layston h't ea' in p'prios usus. Aest. 3 marc. Proc. 7.6d. Syn. 16d.
L.val. nihil 9 Ed.2 nihil.

11

Allyngton 1 Sf 9 Athelington

A personage   valued at 4.14.2 the tenth 9.5d.

Alpheton u Sd 5

A Personage   valued 10.1 the tenth 2s.

(11v)
Spirit.

Ampten t Sd 4

A personage   valued at 5.2.1d the tenth 10.2½

Arwerton n Sf 13   Everwarton

It once appertayned to the Bacons, but now it belongeth to S'r Phillip Parker a worthy knight who by the fathers side cometh of the Barons of Morley, & by the mothers side of the worthy familye of the Calthorps.[6]

Spirit.   A personage   valued at 10.13.4. the tenth 21 4d.

....

13

Ashbye a Sf 1   Askbye

A personage _____(*Blank*) valued at 6 li the tenth 12s.

(13v)
L.val.

Ashe h Sf 10   iuxta Campsey

A personage p'sent. valued at 14.5.0 the tenth 28 6d. subsid. 24s.
Domsd. Comes Marescallus est patronus illius. Rector h't mansu' cu' una acra terre. Proc. 17.6 Syn. 22d.

....

14

Ashfelde l Sf 7   Ashfeld cu' Thorpe

(TA transcript: 'Ashfeild parva alias Badwell Ashfeild q Sd 6')

15

Asyngton u Sd 5

A vicarage valued at 10 li the tenth 20s. The Personage was hertofore appropriated to the Prior and Covent of Hatfeld Peverell.
D'n's Rogerus Corbett 9 Ed.2.
Test.eius Guido Corbet armiger sepelit'r in australi Ala huius eccl'ie obijt 1433. Fuit D'n's manerij de Asington.

16

Aye k Sd 7 Eaye. A market towne

(The market kept on the ('Saturday' *in hand of Tom Martin*). Of some antiquitie where as yet are sene the ruines of an ancient castle which once belonged unto William de Mallet a Norman Baron. In the tyme of K: Hen. 1, it was taken from him & with the dignitie of it bestowed upon Stephen Earle of Bolein who afterward bestowed it upon his sonne William Earle of Warren. When he dyed in the expedition to Tholouze it fell into the kings handes & so remayned untill Richard the 1. K: of Englande gave it unto the Duke of Brabant (then called the Duke of Lotharynge) with the niece of the forenamed William. Long after this when it was agayne fallen into the handes of the kings of Englande, King Edward 3 bestowed the title & dignitie of it upon Robert Ufford Earle of Suff.[7]

Spir.   It is a vicarage valued 11.14.7½. The tenthe 23.5½. The Personage was appropriated to the Prior and Convent of Eye.

17   St.Andros b Sf 2
Spir.   A vicarage valued at 5.13.4. the tenth 11.4d.
All tithes p'd in kinde save lactage which they allowe not & port for w'ch they allowe ijd an orchard and iiijd for an hemplande.

2 mannours. Ilketeshall. Lord therof S'r Nicholas Bacon. Of the other Mr Duke of Keleshall. Of the first the fine arbitrable. They work certayne dayes in harvest.

....

18   Baddingham l Sf 9
A personage   valued at 22.16.5½ the tenth 45.7¾.
1423   Joh'es Carbonell miles sepelitur in cancella eccl'ie S'ti Joh'is Baptiste de Badingham 1423. H'uit maneriu' de Badingham Saxham in Badingham.
1478   Robertus Lyston armig. D'n's manerij de Badi'gha' et patr: eccl'ie eiusdem 1478 testam. eius p'b. 1484.
In this towne are 3 mannours 1. Baddingha' hall hertofore belonging to Bovill, then by his d. & h. to Carbonell, & by his h. to Lyston & by his to Rous of Badingha' who now is Lord thereof. To this mannour belongeth Court baron & Leete. It is holden in knights service by finding divers soldiers in Aye Castell of wh. it is holden by the halfe of a knights fee. The coppyhold fall to the yongest. The dower the third. The fines arbitrable.
2. Coulstons in Edw.2 his tyme belonged to S'r Ralfe Hardrichshull: in S'r W'm Carbonell his tyme to S'r Wakelin Hardrichshull. It afterward belonged to Wingfelds & S'r Anthony now living 1604 sold it to Anthony Pennyng of Ketleburgh in Suff. It is holden by knights service by halfe a knights fee. Fines arbitrable customes & dower as before.
3. Okenhill hall belonging to Mr John Cornwalleys hertofore to Rich'us de Mundevill in 9 Ed.2.[8]

Domsd.   D'n's Oliverus de Ingham patronus.

                Beate Marie   Badley m Sf 8
A vicarage   valued 6 13 4 the tenth 13 4d.

19   Badwellashe q Sd 6
Domsd.   Badwell appr't'r Priori et conventui de Ikesworth.
Edw.2   Badwell magna cu' Ashfeld p'va D'n's Will'us Criketot tempore Regis Edw.2.

27

Baleham m Sf 8   Beylham

Domsd.	Comes Marescallus est p'ronus eiusd. Rector h't mansu' cu' 40 acris terre. Proc. 6.8. Syn. 2s.
L.val.	Rect. val. 12.4.9½. Dec. 24.5¾. Subsid. 22s.
9.Ed.2.	Tempore Ed.2 D'n's de Beylham fuit Joh'es de Burnavill
L.Instit.	Joh'es de Burnavile fuit D'n's et patronus de Beylha' 1317.

20   Barham m Sf 7   Bergham

Domsd.	Prior Eliensis est patronus eiusd. Proc. 7.6. Syn. 2s.
L.val.	Rect. val. 12.10.5 Dec. 25 0½ Subs. 22s.
Ed.2	Tempore Ed.2 D'n's Prior Eliensis fuit.

Bareowe s Sd 2   vid. pag.297

Domsd.	Aest. 36 marc.
L.val.	Rect. val. 23.9.9½. Dec. 46 11¾ Subs. 42s. Patronus D'n's Joh'es Heigha' miles.⁹
Ed.2	Tempore Ed.2 D'na huius ville fuit Comitissa Glocestriae.
Lib.Inst.	12 cal. maij D'n's Hugo le despensier iunior 1325 p's. Joh'em de Fentone.

Ep'us Norw. per lapsum pres: Joh'em de North Kellesey per breve Reg: Edw.3 datu' 27 Apr. anno eius Regni Angl. 15 et Franc. 2 in quo continet'r quod Elisabeth que fuit uxor Aegidii de Badlesmere recuperavit presentationem sua' ad eccl'ia' de Barwe versus W'm Boutruileyn et Margeria uxorem eius.

25 Aug. 1347 D'n's Hugo le despensier p's. cum Elizabetha uxore sua pres: Edm. de Grimdesby per resignat' Joh'is de Northkellesey.

11 Jan. 1354 Guido de Brienne baro pres: Rich: de Hornington.

22 Nov. 1387 D'n's Ph'us le despenser filius D'ni Ph'i le despensier milit. pres. Joh'em Pycheford.

19 Jul. 1398 D'nus Ph'us le despensier p's: Rogeru' le despensier.

2 Dec. 1399 Idem pres. Thomam de Hadley.

28 Feb. 1451 Rogerus Wentworth arm: et Margeria consors sua D'no de Roos p's: Georg: Hawys per mortem Rob: Westington.

Barnebye a Sf 1

Barsham b Sf 2

22   S'ti Michaelis   Beckles b Sf 2

A market towne kept on the Saterdaye. It standeth upon the Waveney. It was pitifully defaced with fire a'o _____ (*blank*)¹⁰ but it hath almost recovered hir former beautye agayne.

Bawdsey e Sf 4

23   Bedfeld l Sf 9

Benhall d Sf 11

(23a?)   Basforth m Sf 8   Batesforth

Maneriu' pertinebat ad Ep'u' Norwicense' It. 12 Hen. 7 computu'. Redd't liber. tene't. 62s 5d nat. tenent. 9.14.2.

....

Belynge magna g Sf 5

Patron Justice Clenche.[11]

The Mannor of Seckford Hall in Belynges belongeth to Mr Seckford and hath continued in the elder house for many years. Keepeth court baron at the place but no leete the fines arbitrable.

24   Bealinge parva g Sf 5

Mr Thomas Seckford patro'.

Belsted parva n Sf 13

L.val.   Rect. val. 7.6.0½d Dec. 14.7¼ Subs. 12s.

D'n's Joh'es de Goldingham est p'ronus illius. Proc. 4s Syn. 12d.

The mannour of Belsted belongeth to Mr Henry Reynolds from his father Henry who bought it of Mr (*blank*) Goldingham.[12] The fine arbitrable.

....

(*TA transcript:*   'Bedingfeild l Sf 9

In this town are four mannors —

1. Bedingfeild hall Lord S'r Henry Bedingfeild.

2. The priory mannor parcell of the priory of Snape. L: Mr Tho: Bedingfield of Darsham bought by his father of the Duke of Norff. 3. Manor of Flemings in Bedingha' ('sic' *TA*) Mr Thomas Bedingfeilds by Inheritance from his ancestors who married the dau'r and heir of Adam Fleming Lord of the manor.

4. Gislinghams in Bedingfeild. Lord Mr Rivett of Rishangles')

....

28   St.Michaelis   Benaker c Sf 3

....

29   Bernyngham q Sd 6

L.val.   Rect.val. 13.9.2. Dec. 26.11. Subs. 24s. The Patro' the E: of Sussex

Caius Colledge in Cambridge hath a mannour in it.

Mr Bradbury of Ashell hath a mannour in it.

....

30   Berton Magna t Sf 8

(*Transcript by Sir Thomas Gage,* sub *Gt.Barton*: 'House and 40 acres of Glebe, all Tythes in kind save for Lactage, 3d each Cow. No tythe of Hemp but 6d per Bushel as sown and for Fire a Hearth Hen at Christmas (MS Neve 4to the 14 t 8 in Sudbury Arch. f.11.59)')

31   Berton r Sd 1   Berto' parva

Domsd.   Commonly called Berton mills. Aest. 30 marc. Domsd.

L.val.   Rect. val. 14.15.10 Dec. 29.7. Subs. 26s

9 E 2   Abbas S'ti Ed'i D'n's 9 Ed.2

Taske 3.10.4.

Ded.10s

red. 3.0.4.

(*Transcript by Thomas Martin*:

'Bilston o Sd 5   Bildestone   30

Spir.   is a personage pr'sentative. Hath belonging to the Rectory a Great House and 50 acres of ground entire about the house and a field of 10 or 12 acres in high street towards Nauton & Briset Magna.

Temp.   It is a market Towne of Great Antiquitie kept on the Wednesday & hath been of more account heretofore than now it is for in the time of Q.Mary in a great dearth by the Com'andment of Mr Doyly of

Task   Pondhall [14] all the Country thereabouts brought their victuals and

58s   other Necessaries to Hadley to be sold whereby this Towne of

Ded. nul's Bilstone hath decayed. It was full of fair Inns which now are neglected. Only in this Towne is some small Quantity of Fish and Flesh sold on the Market day. They have two Fairs in the Year 1 kept on Ashwednesday 2. on Ascension day. The last fair was obtained & their charter renewed for them by Walter Devorax Earl of Essex who was Lord and Patron of the same as heir to the Bourchiers Earls of Essex unto whom it appertained for many years together. Robert the last Earl sold it to —————— (*blank*) a Merchant of London.[15]

Est. 12 Marc. Carnag. 7½.

Thomas de Loveyne D'nus 9 Ed.2.

Rect. val, 12[1] 16.10½ decim. 25s 8d Subs. 22s.')

32   Blakenham magna m Sf 8

alias Blakenham super aquam.

Domsd.   Prior de Okeburne est p'ronus istius. Aest. marc. 7½. Proc. 6 8d Syn. 12d.

L.val.   Rect. val. 6.16.0½ Dec. 13.7¼ Subs. 12s.

9 Ed.2   Abbas de Becherlewyne d'nus 9 Ed.2.

Blakenham sup' mo'tem m Sf 8

Domsd.   D'nus Thomas la Veer est p'ronus eiusd' ratione custodie heredis aest. 15 marc. Proc. 6.8d Sy' 2s.

L.val.   Rect.val. 10.3.4. Dec. 20 4d Subs. 18s.

9 Ed.2   Thomas de Veer d'n's 9 Ed.2.

33

Bliborough c Sf 3   Blyburgh

Henninges in his Theatru' Genealogicu' s'th that Annas king of the East Angles slayne by Penda king of the Mercians was buryed in this towne. [16]

Domsd.   Prior de Bliburgh h't ea' in p'p'os usus. Aest. cu' capella de

L.val.   Walbordeswyk 43 marc. Proc. 7.6d Syn. 2s. L.val. nihil.

9 Ed 2   Joh'es de Claveringe d'n's 9 Ed.2.

34   Blaxall d Sf 11   Blacksale

Domsd.   Comes marescallus est p'ronus eiusdem. Proc. 7.6. Syn. 18d.

L.val.   Rect.val. 20 li. Dec. 40s. Subs. 36s. Patronus Rex. Angl.

9 Ed. 2   To the Rectorie belong convenient houses with 80 acres of glebe by

Richardus the measure of the 18 foote pole. All tithes are p'd in kinde save

de Weyland furres, broome, wood, friuct, doves, hony, waxe, egges & hennes.

D'n's 9   Only 3 houses v'c't the hall — Blaxall hall, Gouldes his house &
Ed.2   Sooke his house pay every yeere ech house 2 chickens for lactage.[17]
           The King is patrone.
           In the towne are 2 mannours 1. Blaxhall Hall belonging to
           _____(Blank) Nevill L.Aburgavenny from his predecessours. It
           appertayned hertofore to William Cleydon, & after to Richard Nevill
Taske cu' E. of Warwicke. By mariage it went from the Nevills & by mariage
p't of   came unto them agayne where it remayneth to this daye. To it is
Tunstall   annexed the patronage of Chesilford. It is holden in soccage of the
54 10d ded.manour of Gristons in Stratford by Glemha' which belongs to S'r
6s red. 48s Henry Glemha' k't.[18] 2. The Mannour of Valence in Blaxsale
10d   apertayneth to Mr Frauncis Saunders from his father Frauncis who
           bought it of Cob & Collymer 2 Marchantes who purchased it of W'm
           Whetcraft of Ypswich to whome the L.Willoughbye of _____
           (blank) sold it being a member of the Mannour of Campse who had
           it of the K: Hen.8 after the dissolution of Religious houses by
           purchase it belonging before to Campse Abbye. It is holden in Capite
           of the Kinge. In both these mannours the woman hath no dower.
           The coppyholdes descend to the yonger son. The fines arbitrable.
           The Leete _____(blank)

           (TA transcript: 'Blyford c Sf 3
Domsd.   Prior de Bliburgh h'et eam in proprios usus. Est ibi capellanus
           perpetuus. Aest. 7 marc' Procur. 6s Syn 12d.
L.val.   L.val. nihil.
9 E.2   Thomas de Bavent et Hamo de Miklefield D'ni 9 Ed.2.')

35   Boulge eh Sf 4   Bulge
Domsd.   W'mus de Rungtone est p'nus (TA transcript: 'istius. Rector h'et
           mansum cum tribus acris terre procur. 3s4d Syn. 2s.
L.val.   Rect.val. 3-12-1 Dec. 7-2½') proc. _____Syn. _____
t.Ed.   Margaretta Regina Ang. d'na 9 Ed.2.

           S'r Henry Seckford lord of the mannour.[19]

                        ....

                        Boxford u Sd 5   Boxforth
Domsd.   Aest. 20 marc. Carnag. 9½d
L.val.   Rect. val. 20 li Dec. 40s Subs. 36s
9 Ed.2   Abbas S't Ed'i D'n's 9 Ed.2.

                        Boxstede u Sd 5
Domsd.   .... de .... (illegible)
9 Ed.2   Will'us de la Lee D'n's 9 Ed.2.

(37)   Blunston a Sf 1   Blundestone
9 Ed.2   Aest. 20 marc. proc. 7.6. Sy. 17s.
L.val.   Rect.val. 13.6.8. Dec. 26.8 Subs. 29s
           Patronus Mr W'm's Sydnor.
           The mannour of Blunston belongeth to Mr Willia' Sydnor who
           bought it of Mr Yermouth now of Benaker late of Blunsto'[20] in
           which towne his predecessors have contynued almost since the

                              31

conquest untill the tymes of K.Edw.4. whose predecess. in Hen.5 his tyme maryed the d. & h. of Blunsto' in whose name it contynued since the conquest untill by this mariage it was translated into the familie of Yarmouth aforesayde. The fines are arbitrable. It only keepeth Court Baron & not Leete for in all Lovinglande is no Leete kept but by Mr Jarnegan of Cossye except in Burgh Castell, which Mr Jarnegan esquier hath the driffts hath waifes strayes felons goodes &c. & hath it in fee farme from the Queene.[21] The whole island is priviledged from assises & sessions.

In this towne was a mannour called Gunviles but is now altogether decayed & hath not any tenaunts.

Mr Willia' Sydnor is patro' of the p'sonage w'ch is presentative.

Rect.val. 13.6.8. Dec. 26 8 Subs. 24s Proc. 7.6. Syn. 17d. All tithes are p'd in kinde only for portmonye they pay ijd.

(*In hand of PLN: Bradfield* 'St.Cleres t Sd 4')

38	Monks Bradfeld t Sd 4

Burnt Bradfelde t Sd 4 alias little Bradfelde

39	Bramfeld c Sf 3 Brounfelde
Domsd.	Prior de Bliburgh habet ea' in p'prios usus. Vicarius eiusd' h't mansu' cu' 2 acris terre. Proc. 7.6d Syn. 12d.
L.val.	Vicar. val. 6.7.6. Dec. 12 9d.
9 Ed.2	Nich'us de Segrave Walterus de Norw'h d'ni 9 Ed.2

L: of the mannour of Bramfeld Mr Edw: Bacon of Shribland from my L: keeper Bacon.[22] The fine arbitrable nowe & many tymes & xijs an acre. Was certayne hertofore & but xijd an acre. The townesmen might have had it enroled in the chauncery by the L: Keeper for the certayntye of ijs an acre & would not: coppyhold falls to the yonger.

Bradley magna x Sd 8

Domsd.	Aest. 30 marc.
L.val.	Rect. val. 17 1 5½ Dec. 34 1½ Subs. 30s.
9 Ed.2.	Joh'es Boutetort D'n's 9 Ed.2.
	(*TA transcript may form part of Chorography text*: 'D'na Joh'na de
Bradley mag. 1332	Botetourte p'ron' E. de Bradley magna 1332 Liber 2dus Institut' fo.55')

....

Bramford m Sf 3

Brantham n Sf 13

| 9 Ed.2 | W'm's de Brah'm d'n's 9 Ed.2 |

Brettenham o Sd 5

A litle towne at the head of the litle river Breton once of great fame called of Antoninus Combretoviu' for as Bretenham with us doth signifye an house or dwelling at Breton so doth Combretoviu' with the Britons signifye a valley or lower place by Breton.[23]

| Domsd. | Aest. 16 mar. Carnag. 7½d. |

L.val.	Rect.val. 11.3.9. Dec. 22.4½ Subs. 20s.
9 Ed.	Comes Glocestre D'n's ville 9 Ed.2.

The king is patron, the L.Chauncelour presenteth. It hath some 12 acres of gleabe. All p'd in specie.

In it are ('2' *crossed out*) mannours 1. the Man: of Bretenha' ('Hall' *crossed out*) cum Rheeses where the fines are arbitrable. The Lord therof S'r Anthony Felton k't [24] to whome it descended from his ancestours unto whome it came by mariage of the d. & h. of Thomas Sampson who many ages together were owners of the same. The Leete is the Kings.

('The Man: of Stansted' *crossed out*)

(*TA transcript*: 'Bredfeild e Sf 4   Bradfeild

Domsday	Una medietas dict' Eccl'iae appropriata Priori et Conventui de Butlee alia priorissae et convent' de Campse. Aest. 10 marc. vic. 40s proc. ex parte priorissae 3-4 altera ignora't. Syn. 2s.
L.val.	Vicar. val. 4-4-2. Dec. 5-5.
9 E 2	Margaretta Regina Angl' D'na 9 Ed.2.
Bredfeild	The mannour of Bredfield cum Winderviles appertaineth to S'r Antony Wingfeild who bought it of S'r Robert Drury of Hawsted to whom it descended from his father. [25] The fines arbitrable the Coppylands holden in Gavelkind.')

44	Briset magna m Sf 8
Domsd.	Prior eiusdem h't eccl'iam in p'prios usus. Aest. 9 marc. Proc. 6.8d Syn. 2s.
	D'n's de Brycet 9 Ed.2 fuit Richardus Lovedaye.

	Briset parva m Sf 8
Domsd.	Prior, monachor' Thetfordie est patronus illius. Pr. 4s Sy. 12d. Aest. cu' Offingtone.
	L.val. (*blank*)

45	Brockford k Sd 7

	Brightwell g Sf 5
Domsd.	Joh'es Lampyt est patronus eiusd. Aest. 5 mar. Proc. 3.4. Sy. 12d. Lib.val. nihil.
9 Ed.2	Joh'es de Lamput D'n's ville tempore Ed.2 a'o 9.

....

Brome k Sd 7

....

Bucklesham f Sf 12

....

Bungaye b Sf 2

A market towne kept upon the Thursdaye.

50	Burntileye u Sd 5

Burgate k Sd 7

Burghe g Sf 5

Domsd.	Heres Thome de Ufforth est patronus illius. Aest. 12 mar.
L.val.	Proc. 7.6. Syn. 2s. Rect. val. 8.3.4. Dec. 16.4. Subs. 14s.
9 Ed.2.	Eva de Ufford D'na 9 Ed.2.
4 lib.	Appropriavit W'm's Ep'us eccl'ia de Burgh cu' o'ibus fructibus &c.
Inst.	custodi et capellanis Cantarie annunciationis virginis marie infra eccl'ia monasterij seu prioratus de Campesse que p'petua cantaria fundata fuit p' D'na' Matildem de Lancastre filia' D'ni Henrici quonda' Comitis de Lancastrie Comitissam Ultonie relictamq' nobilis viri D'ni quo'dam Radulphi de Ufford ad honore' dei &c. p' salute a'i'ar' D'nor' Rad'i p'fati D'ni W'mi de Burgo Comitis Ultonie sui priori mariti, Elisabeth de Burgo et Matildis de Ufford filiar' suar' ad a'i'e sue et d'nor' Joh'is de Ufford & Thome de Hereford militu' cum ingraverunt de hoc mundo, in perpetuam. Non erit ibi vicarius deputatus sed stipendiarius capellanus. Primor' loco fructu' solvet ep'o annua' pensione' duar' marcar' ad sinodos pasche et Michaelis. Datum apud Southelmham 25 Febr. a'o D'ni 1348.

Burgh Castell a Sf 1

Once called Cnobesburgh that is as Bede interpreteth it Cnoberi urbs, Cnobers towne, which as Bede sayth was a castell most pleasant by reason of the neerenes of the sea & of the woodes in the which was once a monasterie built by Furseus a Scot. Now only remayne ruined walles bushes & bryers. Here manye tymes are Romish coyne founde by them that digge in that place.[26]

Domsd.	Aest. 10 marc. Proc. (*blank*) Syn. (*blank*)
L.val.	Rect.val. 6.13.4. Dec. 13.4d.
9 Ed.2	Prior de Bromholme d'n's 9 Ed.2.
	To the rectorie belongeth an old house w'th 32 acres of gleabe wherof 24 are arable. All tithes p'd in kind save tithe calfe they pay none nor yet lactage, but for herbage 3d for cowe & calfe.
'Burgh Castell	(*TA transcript: this fragment may not be of this text*: W'm Roberts Lord the Man'r bought of Q.Mary 120 li p' ann'.')

....

	(*TA transcript*: 'Burstall m Sf 8
Domsd.	Abbas de Bello est p'ronus ejusd. Syn. 12d Lib.val. nihil. 9 E.2 nihil.')

	(*TA transcript*: 'Butley d Sf 10
Domsday	Prior de Butley h'et eccl'iam in proprios usus. Aest. 5 marc. L.val. nihil.
9 E.2	Comes Norff. D'n's 9 E.2
	Butle cum Capell' an Impropriation. Mr Forth[28] hath it, findeth a Curate who medleth with no tithes But all goeth to Mr Forth which all paid in kind save as in Boyton they of both towns being distinct towns yet go all to one Church.

Mr Forth Lord of it.'

(*TA transcript:*   Buxhall p Sd 3

L. val. Rector. val. 20 li 4d Dec. 40s-0½ Subsid. 36s.

Domsd. D'ni villae de Buxhall Richardus Wayland Rogerus Sturmy Robertus Cockerell.

9 E 2 Joh'es Tendring 9 E.w.

Isabella uxor Edmundi Hethersett militis obijt circa 20 Jan. A'o 13 Regis Ed. 4'ti sepel' in hac Eccl'ia.')

56   Candish u Sd 5   Cavendisch

Domsd. Aest. 42 marc. Carnag. 7½

L.val. Rect.val. 26 li Dec. 52s Subs. 46s.

9 Ed.2 Joh'es de Clynton d'n's 9 Ed.2.

(*TA transcript*: 'Capell n Sf 13 Capelles

Will'us fil. Radulphi est patronus istius. Aest. 13 marc. Proc 7s 6d Syn. 2s.

L.val. Rector. val. 13-18-4 Dec. 27-10 Subs. 24s.

9 E.2 Will'us filius Radulphi d'n's 9 E.2.')

57   Capell e Sf 4 Capelles

(*TA transcript:*

'Domsday Prior de Butlee h'et Ecc'am in proprios usus. Aest. 20s Proc. _____(*blank*) Syn. _____(*blank*)

    L.val. nihil.

9 Ed.2 Symon de Ratlesdene D'n's 9 Ed.2.

I take it is united to Butlee the church is down the parishioners go to Butley Church. The town is a distinct town by itself.')

(*TA transcript*:   'Carleton 1 Sf g

Domsday Aest. 4 marc. In Reg'ro D'ni Ep'i Norwici aest. 7 marc.

L. val. Rect. val. 3.11.0½ Dec. 7.1.¼.

9 E.2 Comitissa Marescall. no'i'e (*sic*) dotis D'na 9 Ed.2.')

(58?)   Carleton a Sf 1

Domsd. Aest. 33 marc. Proc. 7.6. Syn. 2s.

L.val. Rect. val. 12.10.7½ Dec. 25.0¾. Subsid. 22s.

    9 Ed.2 nihil.

      ....

(59?)   Cattywade

    9.Ed.2.nihil.

(*TA transcript*:   'Cavenham r Sd 1

Domsd. Appropriatur Priori et convent. de Stokes. Aest. 20 marc.

L.val. Vicar. val. 5.5.10. Dec. 10.7d.

9 E.2 Comes Glocestriae D'n's 9 Ed.2d.')

S'r Edward Lewcknor L: of the towne of Cavenham.[29]

60   Charsfeld h Sf 10

(*TA transcript: original partly illegible*)

'Domsday Prior de Letheringham h'et Ecc'am in proprios usus. Proc. 6 8d Syn 2s.

L.val. nihil. 9 E 2 nihil.
They pay 15 cheeses for lactage.
Mr Thomas Bedinghfeild of Oxborough Lord of the Mannor.')

Chatsham n Sf 13
(TA transcript: original partly illegible::

'Domsday Priorissa de Wykes h'et Eccl'iam in proprios usus. Aest. _____
(*blank*) Rect. 40s Vicar. 5 marc. Proc. 6-8d Syn. 2-4d.

L.val. Vicar. val. 4-13-4 Dec. 9-4d.
9 E 2 nihil.')

61   ### Chelsworth o Sd 5
Domsd.   Aest. 12 marc. Carn. 4d
Rectoria valet 8.8.9. Dec. 16: 10½ Subs. 14s.

9 Ed 2   A p'sonage presentative, the King patron. No customes all p'd in
D'n's   specie. There is a portion of tithes by some esteemed of the third
Joh'es   part of the towne which of old did belong to the abbot of Burie to
de S'to   finde his horses oates. These tythes now belonginge to S'r Henry
Philiberto Gawdye k't. [30] Some say they should go out of the demeanes of the
Mannour.
The Lord of the Mannour w'th the Leete is S'r Anthony Wingfield
k't unto whome it did descende from his grandfather who amongst
other things had it by mariage of the coheire of the E: of Oxford
who came to it by mariage of the heire of Howarde who were long
tymes owners of the same. The fines arbitrable. There be no
demeanes for long since were all the demeanes parcelled out into
coppiholdes in which nature they rest now confirmed by long
prescription. No mention where the mannour house stoode. yet at
the west end of the churche appeareth the seate of a most ancient
house environed w'th ditches or moates according to the forme of
antiquitie + vide p.318

Chempton n Sf 13   Chelmundestone

....

Cheston c Sf 3   Chediston

....

Chillesforde d Sf 11   Chisselforth
Domsd.   Joh'es de Waylound est p'ronus eiusdem. Pro. 6.8. Syn. 2s.
L.val.   Rect. val 5.3.4. Dec. 10.4d
Mr.Sanders The patronage of this towne belonged hertofore to John Russell &
Stephen Farnham tenauntes of W'm Cleydon L: of the mannour of
Chisselforth of whom John Wayland bought it & left it to S'r
Richard Wayland k't his sonne.
Now the patronage is appendant to the mannour of Blaxsale hall &
Mr Frauncis Saunders gent. p'senteth by vertue of the lease of that
mannour from my L: Aburgavennye.

In it are 2 mannours 1. the Mannour of Chiselford hertofore
apertayned to W'm Cleydon but now to S'r Michaell Stanhope k't by
purchase of John Sone gent. who had it from his father Frauncis

whose father John Sone purchased it of the Duke of Norff.[31]

2. The Mannour of Russells in Chiselford belonging to Mr John Hawghfen gent. of Tunstall from his father John to whom it came by gift of the Suffragane of Butley who purchased it of Russells to whome it belonged for manye yeers.[32]

| 64 | Chilton u Sd 5 |

....

<table>
<tr><td>(65?)</td><td>Clare x Sd 8</td></tr>
</table>

a market towne where are as yet to be seene the ruines of a castle. Fro' this towne the honourable familye of the Clares who descended from Gislebert the Norman whose children were called Earles of Clare. From this place also Leonell son to K.Edw.3 tooke his title of Duke of Clarence, having marryed a wife out of the stocke of the Clares. Here in the church lyeth buryed this Lyonell who dyed in Italye after he had taken to his seconde wife the daughter of Galeacius viscount of Millan. Here layeth also enterred Jone D'Acres daughter of K.Edw.I who was wife to Gilbert 2 of Clare Earle of Glocester.[33]

Domsd.   Appropriat'r Priori et convent' de Stokes.
          Vicar. val. 4.18.9. Dec. 9.10½.

66   Cleydon
Domsd.   D'n's Edmundus Bakun est patronus istius, (*TA transcript adds* 'ratione custodiae heredis de Brewes')
          Rect. val. 10 li Dec. 20s Subsid. (*TA transcript*: '18s Proc. 7s 6d Syn. 20d.' *Original partly illegible*)

                               Clopton g Sf 5
Domsd.   D'n's Thomas Latymer est patronus istius.
          Rect. val. 16.13.4. Dec. 33.4. Subsid. 30s Procur. 7.6d Syn. 2s.

67   Cockfeld u Sd 5
L.val.   Rect. val. 30 li Dec. 3 li Subsid. 54s Carnagiu' 7½
Domsd.   Abbas S'ti Ed'i d'n's 9 Ed.2

                             Conyweston q Sd 6
L.val.   Rect.val. 13.0.5. Dec. 26 0½ Subs. 22s.
9 Ed.2   Abbas S'ti Ed'i D'n's 9 Ed.2.

68   +   Cookeley c Sf 3
Domesd.   Rogerus filius D'ni Will'mi de Huntingfeld est patronus eiusdem. Rector h't mansu' cu' 10 acris terre. Proc. 6.8d. Syn. 12d. Rector. valet 6.13.4. Dec. 13.4.
Lib.Inst. Will'mus heres Regeri de Huntingfeld fuit in minori aetate 1348 et tunc p'sentavit Rex Edwardus tertius.
          To the rectorie belongeth an house w'th _____(*blank*) acres of gleabe now in possession of the incumbent. Mr Attorny S'r Edward
9 Ed. 2   Cooke[34] detaynes 2 acres worth 40s yeerly & others in the towne
Joh'es   other p'ts of the gleabe. All tithes are p'd in kinde save that by their
de Fress- custome they pay no haye but 3d for an acre of medowe 5d for

37

cowe & calfe where neyther tenth nor seventh fall & for a tithe calfe 3s 4d & for a seventh after the rate. For a tithe lambe 20d no tithe milke nor cheese 4d for an hempland of a pecke sowing. For firing, an harthen at Christmas. In it are 3 Mannours 1. Cookely Hall L: S'r John Heveningham from his father S'r Arthur &c.[35] The fines arbitrable, services ordinarie. Woman hath no dower. Coppyhold to the eldest. Some of the tenauntes pay rent hennes.

2. Rowells S'r John Lord from his father he from Rowses & they from Heveninghams. 3. Cookeley Graunge belonged to Metingham Colledge Mr Pettes now Lord by purchase of Mr John Smyth of Blickling.[36]

Copdock n Sf 13

L.val.
Domsd.   Rect.val. 9.12.0½. Dec. 14.7¼. Subsid. 12s Proc. 4s Syn. 2.8d
9 Ed.2   Richardus de Copdock est patronus eiusdem et d'n's 9 Ed.2.

69   <center>Cornerd magna u Sd 5</center>

Cornerd parva u Sd 5

....

(*Tanner transcript*: 'Cotton Neve MS 4to p.70.

In the South Chappel is a Tombe wherin are buryed the Hemenhalls whose arms are on the windows right ag'st the Tombe & they bear or on a Fesse between 2 Cheverons g. 3 Escalops arg. There was also a fair Tombe on the North side of the Chancel where lay buryed as Men say S'r Wi'm Wolfe al's Wingfield but is defaced by the rudeness of some.')

(*Transcript by Tom Martin*: 'To the parsonage belongeth a Convenient & well seated house with about 26 acres Glebe. The patron Will'm Pretyman of Bacton who bought it of Tho's Tyrrell of Gipping. All Tythes paid in kind save for Lactage. They pay 2d every Cow, and 1d for every Heifer of one Year, and 2d for every Heifer of two Years. And 4d for the fruit of each Orchard.[37]

MS Q'o 70')

....

(*TA transcript*:   'S.Cove)

72   Covehithe c   al's Northales
           A Vicarage valued at 5.6.8. the tenthe 10.8d.
Domsd.   Prior de Wangforth h't eam in Proprios usus.

(*Note by PLN which may be part of the original text*: 'Ballivus de Blithing capit wrec: maris nomine d'ni R. in tota villa de North aling a portu de Benacre v'su' le south mere'.)

....

73   <center>Combes p Sd 9</center>

....

38

....

Cretyngham h Sf 10

Domsd. Prior eccl'ie S'ti Edmundi de Gypwico h't eccl'ia in p'prios usus. Aest. 20 marc. Vicarius h't mansu' cu' 5 acris terre. Aest. vicar. 40s Proc. 7s 6d Syn. 2s.

L.val. Vicar. val. 9.10.10. Dec. 19.1d Subs. 6.8d.

The Vicarie presentative the King patro'. In it are 1. Mannour of Cretingha' alias Tyes, the L: Mr Rivet of Brandeston from his father Andrew Ryvet (who purchased it _____ (blank) [38] The White rents about 10 li p' ann'. Keeps court baron hath waif & straye.

2. Maneriu' de Harolds. The King Lord hath 4 or 5 tena'ts.

3. Maneriu' de Cretingha' belongth (sic) to th'improp'atio' & is in the handes of Lyonell Wythe yeoman.

3. (sic) Manerium _____ (blank) the L; Mr John Cornwalleys of Earle Soh'm. The fines of all these are arbitrable & the coppyholdes by the custome of them all fall to the yongest sonne.

....

Dalinghoo eh Sf 4

P't of it in Wilford the least p't in Loes hundred.

Domsd. D'n's Robertus de Ufford est p'ronus illius. Aest. 20 marc. Proc. 7.6d Syn. 2s.

L.val. Rect. valet 13.6.8. Dec. 26s 8d Subs. 24s.

9 Ed.2 D'n's Comes Norff. 9 Ed.2.

The patron S'r Anthony Wingfield. All tithes p'd in kind save cheese w'ch they pay not nor ever did nor ough in lieu therof.

In it are 1. the Man: of Dalingho 2. Dalingho Campsee 3. Dalingho Earle 4. Bredfeld Campse. Of the 1 & 4 Lord S'r Anthony Wingfeld of 2 & 3 the heire of Bull a yeoma'. [39] The fines are arbitrable. The custome giveth the coppyholdlandes to the yongest sonne.

....

(TA transcript: 'Debach h Sf 4

Aest. cum Boulge L.val. Domsd. nihil.

D'na Margaretta Regina Angliae D'na villae 9 E.2.

The townesmen pay 15 tithe cheeses.')

The Mannour of Debache belongs to S'r Anthony Wingfeld bought of S'r Robert Drury of Hawsted to whome it descended from his father.

The coppyholdes holden in Gavelkinde.

....

Dynnyngton l Sf 9

Once it belonged to John Phillips L: Bardolph &c but now it appertayneth to the w'shipfull familie of the Rouses.[40]

Domsd. W'mus de Reppes est patronus illius. Aest. 50 marc. Proc. 7.6d Sy' 3s.

L.val.	Rect. val. 36.3.4. Dec. 3.12.4¼ Subs. 3.4.0.
9 Ed.2	W'm's de Bovill et Radulphus de Hardrichshall D'ni 9 Ed.2.

....

Drenkeston t Sd 4   Drenkeston

Domsd.	Aest. 16 marc. Rect. val. 16.17.1. Dec. 33.8½ Subs. ('30s' *TA transcript: illegible in original*)
9 Ed.2	Thomas de Loveyne D'n's 9 Ed.2.

(*TA transcript*:   'Dunnyworth d Sf 11
Comes Marescallus est p'ronus istius. Aest. 6 marc. Proc. 3s 4d
Rect. val. 4.10s Dec. 9s D'n's villae Comes Norff.')

....

88	Easton c Sf 3 Easton nesse

The most easterly p't of all Englande.[41]

Domsd.	Easton Bavent Thomas de Bavent est p'ronus istius. Rector h't mansu' cu' 8 acris terre. Pr. 7.7½. Syn. 2s.
L.val.	Rect. val. 12 li Dec. 14s Subs. 20s.
9 Ed.2	Thomas de Bavent D'n's 9 Ed.2.

Easton h Sf 10

Domsd.	D'n's Edwardus Charles est p'ronus eiusd' Pr. 7.6. Sy. 2.5d.
L.val.	Rect. val. 10.18.6½ Dec. 21.10¼ Subs. 18s.
9 Ed.2	Joh'es Charles D'n's 9 Ed.2.

S'r Anthony Wingfeld patron.

89	Easton Gosbecke m Sf 8

Earle Soham h Sf 10 vide Soham infra pagina
_____(*blank*)

Earle Stonham l Sf 8 vide Stonham infra pagina
_____(*blank*)

90	O'i'u' S'torum Eyke h Sf 10

Edwardeston u Sd 5   a towne now of no great fame but in former tymes it had inhabitants in it of great honour & fame as the Lordes of Montchensy.[42]

91	Eldon r Sd 1
Spir.	Ellow b Sf 2

Rect. val. 12 li Dec. 24s Subsid. 20s. the patro' Mr Platers of Saterley.[43] To it belongeth a convenient house & a fayre new barne with about 25 acres of gleabe all tithes p'd in custome save for hartsilver they pay 1d as much for port. For lactage for every cowe 1d.
Thomas Lone Yeoma' built a new church porche at his owne proper charges.[44]
There is only the Mannour of Ellowe in this towne which belongeth to Mr Platers of Saterlye.

Temp.	The Mannour of Ellowe once belonged to Wachesha' who also was

L: of Oxnedes & Marlingford in Norff. whose d. & h. was mar. to S'r
Thomas Gerbridge & by his d. & sole heire it descended to Edmond
Barrye by (*sic*) whose 2 d'r & heire was maryed to Bardolph sans
yssue & then to Aslack who by hir had yssue one d. marryed to
Plater of Saterlye to whome in right of his wife this mannour fell, of
who'e is lineally descended _____ (*blank*) Plater now of
Saterley.[45]

South Elmham

Manerium pertinebat Ep'o Norwicens' ante p'mutatione' facta' a
Ruggo Ep'o ad Henr. 8 Reg. Angl. terrar' ep'atus p' terris Monasterij
S'ti Benedicti de Hulme. Ten't 12 Hen. 7 Computu' Reddit. Assis.
liber. tenent. et nat. 34.7.3¼. Firma fedi. ter. decassat. 13 17 11.
Firma piscarie p' totu' domu' de Southelmha' 2s. Firma fedi terrar'
dominical' 8.11.9. Reddit. Alteri 15.5d.

(*Note by PLN which may be part of the original text*: 'In & about
this town are the parishes of Elmham St.James St.Crosse All Saints
Saint Nicolas St.Mich. archangel Homersfeld St.Margaret Saint Peter
all valewed in the Kings books & paying tenths.')

....

(94)
S'te Genefeve Ewston q Sd 6

(*Note by PLN which may be part of original text*: 'See Fakenham
both together valewed at 3:7:11 decimae 26 sol. and nine pence half
penny.')

Exnynge r Sd 1

A towne of greater fame hertofore then nowe For it was famous for
the birth of Etheldred the virgin, daughter unto the kinge Annas.
also for the conspiracie of Ralfe earle of the Eastangles against
William the Norman, lastly for the way which Hervay the first
Bishop of Elye caused to be made from hence to Elye, but now by
reason of the neereness of Newmarket, it beginneth to decrease.[46]
(*Note by PLN which may be part of original text*: 'Vicaria in
Fordham deanry valor 13:7:6d Dec. 26 9d ad no'i'u' ep'i.')

95
Fakenham Magna q Sd 6

Fakenham parva q Sd 6

*Note by PLN on another fragment may be a version of the original
text*: 'Fakenham parva by Euston the valew of both together in the
Kings books £3 7s 11d decimae 26 sol. 9d obol.')

(96)
Farnham d Sf 11

....

97
Felsham t Sd 4

....

98
Fernham Martyn t Sd 4

Fernham o'i'u' S'tor' t Sd 4

99   Felixstow f Sf 12   Filchestowe

(Note by PLN which may form part of original text: 'Valor 5.9.7. Dec: 10:11d ob.')

Finboro magna p Sd 3   Fynburgh

(100)   Finboro Parva p Sd 3   Fyneburgh

(Note by PLN on another fragment may form part of original text: 'Finboro Fynebergh Fyneburgh parva called the chappell of little Finborow valued in the Kings books at 33 shill. 4d decimae 3: shill. 4d'. *Original text crossed out and illegible)*

Fynningham k Sd 7

101   +   Flempton s Sd 2

Domsd.   Aest. 8 marc. Rect. val. 5 li Dec. 10s Patr. D'n's Thomas Kytso'

L.val.   Abbas S'ti Ed'i D'n's 9 Ed.2.

My Lady Kitson Lady of the towne.[47]

Flixton a Sf 1

Domsd.   Aest. marc. 6½ Proc. 5s Syn. 11d.

Lib. val. nihil.

9 Ed.2   D'n's vel Edmundus Bacon vel W'm's del Auncy.

102   Flixton b Sf 2 instead of Felixto' so named of Felix the first Bishop of these p'ts.[48]

L.val.   Flixton vicar. val. 6 li Dec. 12s.

Flouton n Sf 8   Floketon

(TA transcript:

'Domsday Joh'es Boun est p'ronus istius Aest. 6 marc. Proc. 4s Syn. 12d Rect. val. 31-9-9½ Dec. 6-11½ vel ¾.')

103   Fordham r Sd 1

(PLN note which may be part of original text: 'Vicarie valor 13.6.8. Dec. 26.8.')

Fordley c Sf 3

In Fordley besides the Mannour of Middleton & Fordley which belongeth to Mr Page of Framyngha' who bought it of Mr Hunings of Aye who had it of Mr.Tylney who bought it of Mr.Bedingfeld of Dichingha' to whome he had solde it before (it continued in the Tylneys for many years together) is also the Mannour of Brenfenne belonging to Mr.Brooke of London who bought it of S'r Owen Hopton. [49] Both the townes of Middleton & Fordley are but one towne & in every rate Midleton beareth 2 parts, Fordley 1. Fordley is a personage p'sentative of Mr.Page. In these townes is a mannour called Austens belonging to Mr.Jenny of Knatshall.[50]

....

Framisden l Sf 7

4 Lib.Inst. Ep'us W'm's appropriavit Abbatisse et convent. minorissar' London de regula S'te Clare eccl'ia de Framisden ad instantia' Isabelle Regine Angl. reservata canonica obedientia iurisdictio'e visitiatio'e &c.

pensione unius marce annua et eccl'ie Cathedrali Nor'ci 2 solid. et 8 denarior' p' equales portio'es solvend' ad sinodos pasche et michaelis, vicaria et portio'e assignanda vicarie et eius primis fructibus. Dat' Londo' 31 Maij 1348.

....

Fresenfeld l Sf 9

(*TA transcript which may form part of Chorography text*:

'Freston
There is part of an house loftily built not far from the channell called commonly Freston Tower.')

....

Fritton a Sf 1
(*PLN note*: 'val. 3¹:3s:4d dec.13:4d')

....

(*PLN heading on Chorography paper*:
'Gadgrave'

....

Geddinge t Sd 4

....

Glemham magna d Sf 11

Glemham parva d Sf 11
Of theise townes have the ancient familye of the Glemhams in Suff. taken their cognomination.[51]

113   Gorleston a Sf 1
A towne by Yarmouth wheras yet is seene a tower the remnant of an ancient monasterye[52] (*TA transcript adds* 'called little Yarmouth Gorleston and Southtowne al's Gernemuth p'va valor 11 li Dec. 22 sol. annexa vicaria')

Groton u Sd 5

(114)   Grundesboro g Sf 5
(*Note by PLN which may be part of original text*: 'in the church partie per chevron azure & gules 3 standing covered cups or')[53]

....

115   Hacheston h Sf 10
Commonly called Parham Hason.

(*Note by PLN on Chorography paper*:
'Herthurste cum capella de Boxted 29:14:2d dec: 59s 5d')

116   Hadley o Sd 5
A market towne kept on the Monday famous for the wolling cloth that is made there in great abundance. It is also renowned for the buryall of Guthrum (Stow calleth him Gythram) or as others call him Gormo a danish king, who was interred in this towne. For when

43

as Alfred had brought him to be a Christian & to be baptised (whose name was then called Athelstane) he appointed him to rule these countryes of the East Angles. It was then called Headleaga. This Gythram or Athelstane dyed a'o D'ni 890.[54]

117
Temp.

Halesworth

A market towne kept on the tuesday the priviledge wherof was purchased by Richard Argentein in the tyme of Henry 3d. This towne for many yeares together belonged unto the Argenteins[55] who were Lordes & patrons therof untill by a daughter & heire who matched with the Alingtons it was with other mannours translated into the familye of the Allingtons wherin it continueth to this daye. The Lord keepeth Court and Leete. The fines are at the Lordes pleasure. This towne hath the priviledge & keepeth a fayre 3 whole dayes, to wit St.Lukes eeve, St.Lukes day & the day followinge. In this towne was a parke & in it a goodly house, the one nowe ruinated & the other disparked, the parke was let out by Coppye by old S'r Giles Allington knight[56] when he left Suffolke to dwell at Horsheath Hall in Cambridgeshire, who was great grandfather to Giles Allington Esquier who now is possessed therof.
The taske of this towne is _____ (blank)

Spir.

It is a personage p'sentative valued at xx^li the tenth 40s the proxies 7s 6d. Synodalls 12d.
The Patron is Mr.Alington of Horsheath in Cambridgshire. To the parsonage belongeth a' house moated with outhouses garden & orchard & 22 acres of gleabe, 12 acres wherof are mostly pastour, 10 medow grounde all laying about & neere his house except 5 acres which lay in the parishe of Holton about a myle from the house, which 5 acres though they are in Parochia de Holton yet are they inter loc(a) decimabilia de Halesworth. Unto the Parsonage or Rectorie belongeth a Mannour called the Rectorye Mannour wherunto appertayne 20 Copyhold Tenants, ten of them having mansion houses.
The p'sent incumbent this yeare 1602 is John Argall a gentleman borne & an ancient batchelour of Divinitie, who beareth parti per fesse argent & vert a pale co'nterchanged, on the first 3 lions heads arrached gules, a mullet sable for difference.

118

Hargrave s Sd 2
A Personage valued at 4.11.8d the tenth 9s 2d.

	Harcksted n Sf 13	Herkestead
A p'sonage	valued at 11.3.9. the tenth 22.4½.	

119

Harleston p Sd 3

Hasylwood d Sf 11

120

Hasketon c Sf 5
Called ordinarily Woodbridge Hason.

Haverill x Sd 8
A market towne

44

(121)	Hawkden x Sd 8
	Helmyngham m Sf 7

122	Hawsted s Sd 2 Hasted

....

123   Hemyngton m Sf 8

Camden   In this towne Baldwin le Petteur held certayne landes per seriantiam pro qua debuit facere die natali D'ni singulis annis coram D'no Rege Anglie unu' saltu', unu' suffletu' et unu' bombulum (vel ut aliter legitur) per saltu' sufflu' et Pettu'.[57]

124   Hemley f Sf 12   Helmelee

Spir.   Hengrave s Sd 2   Hongrave
A parsonage valued at 9.7.1. The tenth 18.8½ the subsid. 16s.
The patron S'r Thomas Kitson.

(125)   Henlye m Sf 7

Spir.   A vicarage valued at 10 li 10d the tenth 20s 1d the subsidie 18s.

Domesd.   Sacrista Norwici hab't eam in proprios usus.

Spir.   Hevenyngham c Sf 3
A p'sonage valued at 11 6 8 the tenth 22 8d the subsidye 20s.

Domesd.   Prior S'ti Neoti est patronus illius. Rector h't mansu' cu' 12 acris terre.
The Patron now is the Queenes Ma'tie.

Henham b Sf 2

....

Spirit.   Hensted b Sf 3
It is a p'sonage p'sentative valued at 12 li the tenth 24s the subsidie 20s the Procur. 7s 6d the Synod. 2s.

The Patron Mr.William Sydnor esquier who purchased the patronage therof together with the Mannour of Henstead of Mr.Humfrey Yermouth of Benacre. The p'sent incumbent 1602 Mr.Laurence Beighton.

The gleabes are 7 acres of hardland pastures & 25 acres of arrable in all 32 acres a convenient dwelling house a barne stable & other necessarie houses of office.

All tithes are p'd in their kinde as they fall savinge for lactage they pay a penny for every cowe & if they have 7 piggs, calves or geese, the p'son hath one for tithe, allowing unto the p'tie soe paying the same 1½d & if he hath but 6 or under that nomber then the p'son hath no tithe but for every of them an ½d & for every colt unwrought 1d whether they be fedde on common or elsewhere within the sayd parishe.

Temp.   There are within the sayed towne 2 Mannours suite v'c't the Mannor of Henstead Parpoundes purchased by the sayd Mr.Will'm Sydnor of Mr _____ (blank) Brewster of Wrentha'[58] which sayd Mannour some saye was sometyme a member of the Mannour of Wrentham &

45

was then called Wrentham Parpoundes but is not true but is a mannour absolute, unto which now belongeth Court leet & Court Baron. The other is the Mannour of Henstead Bounds purchased by the sayd Mr.Willia' Sydnour of Mr.Humfry Yermouth abovesayd of Beanacre, he holdeth Court Baron upon the same. The L. hath fishing of the Rivers fowling hauking &c. to himselfe wayf & estrayes felons goodes &c. The Tenauntes owe suite & service at every court. The Copye & free Rents are differing & not all after one rate but some more some lesse, the fine at the will of the Lord. It payeth Taske _____ (*blank*)

(*See continuation in Appendix*)

(*Note by PLN on Chorography paper*:
'Horningsherth mag. valor 10:17:8½ Dec: 21 9¼
Horningsherth p'va 5:5:6½ Dec: 5s 7¼')

Spir.	Hesset Sd 4

A p'sonage valued at 12.17.1 the tenthe 25 9¼ the subsidie 22s the Proc. _____ (*blank*) Synod. _____ (*blank*)

Hintlesham n Sf 13   Hynclesha'

Domsd.	D'n's Rex Angl. patronus eiusdem. Aest. 34 marc. Synod. 4s.
L.val.	Rect. val. 33 9.7. Dec. 3.6.11½ Subs. 3li
Inq.	Hintlesham D'ni Joh'es Talbott: Margeria Pipparde temp. Ed.2.
L.4 Inst.	Appropriata fuit eccl'ia custodi et scolaribus Regis Universitatis Cantabrigiensis p' W'm Ep'u' salva vicaria et habitatio'e et congrua portior' p' vicario. D'no Ep'o et successoribus suis et eiusde' no'i'atio'e reservata pensio'e duar' marcar' annue Ep'o. Dat. Norwici 6 Jan. 1349.

Hoo h Sf 10

In it is an ancient house belonging to Sir Anthonye Wingfeld called Godwins.

Honington q Sd 6   Honewetene

130   Higham n Sf 13

(*TA transcript*:

'Spirit.	Hepworth q Sd 6
Domsd.	A parsonage valued at 13-17-3½ the tenth 27-8-¾ subsid. 24s')

131   Hinderclay q Sd 6   Hilderkele

L.val.	Rect. val. 9.19.4½ Dec. 19.11¼ Subs. 16s.
Inq.	The L. therof in the tyme of E:2 was Abbas S'ti Ed'i.

....

(*Tanner transcript*: 'Holton Neve MS 4to p.132 (*Holton St.Peter*)
In the Southside of the Church is a Chapel where are 2 graves, the one never had any brass, the other is reaved. In the Windows is this Coate arg. fretty of 8 p..... azur charged w'th a fleur de Lis on each crossing or, on a canton g. a Soleil of the 3d.')[59]

Domsd.   Will'mus de Boyton est patronus illius. Aest. 6 mar. Proc. 6.8d. Syn. 2s.

Lib.val.   Rect. val. 7.14.7.Dec. 15.5½ Subs. 12s.

Holton D'n's Will'mus de Boyton tempore Regis Edw.2.

(*TA transcript*:   'Holbroke n Sf 13

Domsd.   Joh'es de Holbroke quondam erat patronus ejusd' postea vero appropriata est Abbati et Conventui de Almarlia. Proc. 7-6d Sy. 12d.

L.val.   Rector. val. 11-11-3. Dec. 23-1½ Subs. 20s.')

Hopton a Sf 1

Domsd.   Prior Norwici h'et ea' in proprios usus.

+   Hopton q Sd 6

Rector. val. 13.4.2. Dec. 26.5. Subs. 22s.

In it are 2 mannours 1. the mannour of Browns w'h hertofore belonged to the L.Bourchier E: of Essex & so descended by right of inheritance to Robert the Last E: of Essex who sold it to Mr. ——— (*blank*) Ashfield to whose sonne & heire it now appertayneth.60

2. the mannour of Cockets.

The Freehold holden of the Kinge.

No epitaphe in the church or chauncell.

....

Horyngflete a Sf 1   Heringflete

Domsd.   Prior S'ti Olavi h't eam in p'p'ios usus. Aest. 10 marc. Proc. ...... Sy' 13d. L.val. nihil.

9 E 2   Catherina filia Osberti d'na 9 E.2

(*TA transcript:*   Homersfield b

Rect. val. 5-6-8 Dec. 10-8d.')

136   Hoorham l Sf 9

(*Original illegible: TA transcript:*

'Domsday Petrus Jernegan est patronus illius aest. 18 marc. Proc. 6s 8d Syn. 3s 4d.

L.val.   Rect. val. 12-7-1. Dec. 24-8½ Subs. 22s

Rog'us filius et haeres Will'i de Hungerford in custodia Joh'is de Grey et Petr. Gernegan 9 Ed.2.')

Hosely c Sf 4   Houslie

(*Original partly illegible: TA transcript:*

'Domsd.   Comes Marescallus est patronus istius. Rector h'et mansum cum duodecim acris terre. Aest. 18 marc. proc. 7-6d Syn. 2s 8d.

L.val.   Rector. val. 12-6-8d Dec. 25-8 Subs. 22s.

Comes Norff. D'n's 9 E.2

Tax. cum Shatsham 43s 4d ded. 30s redd. 13-4.

In it are 1. the man. of Holeslee belonging to the Duke of Norff. by whose attaynder it fell into the Kings hands who gave it to Tho. Howard now E. of Suff.

2. Mannor. of Sutton in Holeslee the Dukes heretofore now the Earl of Suff. as the others before.

3. Mannor of Cadwellhall belongeth to John Harbert a yeoman his sonn by purchase of ———— (*blank*) Purpett of Newborne in Colneys.')

137   Hoxon l Sf 9   A towne hertofore called Hegilsdon, notable & famous for the martyrdome of Edmond the King whome the danes (because he would not renounce the Christian Religion) bounde fast unto a tree & shotte his bodye full of arrowes & so most cruelly martyred him. In this place afterward was a Palace belonging to the Bishop of Norwich very fayre & gallant untill they not long since changed it & other the lands of the Bishopricke for them of the monasterie of St.Benets in Norff.[61]

Hundred of Hoxon by the bishop of Norw'ch 12 Hen. 7 let out to farms of xls. p' ann'. Rents of Assises of freeholders 12.4.10½ for their work iiis iiijd p' terris assertis 2.5.3½. Reddit. Assis. nat. tenent. 10.19.ob. q'rt' & (*blank*)d. Reddit. diversoru' cotagioru' 8.4d de operibus liber. tene't. 9d. All these are to the mannour of Hoxon.

Maneriu' Rectorie de Hoxon. Ep'us d'n's. Reddit. assis. liber. tenent.

Nund. 1.   3.3.1¼. Reddit. assis. nat. tenent. 3.9.3¾. Reddit. assis. diversoru'
Fest. St.   cotagioru' 4s 6d. Reddit. diversoru' tenent. pro quada' consuetudine'
Ed'i Regis   vocata cornuculu' nunc in denarios 9 3¾. Fedi firma 29.4.5¾. Firma
2. S'ti   terraru' decassat. 2.16.4. novus reddit. ter. decassat. 1.10d. Reddit.
Laurentij   mobiles 1 q'rteriu' fr'i 7 bushells avenaru' 11 capones 56 galline, 180 ova. Egestiamentu' veteris p'ci 4 li Firma Tolneti 3 nundinates 10s. Firma Piscarie 6.8d.

((*Note by PLN which may form part of original text:* 'Hoxne vicaria valor 17:3:6d ob. dec. 34s 4d p'end. ad Collat' Ep'i.')

....

(138)   Huntingfeld b Sf 3
(*Original partly illegible: TA transcript:*
There were in the time of King Edw. the 1st Barons that took their denomination of this town.[62]

Spirit.   Haeres d'ni Will'i de Huntingfeild militis est patronus ejusd.
Domsd.   Rector h'et mansum cum 30 acris terre. Proc. 7s 6d Syn. 2s.
Lib.val.   Rect. val. 13-6-8. Dec. 26-8d Subs. 24s. Cantaria ib'm 4 li 17-6d Dec. 9-9-½.

Rog'us Huntingfeild filius et haer. D'ni Will'i Huntingfeild praesent. A'o 1328. Ejus haeres Will'us fuit in minori aetate 1348 et praesentavit Rex Edwardus tertius. D'n's Will'us de Huntingfeild miles praesent. 1361 et 1367.

Comitissa Suffolciae D'na Isabella p'sent. 1396. D'n's Will'us de la Pole Comes et March. Suff. p'sent. 1446. Joh'es de la Pole Dux. Suffolc. 1487. Margaretta de le Pole d'na manerij de Huntingfeild ratione dotis suae 1510 Carolus Brandonius Dux Suff. 1546. Henricus Carew Baro Hunsdon 1571.')

139	Icklingham r Sd 1
Domsd.	S'ti Jacobi aest. 16 mar. O'i'u' S'tor' 20 marc.
Lib.val.	Rect. S'ti Jacobi val. 11.11.5½. Dec.23 1¾ Subs. 20s.
	Rect. S'tor' 12.17.2. Dec. 25 9½ Subs. 22s.
9 Ed.2	Abbas S'ti Ed'i D'n's 9 Ed.2.

Southelmham St.James b Sf 2

Domsd.	Aest. 12 marc.
L.val.	Rect.val. 8¹ Dec. 16s Subs. 14s.
9 Ed.2	Ep'us Norwici D'n's de Southelmha' 9 Ed.2

(*Note by PLN which may form part of original text:*
'S'ct. Mich'is arch'i 4.18.9d Dec: 9:10 ob.
S'c'i Petri ib'm 8¹ dec: 16 sol.
S'ctae Margaretae ib'm 6:3:11: dec: 12:3d ob.
S'c'i Nicholai ib'm 6 li dec: 12.
Omnium s'c'or' ib'm 8 li dec. 16 sol.')

140	Ilketeshalle St Johns
Domsd.	(*Partly illegible entry: TA transcript:*
	Aestimat. 13 marc. Syn. 9d L: val: nihil.
9 E'2	D'ni de Ilketshalle Comitissa Marescalla Guido Ferre Jacobus Ilketshall 9 E.2.
	Ilketshall St Andreae in Decanatu Wangford Valor 5 li 13s 4d. Dec. 11-4d.
	Ilketishale S'ae Margarettae Vicaria 5-13-9 Dec. 11-4-ob. S'c'i Laur. S'c'i Joh'is')

Iken d Sf 11

(*Original partly illegible: TA transcript:*

'Domesd.	Comes Marescallus est patronus ejusd. Rector h't mansum cum 6 acris terrae. Aest. 10 marc. Syn. 23d. Rect. val. 6-13-4. Dec. 13-4d.
9 Ed.2.	Rogerus Shirmyon vel Comes Norff. D'n'i 9 E.2.')

141	++	Ikesworth q Sd 6	Ixworth

In this towne was an ancient Priorye founded by Gilbert Blunt baron of Ikesworth who of this towne had the title of his Baronye. the last of which Barons was slayne at Lewes a'o 48 Hen.3 & left behinde him as heires his two sisters Agnes wife of William Creketot & Rose wife of Robert de Valens. Camden.63

Domsd.	Ikesworth app'at'r priori et convent' de eade' Aest. 20 marc.
9 Ed.2	L.val. nihil. Edmundus de Pakenham et W'm's de Criketot d'ni 9 Ed.2.

The church is impropriatt without vicarie. The p'sonage is donative & the minister stipendiarie. All tithes are p'd in kinde save for haye they pay 4d an acre in medowes. 4d cowe & calfe & no lactage. If their wood be bound they pay tithe, if loose none.

The market is kept on the Frydaye. In it are 2 fayres in the yeere 1. May day 2. Lukes day. Taske 55.4d no deduct. The Mannour of Ikesworth belongeth to S'r John Carrell of Sussex from his father to whome it came by his wife being d. & h. of Mrs.Cuddington to whome Mr.Cuddingto' hir husband gave it by his testament

49

absolutely.[64] Who had of King Hen.8 in exchaunge of the Mannour of Cuddingto' in Surrey now called Nonesuch. It belonged before the dissolution of abbyes to the Prior of Ikesworth. This Man'our is held in capite the fine arbitrable. No extraordinary service done by the tenauntes. It is called the Priorye man: keeps court & leete hath wayfes & straye. S'r Nicholas Bacon as Steward of the libertye of St Edmund of Burye keepeth a leete in the towne by force for he hath usually kept it on Buckton greene & not in the towne as appeareth by his rolles & streat.

Ikesworth thorp q Sd 6

Domsd.	App'at'r Pr. et Conv. de Ixworth. Aest. 8 marc. L.val. nihil.
9 Ed 2	Thomas de Pakenham d'n's 9 Ed.2. Taske 36.4d. no deduct.

142

Ikeworth s Sd 2

(*TA transcript:* 'Aest. 16 marc. Rect. val. 7-11-5½. Dec. 15-1¾ Subs. 12s.
Patr. D'n's Will.Harvy. Tho. de Ikesworth D'n's 9 Ed.2.')

Burnt Ileye u Sd 5

(*Original partly illegible and incomplete; TA transcript:*

'Domsd.	Appropriatur Abb'i et Conv. S'c'ae Osythae. Aest. 15 marc. Vic.
Lib.val.	13 marc. Carn. 7½d Vicar. val. 8 li Dec. 16 Subs. 6s8d.
9 E.2.	Abbas S'c'ae Osithae et Joh'es de Shelton D'ni 9 E.2.

The patron of the Vicarie is Antony Roper of Farningham in Kent Esq. from his father who hath also the Impropriation and bought it of Mr.Hunnyngs.

To the vicary belongeth now only an house and one acre of gleabe. There ought to be 10 or 12 acres and a pension of 8 marc. p' ann' paid to the Vicar but if the Vicar can keep himself honest they that detayne those gleabes and marks from him will take order he shall be an honest poor vicar.[65]

All the small tithes are paid in kinde.

The mannor of Burnt Illey belongeth to S'r Robert Jermyn from his father S'r Ambrose who bought it of Mr.Thorp a lawyer and he of _____ (*blank*)[66] It belonged heretofore (*sic*) and was called Sheltonhall. This mannour keeps Court and lete. In it was a Chappell S'ti Jacobi. They say it was a markett town before it was burnt.')

143

Moncks Ileye u Sd 5

The Whole & only Mannour belongeth to the deane & Chapter of Canterbury who w'th the Lordship keepe also the Leete. The customes to the eldest. The fines arbitrable.

Domsd.	Aest. 30 marc.
L.val.	Rect. val. 13.18.9. Dec. 27.10¾ Subs. 24s. Prior Cantuarie D'n's 9 Ed.2.

The Archbishop of Canterburie is patron. It hath 20 acres of glebe. No customes for all tithes p'd in specie.

This towne is not of the diocese of Norw'ch but a peculiar to the Bishop of London.[67] So in all lawe matters the towne had a iurisdiction in it selfe not subiet to the Abbot of Burye which first of all was agreed upon for a certayn yeerly rent to be p'd to the Abbot by the Prior of Canterbury. But all these since the suppression cease & are not in Use.

In the church is not one escutcheon or monument & yet in the towne are many fayre houses & sweet dwellings for ayer. From this Towne came S'r James Hobart attorny generall to K.Hen.7 here were his ancestors borne. Of him are descended the Hobartes in Norff.[68]

Ingham q Sd 6

Domsd.	Aest. 18 marc. Rect. val. 12.16.0½ Dec. 25 7¼ Subs. 22s
	L.val. (*blank*)
9 Ed.2	Abbas S'ti Ed'i D'n's 9 Ed.2.

....

Kenton 8 (*sic. should be h*) Sf 10

Domsd.	Prior de Butlee h't eccl'iam in proprios usus.
L.val.	Vic. val. 8 li Dec. 16s Subsid. 6s 8d.
Ed.2	Tempore Ed.2 D'n's ville Nigellus de Kenetone.
20 Ed.3	De Margaretta de Kenton tenente maneriu' de Kenton p' servicio unius feodi militis de Eva de Ufford q'd Ivo de Kenton nup' tenuit de Rogero Fil: Osberti: xls.

....

(*TA transcript*: 'Kessgrave g S f 5   Kessingrave'
Original text partly illegible: TA transcript:
Prior de Butley h'et Ec'iarn (*sic*) in p'p'os usus et facit deservire Eccl'ie per capellanu'. Syn. 2s.
Nihil h'et'r in lib.val.
Tempore Edwarde 2di Dominus villae D'n's Joh'es Holbroke.')

Kesland a Sf 1   Kesinglande

4 Lib.	W'm's Ep'us appropriavit eccl'ia de Kesland Abbatisse et monialibus
Inst.	domus minorissaru' London de regula S'te Clare ad instantia' Isabelle Anglie regine (qua' domu' minorissar' fundavit Edmundus Comes Lancastrie) reservata vicaria et portione assignando vicario Ep'o, canonica obedientia, iurisdictio'e, visitatio'e &c. loco primor' fruct'm pensione duar' marcar' annua, ep'o eccl'ie cathedrali 4 solidor' in sinodis michaelis et pasche equalibus porcio'ibus, salvis primis fructibus vicariar'. Dat' London 31 Maij 1348.

Kettlebaston o Sd 3   Ketelmerston

Domsd.	Kettelverstone aest. 20 marc. Carn. 7½d.
	Rectoria valet 13.6.8. Dec. 26s 8d Subsid. 24s.

The Lord is patron of the Parsonage presentative. To the p'sonage belongeth 16 acres of gleabe. All p'd in specie. The Mannour belongeth to W'm Appleton gent. given unto him by his mothers brother, Edward Clarke esq: late Lord of the same who had it from the Kinge.[69] It is called Kettlebarston Hall, the fines arbitrable, customes to the eldest.

The Leet is the Kings.

There was also somtymes another Mannour called Barrards but long since so suppressed & dispersed that no tract visible therof at this day appeareth.

Knatshall q Sd 6

....

151   Kirtlow a Sf 1   Kirkeley

(152)   Kirton f Sf 13

(PLN note which may form part of Chorography text: on separate fragment: 'Kirkton in Colneys deanry 10:13:4 dec: 21 sol. 4d.'

PLN note which may form part of Chorography text: 'Kirketon al's Sholey Saumforth deanry valor 20 li dec. 40 sol.')

....

154   Langham q Sd 6

(Original crossed out and illegible: TA transcript:

Domsd.   Aestimat. 10 marc.

L.val.   Rector. val. 5-6-10½. Dec. 11-8-¼

9 Ed.2   Will'us de Criketot D'n's 9 E.2.')

          Lanham u Sd 5   Lavenham

A market towne.

Domsd.   Aest. 28 Marc. Carnag. 7½.

L.val.   Rect.val. 20 li 2 11 Dec. 40.3½ Subs. 36s.

9 Edw. 2 Comes Oxonie D'n's.

Spir.   A p'sonage presentative by the L: of the Mannour of Lavenha'.

To the p'sonage belongeth a Seignorie or Mannore called Maneriu' Rectorie de Lavenham unto which belonge divers tenantes. The Parson incombent keepeth courtes, the fines at the alienation are arbitrarie. There belonge 140 acres of demeanes or gleabe. All tithes p'd in specie save a small portion of tythe corne belonging now to a barne called Monkes barne & is still the Earle of Oxfords somtyme belonging to the Priorie of Colne in Essex and as by tradition is receyved was proportioned first for the allowance of certayn monks in Colne priorie which yeerlye at certayne tymes came to Lanham to preache. There was a parke about 30 yeers since now disparked contay'ing some 900 acres of ground for w'ch the Parson had tithe a fee bucke & a fee doe, but of late dayes after a long suyte he hath recovered xx^{li} p' ann'.[70]

Temp.   There is but one Lordship in the towne called Maneriu' de Lavenham

1. Lanham where there be 2 sortes of coppyholders. The one called Burgage

2. Overhall holde where the fines are certayne as double the Lordes rent without

3. Nether impeachment of wast: the other are such as dwell w'thout the

Hall   Burrough for whome the fines are arbitrarie at the will of the Lorde. The Leete belongeth to the Lord who also giveth the benefice.

Vide p.317

Lawshall u Sd 5

Domsd.   Lausele aest. 30 marc. Vicar. 8 marc. Carnag. 7½d. Rectoria valet 20
              li 2s 8½d Dec. 40s 3¼d Subsid. 36s.
              The Lord is patron. The parsonage hath 40 acres of gleabe. Their
              custome is to pay for an acre of Bullemonge iiijd for an acre of
              medowe haye iiijd for a cowe iiijd ob. for cheese & a tithe calfe xxd.
              In it are 2 mannours the chief Lawshall Hall unto which belongeth
              the Leete of the whole towne. The customes of this mannour to the
              eldest, the fines arbitrable, the Lord is S'r Robert Lee alderman of
              London who bought it of Edward Rookwood of Euston who
              purchased it of Henry Drury of Lawshall[71] whose ancestors after
              the generall suppression of Monasteries had it of the Kinge, before
              which tyme it somtyme did belong to the Abbot of Ramsye a
              monastery in Essex whose armes I finde there carved in wood
              w'thout coullours. Or on a bend azure 3 rams: heads cabashed arg.
              horned of the first. The other Mannour called Hennyngfieldes Hall
              is but litle. The Lord S'r Rob: Drury desc. to him fro' his ancestours
              in whose name it hath long continued.

                              Laxfield r Sf 9

                          ....•......

                              Layston c Sf 3
              In this towne was once an abbey of much beautye called Layston
              abbye.

                          ....•

                              Lemington f Sf 13
              (*Note by PLN may be Chorography text:* 'In the church arg't on a
              bend between 2 cotizes dancett. sab. 3 cressents or q're if not
              Gonvile.')[72]

158   Lestoft a Sf 1
              A market towne.

                              Letheryngham h Sf 10
              This towne & the Parke in it appertayneth to that worthy knight S'r
              Anthony Wingfeld who hath a goodly house in it called
              Letheryngham hall.

159   +   Levermere magna t Sd 4
Domsd.   Aest. 22 marc. Rect. val. 15 8 11½. Dec. 30.10¾ Subs. 26s.
L.val.
9 Ed 2   Abbas S'ti Ed'i D'n's 9 Ed.2.
Mr.Ward   Mr.W'm Webbe the patro' ready to be sold to Mr.John Claxton of
incumbent   Livermere magna. To it belongeth a convenient dwelling house with
              outhouses & 44 acres of gleabe wherof are pasture 10 the other
              arrable. All tithes are payd in kind save in stead of lactage they pay
              3½d for a cowe that hath a calfe, for every fallowe cowe & bullocke
              2½. Certayne houses pay a lockhenne at Christmas & are therby
              discharged of all tithes that growe in loco excepting pigge & calfe.
              No cheese. They pay for every calfe if killed & eaten 1d if weaned

ob. if all or any p't be sold the tenth pennye.

The fines arbitrable copyholdes fall to the yongest. Taske 19. 5d Deduct. 6s Reduct. 73s 5d.

In it are 2 mannours 1. Broomehall L. Mr.W'm Webbe from S'r John Carell who had it by his wife & she from the Bokenhams hir p'decessors who were Lordes therof for many yeers. Mr.Webbe selleth it to Mr.John Claxto'.
2. The Man. of Uphall L. Mr.Claxto' aboves'd from his father Hamond Claxto' of Norw'h who had it in right of his wife d. & h. of Clement Clercke clerck of the crowne office. This mannour hath no coppyholders. The free tenaunts of both mannours doe 1 dayes worke in harvest. Uphall hath besides 2 iourneys of the plough 1 duas aruras. The king keepeth Leete & hath wayf & straye.

Levermere parva q Sd 6

Domsd.	Aest. 10 marc.
L.val.	Rect. val. 6.12.11. Dec. 13.3½
9 Ed.2	Barth'us de Lyvermere d'n's 9 Ed.2.
	Taske 52.5d Deduct. 10s Reduct. 42.5d.

....

162   Lounde a Sf 1

Loudham

It is an hamlet of Petistree.
The L: therof hertofore in 9 Ed.2 was John Lowdha'.
Priorissa de Campse h't ea' in p'prios usus. Aest. Rect. 5 marc. vic. 40s. Proc. 7 6d Syn. 2s.

163   Marlesford h Sf 10

Domsd.	Thomas Saukevile est p'ronus eiusdem. Rector h't mansu' cum duodecem acris terre. Proc. 7.6. Syn. 22d.
L.val.	Rect. val. 9.6.8. Dec. 18.8d. Subs. 16s.

All tithes are p'd in kinde save for lactage they pay 1d for every cowe. Tithe wood they pay none, only an harthen at Christmas.

In it is only the Mannour of Marlesforth now appertayning to S'r Walter Devorax k't.[73]
The Woman hath no dower. The coppyhold falls to the yonger. The fine at the will of the Lorde.

....

(164)   St.Margarett of Akers b Sf 2

Melles k Sd 7

165   Melton h Sf 4

Domsd.	Prior de Ely est p'ronus illius. Proc. 6.7d Syn. 2s
L.val.	Rect. val. 9.6.8. Dec. 18.8. Subs. 16s.
9 Ed.2	Prior Eliensis D'n's 9 Ed.2.

Mannour of Melton belongs to the Deane of Elye. Keepeth court & Leete (*PLN note: part of Chorography text?:* 'hath a prison')

++   **Melford u Sd 5**   Melesford

Comonly **called Long** Melford. Here S'r Willia' Cordall mayster of

54

ab't 1573	the Rolles built a very fayre & pleasant house a'o _____ (*blank*) but now it beginneth to be ruinous.[74]
L.val.	Rect. val. 28.2.6. Dec. 56.3d. Subsid. 50s.
	Jane Allington widow sister & h. of Edward Cordall Esq. brother & heire of S'r Willia' Cordall knight M'r of the Rolles deceased is patron.[75] To the Rectorie belongeth an C acres of gleabe belonging to the p'sonage & more & 2 houses the one called the p'sonage the other the Colledge. All tithes are p'd in kinde save the herbage or pasturage of kine which is by custome.
	To the p'sonage belongeth a Mannour vid. infra & many Tenants belonging to the same. The incumbent William Gilbert.
Temp.	In this towne are 7 mannours Melford Hall, Fordall, Kentwell, Mostande, Paytons, Moncks & the Rectorie Mannour.
	Of the Mannours of Kentwell, Mostand & Payton is Lord Willia' Clopton sonne & h. of Thomas Clopton esq. deceased & the sayd Mannours have bene in the poss'ions of the Cloptons about CC yeers:[76] the Mannour of Monks belonged also to them ever since the suppression of Abbyes at what tyme they bought it of the Kinge being before in the poss'ion of the Abbot of Bury S'ti Edmond. The Mannours of Fordhall & Melford Hall were purchased by S'r Will'm Cordall aforesayd Fordhall of _____ (*blank*) and Melford Hall of Queene Marie & now by right of inheritance app'tayne to Jane Allington aforesayd. Of the Rectorie Mannour is Lord the incumbent by v'tue of his p'sentation. Unto these mannours by the Tenants is no extraordinarie service done neyther have they any Royalties belonging unto them but as accustomably all mannours have the Mannour of Melfordhall excepted which keepeth Court Baron & Leete & hath all wayfes, strayes, felons & fugitives goodes &c. The fines of Melfordhall & the Rectorie manour are certayne, of all the rest at the Lordes will.
	The Taske of this towne is L7.6.5d.

(166)   Mendham l Sf 9

....

167   Mertlesham g Sf 5

(*PLN note:* 'See Newborne')

(*TA transcript:* 'Capella de Newborne annex' Eccl'iae de Martlesham')

(*PLN note based on Chorography text:* 'bar't' *is a misreading of the original's* 'k't':

'Mettyngham b Sf 2   Castle
In this towne is an ancient castle seated upon the Grene. Which castle appertained to Mr.Bacon son of S'r Nicholas Bacon bar't about the year 1602.[77]
In the year 1613 it belonged to Mr.Hunt of _____ (*blank*)')

168   Metfeld l Sf 9

In this towne is that famous lane so much spoken of for myre & dirt it is in the common rode called Christmas Lane from Harleston market in Norff. to Halesworth Market in Suff.

Mickfeld k Sf 8

169
Temp.
Thom.
Feltham
inf.

++   Mildinge u Sd 5

This towne is in the Fraunchise of Burye wherof S'r Nicholas Bacon is Steward by a lease from our late Soveraigne Elisabeth. In it are divers mannours 1. the Mannour of Milding which is the chiefe mannour & only keepeth leete & court baron. It once belonged to Jeffrey Michell of Yeldham in Essex & after to James Hobart & from him came it by exchange for other lands to S'r John Springe this man his great grandfather & by S'r William Springe sold to John Mendham whose sonne John exchaunged it for landes lying in Halsworth in this Countye with Mr.Thomas Feltham in whose possession it now remayneth. It hath charter warrant. To it belongeth not one coppyholder.

2. The Man. of Tewe belongeth to Mr.Edward Waldegrave iure uxoris the reversion therof bel. to ('S'r' *inserted*) Isaac Apleton & his heires (*Later 17th cent. hand:* 'Mrs.Walgrave dead the possession in S'r Isaak').[79]

4. Man. of Bowers The L. Mr.Cutler of Ypswich purchased of S'r W'm Springe.[80]

Spir.

Rect. val. 10.13.4. Dec. 21 4d Subs. 18s the patron Mr.Feltha' aboves'd. The patronage annexed alwayes since Hen.6 tyme to the Mannour of Milding. To it belongeth a little house with barne & stable & 20 acres of gleabe all tithes p'd in specie. (*Note in early 17th cent. hand:* 'The mannour of Welshall was purchased by Thomas Sherland of Thomas Webbe of Yxworth & by him of Fosset. The patronage and Mannour of Milding sold to Mr.James Allington esq. of Wethersfeld.')

Mildenhall r Sd 1   Beate Marie.

A market towne kept on the _____ (*blank*). In this towne on

Stow

the 17 may 1567 was a great fyre which consumed 37 houses besides barnes stables & outhouses in the space of 2 houres.

....

172

Muncksyley vide Ileye monachor'
Muncksoham vide Soham monachor'

S'ti Andreae   Mutforde a Sf 1

173

Nacton f Sf 12

Naughton o Sd 5

(174)

Nedginge o Sd 5   Neddinge

Aest. 11 marc. Carn. 4½d.

Rectoria valet 8.12.11. Dec. 17.3½ Subsid. 14s.

9 Ed.2. D'n's Henricus de Stanton.

20 Ed.3 Rec. de Joh's de Insula tenent. in Neddinge una' fedu' militis de Ep'o Eliensis q'd Henricus Stanton quonda' tenuit de Ep'o Eliensis xl.

56

The Lord patron. It hath 8 acres of gleabe. No customes. No monuments in the churche.

S'r John Higham L. of the Mannour of Neddinghall the fines arbitrable. The customes to the eldest. This mannour hertofore did belong to the familie of Delapole after whose attaindure the King Hen.8 gave it to Charles Brandon d: of Suff' who againe passed it to the Kinge in exchange for other landes. Queene Marie at lenght by the ayde & meanes of Stephen Gardyner gave it unto S'r Clement Higha' father to the now owner S'r John Higham.[81]

Nedeham

A market towne.

175
Nettlestead n Sf 8

From this town came the Lord Wentworth whome Hen.8 honoured with the dignitie of Barons.[82]

Newborn g Sf 4

(*Note by PLN:* 'Rectoria Capella de Newborne cum Eccl'ia de Martlesham eidem annexa Carleford deanry 7:4:2d dec: 14:5d.')

176
Newton (?) u Sd 5

Newmarket r Sd 1

A market towne the one side of which is in Suffolk the other in Cambridgeshire, for it hath but one streete.

(177)
Gipping Newton p Sd 3   resp. pag.111

Newton s Sd 2

Newton p Sd 3

Neylande u Sd 5

(*Note by PLN:* 'lib'a capella valor 5 li dec: 10 sol.')

It is a chappell of Stoke. It hath tithes as a p'sonage & was hertofore allotted to the vicar of Stoke & in the p'sonall tithes therof & the small tithes of Stoke did the vicarage of Stoke consist. To it belongeth neyther house nor gleabe. But now the Vicar hyreth the p'sonall tithes of Nayland of the Patro' of Stoke. All tithes p'd in kinde save in a common fenne where for the neat goinge is allowed in stead of lactage for cowe & calfe xijd.

The Mannour of Neyland

178
St.Nicholas b Sf 2

Nowton q Sd 6

179
Olton a Sf 1

L.val.
Rect. val. 14.13.4 Dec. 29.4d Subs. 26s.

To the Rectorie belong ancient hanesome houses with 32 acres of gleabe. All tithes payd in kinde save 1d for every cowe for lactage. For a fole 1d. Mr.Archdeaco' Maplesdon.

The patron Mr.Hobart of Haleshall in Norff.[83]

In it is only the Mannour of Oldton belonging to Mr.Hobart afors'd as descended to him by inheritance from his predecessour S'r James Hobart the Kings Atturny generall in the right line, who (as is supposed) purchased it of Fastolffe.

Olton

In the chauncell   Sire Adam Bacon p'sbiter[84]

S'ti Nicholai   Oclee k Sd 7

It appertayneth to S'r Thomas Cornwalleis knight[85]

(TA transcript which may be part of Chorography text: 'One house D'na Joh'n'a relicta D'ni Barth' Davillers mil' def' p'ron' E. de Onehouse 1333. Liber Instit. fo.58')

....

182   Orford d Sf 11
(Note by PLN: 'Sudborne cum capella de Orford in Orford deanry valor 33:6:8 dec. 6 sol. 8d.')
A market & a Mayor towne so called of the river Or, which there falleth into the sea. It was once a large & well peopled towne fortifyed with a castle which first appertayned to the Valoins & afterward unto the Willoughbyes, but now the sea withdrawing it selfe hath spoyled the com'oditye & handsomnes of the haven. Ralphe of Coggeshall an ancient wrighter hath written that in the tyme of Henry the King when as Bartholomye of Glanvile kept the castle of Orford it happened that fishers of this towne to catch in their nets a wild man who in everye part & member of his represented an humane shape & forme, he had heare upon his head, a long bearde, about his brest he was very rough & hearye, who at length secretly fled unto the sea & was never seene after. Why may not this be an illusion to the Devill?[86]

(183)   Otley g Sf 5
(Original largely illegible: TA transcript:
'Domsd.   D'n's Joh'es Hastings est patronus ejusd' Proc. 7s 6d Syn. 2s.
L.val.   Rect. val. 16-6-5½ Dec. 32-7¾ Subs. 28s.

The mannor of Otteley belongeth to _____ *(blank)* Nevill L. of Aburgavenny.[87]

Ouesden x Sd 8

....

Pakefeld a Sf 1   Pageffeld

....

Parham d Sf 11
The L. of this towne Willia' Willoughbye created by K.Henry 8 Baron of Parham.[88] In it is an ancient & goodly house seated in the parke.

....

St.Peters b Sf 2

                              Petaugh h Sf 7

187   Petistre eh Sf 4
Domsd.   Heres D'n's W'mi de Huntingfeld militis est patronus eiusd. Proc.
             6.8d Syn. 2s. Lib.val. nihil.
9 Ed.2   Robertus de Ufford est D'n's 9 Ed.2.
             To the Vicarie the King p'senteth. The Impropriatio' Mr._____
             (*blank*) Lane bought of Queene Elisabeth. To the vicarie belongeth
             an house & an hempland. Hath in tithes the same customes which
             Wickham Market hath.
             In it are 1. the Mannour of Bynge. The Lord therof S'r Anthony
             Wingfeld in the same sort as of Gelha' and Horpoul in Wickham
             Market. The fines arbitrable.
             2. the Mannour of Lowdham the L: therof Mr.Samuell Blenerhasset.
             Of this Mannour was L: in 9 Ed.2 Joh'es Lowdham. In it was a
             chappell hertofore as appeareth by Domsd. booke. Ludham.
             Priorissa de Campse h't eam in proprios usus. Rect. aest. 5 marc.
             Vicar. 40s Proc. 7.6d Syn. 2s. The chappell is ruined & they go to
             Petistre churche. Lowdham an hamlet of Petistree.

                         Playforde g Sf 5   Playforth
Domsd.   Prior de Eya h't eccl'iam in p'prios usus et facit deservire eccl'ie per
             capellanu' secularem. Aest. 12 marc. pr. 6.8. Sy. 12d.
9 Ed.2   Lib. val. nihil. D'n's Joh'es de Playford 9 Ed.2.

188   Polsted u Sd 5
             (*Original partly illegible: TA transcript:*
'Domsd.   Aestimat. 56 marc. Carnag. 9½d.
Lib.val.   Rect. val. 22 li Dec. 44s Subs. 38s. Patronus D'nus Will'us Walgrave
              miles.[89]
9 Ed.2   D'n's Jacobus de Lamburne 9 Ed.2.')

                         Poslingford x Sd 8   Pos.....
Domsd.   Appropriat'r Priori et Conventui de eadem (?) ....
L.val.   Rect. val. 6.10s Dec. 13s. 9 Ed.2
9 Ed.2   D'n's Richardus de Cornerde 9 Ed.2.

189   ++   Preston u Sd 5
Domsd.   Appropriatur Priori et convent' S'te Trinitatis de Gipwico. Aest. 18
             marc. Carnagiu' 7½d.
L.val.   Vicar. val. 5.6.0½ Dec. 10.7¼ Patronus Mr.Reyse.
9 Ed 2   Prior hospitalis S'ti Joh'is Jerusalem D'n's 9 Ed.2.
             The Impropriation belongeth to Mr.Ryece whose father purchased it
             of Mr.Robert Spring of Icklingham & his grandfather of S'r Andrew
             Judde L'd Mayour of London & he of the Kinge who tooke it into
             his handes at the suppression of Religious houses unto one of which
             it belonged at that tyme as appeareth by the record above taken out
             of Domsday booke.[90] It hath only sheafe. The gleabe Mr.Spring sold
             to S'r Ambrose Jermyn being in all 140 acres & an house. Of the
             Vicarie Mr.Riece abovesayd is patron, to it belongeth an house & 2

acres of gleabe. All small tithes are p'd in kinde save for a cowe 4½d in silva cedua tithe, otherwise a locke henne at Christmas or in stead therof iiijd for the fire they burne.
In the church no epitaph.
1. In this towne are 4 mannours 1. Preston Hall belonging to S'r Anthony Wingfeld descended to him from the house of Oxford. The fine arbitrable.
2. Mannour of Mortymers Lord therof Mr.Roockwood of Stannyngfeld by descent from his father who purchased it of Mr.Pooley.[91]
3. Mannour of Swyfts L'd Mr.John Jermyn of Debden who left it to his sonne who sold it to his brother in lawe Mr.Burrells. Mr.Jermyn bought it of Mr.Corbett & he of the King to whome it fell at the supression of Abbyes it then belonged to Jesus Colledge in Burye.[92]
4. Mannour of St.Johns of Jerusalem belongeth to Mr.Rookwood & purchased by his father. It belonged to the knightes of the Rhodes.

190   Rammesholt e Sf 4
Domsd. Prior de Butlee h't eccl'iam in Proprios usus et facit deservire eccl'ie per capellanu' secularem. Aest. 5 marc. Syn. 2-8.
9 Ed.2 Joh'es de Payton d'n's 9 Ed.2.
(*TA transcript may be Chorography text:*
'Peyton hall in Ramesholt was an ancient seat of the family of Ufford after called Peyton & after that called Howard. It lyes neer the Channell off the hooking grounds for whitings whither the Woodbrigg fishermen resort at their season and being of late accounted no good air it has usuall been tenanted so the house looks not great now whatever it has been.')

....

191   Raydon n Sf 13

....

192   Redsham b Sf 2
The mannour of Therbernes in this towne belonged hertofore to the predecessours of W'm Therberne gent. of Cotton in Suff.

(*Note by PLN on Chorography paper:*
'Redsham p'va church united to Ringsfeld see blue book p.196 valew 25:17:1 Dec. 50:0d'. *Ringsfield can be found at p.196 in the Chorography*)

(*Partly visible below:*)   Redgrave k Sd 7
193   Redlingfield k Sd 7

....

Rendlesham h Sf 10
In this towne was Redwald the King of the East Angles mostly resident & first of all his people became a Christian & in this towne was baptised but afterward being seduced by his wife (as Bede sayth) he had in the one & the same church one altar for the Christian

60

religion & another for the sacrifice of devils. In this towne was afterward Swidesham king of the eastangles christned by Cedda the Christian Bishop.[93]

Spir.
A p'sonage to it belongeth a fayre p'sonage insett house with convenient outhouses & 50 acres of gleabe all tithes are p'd in kinde save for port ijd for lactage iijd for every cowe a port henne in discharge of wood & broome burned, but being sold yeeldeth tithe.. Joh'es de Holbrook patronus eiusd. pr. 7.6. Sy. 2.5. Domsed. Rect. val. 24.13.4. Dec. 49.4d. Subs. 44 Lib. val.

Temp.
In it are 3 Mannours 1. Mannour of Rendlesham alias Naunton Hall in Rendlesham which belonged unto Holbrook hertofore & after to Naunton & from Naunton by the d.& h. Margaret of Bartholome Naunton K't maryed to Robert Bokenham who dyed 6 Hen 5 came to him & his d. & h. Margaret mar. to Bartholomew Baron & his d. & h. Margaret maryed to Robert Fitzraulf esquier in which name it contynued untill Herman le Fitz Raulf sold it to Mr. _____ (*blank*) Spenser father to _____(*blank*) Spenser who now is L: therof.[94] The fine arbitrable the coppyholdes fall to the yongest.
Vide plura pag. 312.

Rickinghale ('Magna *etc. missing*)

195
Rickinghale Parva q *(should be k)* Sd 7

....

(196)
Ringesfelde b Sf 2
(*PLN note:* 'Ringsfeld cum Redsham p'va Wangford 12 li dec. 24 sol'

(197)
Rougham t Sd 4

....

198
Roydon c Sf 3

Rumboro c Sf 3

....

199
Rusbrock t Sd 4
The seate of the w'shipfull familie of the Jermines.[95]

Rushmere g Sf 5

....

Saterley g Sf 2   Soterley

A'o 8
R. Rich.
2
Margareta que fuit uxor Ed'i Soterley tenuit die que obijt maner. de Soterle ac advocatio'e' eccl'ie eiusdem ad termi'u' vite de Rege ut de comitatu h'no' Cestrie per ser. 1 fed milit. et non de corona et eadem Margareta obijt dominica ante festu' S'ti Michaelis ultimo elapso. Et Rogerus est filius et heres eorundem Ed'i et Margarete et est aetatis 30 annor' et a'plius.

(*Note by PLN on Chorography paper:* 'Saxham mag. magna in Thingo deanry valew 5:13:11d ob. decimae 23s 4d 3 ferd'.)

Saxham parva s Sd 2

(Original has note by PLN crossed out: 'Valor 8.11.5 ob. Dec. ...' *completed by a PLN transcript as* '17 shill. one penny 3 ferd.')

202 Saxstede l Sf 9   Sastede

(Note by PLN: 'capella, see Framingham castle'.)

Saxmundham d Sf 4

A market towne.

203 Seckford g Sf 5

Semer o Sd 5

Domsd. Aest. 17 marc. Carn. 4½d.
Rectoria valet 11.7.1. Dec. 22.8½ Subsid. 20s.
9 Ed.2. D'n's Abbas S't Edmundi.
To the parsonage presentative belongeth 60 acres of gleabe. No customes, for all tithes are p'd in specie. No armes nor monumentes in the churche. The Lord patron.
Of the mannour is Lord S'r John Higham from his father S'r Clement who bought it of the King for £340 after the suppression of Religious houses it before belonging to the Abbot of Burye. The fines arbitrable.

....

Sheepmede b Sf 2

Shelley u Sf 13

(Note by PLN on Chorography paper headed 'Shympling')

....

208 Sisewell c Sf 3

Smalbridge u Sd 5

209 S'ti Joh'is Baptiste   Snape d Sf 11

Somerleytowne a Sf 1

Once the habitation of Fitz Osbert & Jarnegan now of Mr.Quayntforthe.[96]

....

212 Sotherton c Sf 3

Southolde l Sf 9

S'ti Edmundi Regis et Martyris *(No; this is the dedication of Southwold)* Abbas S'ti Ed'i est patronus eiusdem. Aestimat'r cum Wyrlingworth proc. 7:6d Synod. 9d.

213 Sowoulde c Sf 3

A market towne by the sea, kept on the Thursdaye. It standeth in the east p't of Suff. It is a corporation governed by 2 Balifes. It was pitifully defaced with fire 1596, upon a Fridaye. The haven to this towne is at Walderswick.

Specksall c Sf 3   Speckeshall

(*Original partly illegible: TA transcript:* 'In it is the mannor of
Burghards al's Burghhards which heretofore belonged to the
Banyards and before them to Burghards which descended unto two
dau'rs and heirs of Henry Banyard the one of which was married to
Thomas Duke Esq. the other to John Throgmorton gent. who both
joyntly sold it to Roger Bell of Haughley (and Thomas Talbot of
Bacton) yeoman and he (*sic*) to John Brown of Halsworth gent.,
whose eldest sonne John sold it to Paul Bayning of London Esq. in
whose hands it now remaineth.[97] It is holden of the man' of
Wyssette'.)

(215)   Stanfelde x Sd 8

                               Stansted u Sd 5

Domsd.   Aestimat'r 15 markes Carnagium 7½d.

Rectoria valet 10 li Dec. 20s Subsid. 18s.

The Patrone to the p'sonage presentative is Mrs.Allington. To the
parsonage belong 20 acres of gleabe. All tithes p'd in kinde save that
they have a custome to pay iiijd an acre for medowe & iiijd a cowe
for tithe cheese.

In the church no monumentes for there have no gent. dwelled in the
towne. Only 2 coates Arg. a fesse 2 (*crescents drawn*) in chief gul. &
arg. a chevron entre 3 beares heades musled & coupe sable the one
Mohell the other Wachesham.

The Mannour belongeth to Roger Martyn of Melford Esq.[98] The
fines arbitrable. The custome to the eldest. The Leete the Kings.

216   ++   Stanton q Sd 6

In this towne are two churches which make 2 parishes but yet one
towne.

Rector. Stanto' o'i'u' S'tor' 9.6.10½ Dec. 18.5¾ Subs. 16s.

Rect. val. Stanto' S'ti Joh'is 9.4.9½. Dec. 18.5¾ Subs. 16s.

Of both these is patron S'r Robert Jermyn of Rushbroke. To
Alsaints belongeth a convenient house & 16 acres which the
incumbent hath in possession. But more ought he to have which is
detayned. All are errable. All tithes p'd in kinde save cheese for
whiche they paye only 1d for every cowe. Stanton Joh'is hath all in
specie only ijd for locage. To it belongeth an house with _____
(*blank*) acres of grounde.

In it are the mannours of 1. Stanton hall w'ch keeps court &
Leete it belonged to Bury abbye. S'r Thomas Jermyn bought it of
K.Hen.8. The coppyholders pay for bend dayes. The fine is
arbitrable. Some Freeholders pay rent egges & hennes. The L: S'r
Robert Jermin.

2. Mickfeld Hall hertofore belonged to the Ashfeldes of whome S'r
Thomas Jermin bought it & now app'tayneth to his grandchild S'r

Robert Jermin. It is about 60 yeeres since the purchase. The fine is arbitrable. The copyhold goeth to the yongest. The head houses wherof there are many gather the rents of the branches belonging to them. The leete of this towne the Jermins bought of the King. S'r Nicholas Bacon hath nought to doe therin.

3. Man. of Badwell. S'r Robert Jermin bought it of Willia' Poley father to S'r Willia' Poley of Boxted.[99] It belonged to the Pooleys 300 yeers. To it belong 14 score acres of demeanes. No court kept.

4. Mannour of Nichols extinct.

Sternfeld d Sf 11

Stoke Ash k Sd 7

217

Neyther coate nor gravestone in the churche.

Rect. de Stoke Ash val. 11.1.2. Dec. 221½. Subsid. 18s Proc. syn. there belong to the Rectorie.

Tempore Ed.2. D'n's de Stoke Ash fuit Prior de Ely.

Every house pay 14 cheeses of their ordinarie make.

Stokehall Lord therof now Mr.Edmond Bokenham of Thornha' by purchase.[100] The fine arbitrable. The coppylandes to the yongest. No dower to the widowe.

Stoke n Sf 6 ('13' crossed out)   It is in

Ipswich dea.

Domsd. Eccl'ia S'te Marie de Stoke. Prior Eliensis est p'nus eiusd. Proc. 6.8. Syn. 16s.

L.val. Rect. val. 12 li Dec. 24s Subs. 20s (rest cut away)

++   Stoke u Sd 5   iuxta Nayland

Domsd. Carnagiu' 26½d.

L.val. Vicar. val. 19.0.10. Dec. 38.1d Subs. 34s.

Tempore Ed.2 D'na ville fuit Margareta Regina Anglie.

This towne is in the franchise of Burye.

The patron of the vicarie is Mr.Mannocke resident in the towne to whome also belongeth the impropriat Rectorie descended to him from his father Frauncis Mannock who bought it of iudge Bell & he of Wiseman & he of Throughgood & he of King Hen.8 to whome it came by the suppression of abbyes belonging before to Prittewell Priorie in Essex.[101] To the Vicarie hertofore belonged a fayre & stately vicarie house built of tymber wherin at one tyme have bene lodged 2 Dukes 2 Earles & their duchesses & Countesses. It was alienated from the church in the tyme of King Edw. 6 by an irreligious & unconscionable compostion betwene the Bishop patron & incumbent & instead therof was allotted unto the vicar a little house in the streete not farre from the churche without foot or furrowe of gleabe belonging to the same. All small tithes are p'd in kinde save for every cowe in lieu of lactage the vicar hath xijd.

Looke the mannours in this towne page 296 followinge.

Earle Stonham m Sf 8

(TA transcript: original is partly illegible: 'Because the Earl Marshall was patron of it.

Domsd. Comes Marescallus est patronus eiusdem. Proc. 7-6d Synod. 12d.
L.val. Rect. val. 17-2-6. Dec. 34-3 Subs. 30s.
In Edw. 2d's time the Lord of the man. was the Earl of Norff.')

Stonham Aspall m Sf 8

(*Original partly illegible: TA transcript:* 'Because Aspalle was patron of it otherwise Stonham Antegan St.Lambert.

Domsd. Robertus de Aspall est patronus ejusd'. Proc. 7-6d Syn. 12d.
L.val. REct. val. 19-10-2½ Dec. 39 0¼ Subs. 34s.')

Stonham parva m Sf 8   Stonham Jernegan

Domsd. Bycause Peter Gernegan was patron of it. Petrus de Gernegan est p'nus eiusdem. Proc. 6.8. Sy. 2s.
L.v. Rect. val. 9.17.11 Dec. 19.9½ Subsid. 16s.
Ed.2 Tempore Ed.2 D'n's de Stonha' fuit Petrus Gernegan.

Stowe p Sd 3

A Market Towne. (*TA transcript adds* 'Mariae vicar. val. 6 li 10d Dec. 12.10d.' *Another has* 'Stow S'c'i Petri vicar. Stow Deanry 10-18-4 Dec. 21s 4d')

....

Stowlangtoft q Sd 6

L.val. Rect. val. 8.7.8. Dec. 16.9¼ Subs. 14s.
In Ed.2 tyme the Lord of Stowe Galfridus Peche.

....

O'i'u S'torum   Stradbrooke l Sf 9

....

Stratford d Sf 11   Stratforth

L.val. Rect. val. 5 li Dec. 10s.
The Mannour of Gristons in Stretforth belongeth to S'r Henry Glemham of Glemha' k't 102 whose father purchased it of our late soveraigne Queene Elisabeth.

....

126 (*sic*)   ### Sudburye u Sd 5

Once one of the chiefest townes in those p'ts & so called in respect of Norwich for Sudburye is as it were South burgh, as Norwich is as it were North wic. It is now of no small reputation it is populous & riche in making of wolling cloth. It is a Mayour towne. It was called Sceabridge. 103 In this towne was borne Simon Thibald alias Sudburye ArchB. of Canterburye who was beheaded by the Kentish Rebells Wat Tiler & others a'o 1381. He was son to Nicholas Tibald gentleman. In the tyme of his being Bishop of London which was 18 yeers, he built a colledge where his fathers house stoode, endued it with great possessions, furnisht it with secular clarcks & other ministers valued at the suppression L 122.18.0 in landes by the yeere. He builded the upper end of St.Gregories church in Sudburye.

Sutton c Sf 4

....

Sylham l Sf 9

....

(*Note by PLN on Chorography paper:* 'Tattington cum capella de Brundish vicar. valor 17.11.3 ob. decimae 34 sol. 8d. Hoxne deanry.')

Tattyngstone n Sf 13
(*Note by PLN:* 'Valor 6:13:4 Dec: 13:4d')

....

Thelnetham q Sd 6
The mannour of Thelnetha' belonged hertofore to the Thelnethams by whose d. & h. Juliana it came to the Bokenhams & now remayneth in the possession of Mr.Edmond Bokenha' of great Thornha' esq. The Woman hath no dower. The coppylandes to the yongest. Fines arbitrable.

....

Thirlow parva x Sd 8
Rect. val. 7.10.5. Dec. 15 0½ Subs. 12s.

....

(*PLN transcript:* 'Thorndon in Suff. k Sd 7
See the addenda pag. 277.
Every house payeth 14 cheeses of their ordinary make for lactage.')

....

Thorp l Sf 7

....

Thrandeston k Sd 7

....

Thwate k Sd 7   Thweyt
Neither coate nor gravestone

....

Trymleys f Sf 12
(*PLN note:* 'Trimley Marie Colneys deanry valor. 16:13:4 dec: 33:4d Martini 12.6.5 dec. 33: ob.')

....

Troston q Sd 6

Tudenham g Sf 5

Tudenham r Sd 1
Left out of the Map by Saxton.

Tunstall d Sf 11

Ufford h Sf 4

The place of Robert Ufford Earle of Suff.[104]

....

Uppeston c Sf 3

....

242   Walton f Sf 12

Walpole c Sf 3

243   S'ti Andreae   Walderswick c Sf 3

Walsha' in the willowes q Sd 6

One only mannour the L: therof S'r Nicholas Bacon.
The fines arbitrable. The woman hath no dower. The coppyholdes
are of Gavellkinde.
The benefice merely appropriated & S'r Nicholas Bacon hath it &
findeth a stipendiarie Curat.

244   Waldingfelde Magna u Sd 5

Waldingfelde parva u Sd 5

John Wincoll son of Roger Wincoll is Lord of this towne. No
coppyholders belonging to the mannour.

245   Waldringfield g Sf 5

(*Note by PLN on separate sheet:* 'Waldringfeild is a distinct town
from Waldingfeild Magna and parva g Sf 5')

Whatfeld......

246   Wangford c Sd 1

Wangford c Sf 3

247   Wantisden d Sf 11

Warlingworth l Sf 9

Wyrlingworth Abbas S'ti Ed'i est patronus illius. Aestimatur cu'
capella de Southolt 28 marc. Proc. 7.6d. Syn. 9d.
Rectoria cum capella de Southolt val. 19.12.3½ Dec. 39.2¾. Subs.
34.

248   Wattesham u (*should be* o) Sf 5

....

(249)   Waybred l Sf 9

....

250   Wenham Parva n Sf 13

....

251   Wesselton c Sf 3

Westletoun cu' capella de Syngle. Abbas de Sybtone est p'ronus
illius. Rector h't mansu' cu' 40 acris terre. Proc. 7.6d Syn. 2s

vid. 281   Westall c Sf 3   S'ti Andreae

Domsd.   Prior Norwici h't eam in p'p'ios usus non h't mansu' nisi unica' grangeam. Vicarius h't mansu' pertinens eccl'ie cu' 60 acris terre et est residens. Proc. 7.6d non solvit' synodalia.

Vicar. val. 10.2.3½ Dec. 20.2¾ Subsid. 18s. Patronus Decanus et capitulum Norwici.

(*TA transcript:*   'Weston b Sf 2
Rect. val. 13-6-8d. Dec. 26.8. Subs. 24s Syn. 16d.
To it belongeth a house with a barn and about them about an acre of ground besides the Churchyard all tithes are paid in kind save for hartsilver 1d and for lactage for every Cowe 1d.

Mr.Kempe of Brisete bought the Mannor of Weston of Mr.Garneys of Kenton.')

....

(*TA transcript:*   'Weston m'cate q Sd 6
L.val.   Rect. val. 8-19-7 Dec. 17s 11½ Subsid. 16s.
In the Church on a Stone Orate p' a'i'a D'ni Joh'is Muryall cujus a'i'ae p'pitiet' Deus.')

Mr.Nunne was L: of Weston whose sonne sold it to Mr.Edmonde Bokenham of Thornha' Mag. esq. [105] Mr.Nonne bought it of Fastolff & he of Waldegrave & he of S'r Hugh Hovell k't. The woman hath no dower. The fines arbitrable the coppylands fall to the yongest.

....

254   Westley s Sd 2
Domsd. nihil Aest. 14 marc.
L.val.   Rect. val. 9.15.5. Dec. 19.6½ Subs. 16s.
9 Ed.2   Abbas S'ti Ed'i D'nus de Westly tempore Ed.2.

....

255   Wethersdale l Sf 9

....

256   Wetherden p Sd 5

                                     Wheltham magna t Sd 4
Qwelnitham magna

257   Wheltham parva t Sd 4
Qwelnitham parva.

                                     Whepsted s Sd 2

258   Whersted n Sf 6   Quersted

                                     Wixsoo x Sd 8

259   Wickham h Sf 4   Wycham
A market towne kept on the Tuesdaye.
Domsd.   D'n's Robertus de Ufford est p'ronus eiusd. Proc. 7.6. Syn. 2s.
Lib.val. Vic. val. 6.16.8d Dec. 13.8d. 9 Edw.2 D'n's Robertus de Ufford.

The impropriat p'sonage belonged hertofore to Campsee abbye. At the dissolution of relligious houses the King tooke it into his handes. Queene Elizabeth sold the reversion in fee to Mr.John Lane of Campsee Asch.[106] The King p'sentes to the vicarie & hath a little house & 6 or 7 acres of gleabe belonging to the same. It rec. all the small tithes & hath them in specie save tithe haye for w'ch they paye iiijd an acre for medowe. No tithe hempe but iiijd for an hempland of a bushell sowing. They pay goose pigge calfe woll lambe wood &c. In this towne are 3 mannours 1. the Man. of Wickham belonging to S'r Anthony Wingfield. 2. Man: of Gelham 3. Man: of Horpoul both which hertofore belonged to Ufford E: of Suff. After to the Abbesse of Campse, which the King tooke into his handes at the dissolution of Abbyes & sold to S'r Anthony Wingfield K't by whose sonne & h. S'r Robert they are descended to S'r Anthony Wingfeld k't who now enioyeth them. The fines of all these mannours are at the will of the Lord. The customes ⸺⸺ (*blank*) It was a market in Uffords tyme. Their charter renewed by the last S'r Robert Wingfeld.[107]

(*Partly visible below:*) Wickham ....

....

(*TA transcript:*)   'Wingfield l Sf 9
From this town have that worthy and ancient stock of the Wyngfields taken their denomination.[108] It for many years belonged unto the same family of the Wingfeild (*sic*) untill it with all the lands of S'r John Wingfeild Knight were with his daughter Elizabeth translated into the family of De La Pole. This Elizabeth Wingfeild was married to S'r Michael de la Pole who by King Richard 2 was created L.Wingfeild and after Earl of Suffolk.')

<table>
<tr><td></td><td>Whitton m Sf 7</td><td>Qwittendone</td></tr>
</table>

Domsd.   Ep'us Eliensis est p'ronus eiusdem. Aest. 8 marc. proc. 6.8. Sy. 20d. Rect. cu' Thurleton val. 6.11.5½. Dec. 13.1¾. D'n's Ep'us Eliensis tempore Edw.2 eius a'o 9.

262   Willingham b Sf 2
There were eyther two townes of this name or there were in this towne 2 churches St.Marie & Alsaints.
Willingham Alsaints is otherwise called Ellow & Elgh.
Rect. val. 12 li Dec. 24s Subsid. 20s. O'i'u' S'tor' alias Ellowe the other towne called commonly Willingha' & is Marie hath no church but p't of the inhabitaunts come to Ellowe church & p't to Shanfeld.

                             Winston l Sf 7
263   Wisset C Sf 3
(*Original partly illegible: TA transcript:* 'Wysett cum capella
Domsday   Rumburgh Prior Rumburgh h't eam in proprios usus. Aest. cu' Rumburgh 36 m'c'. Proc. 7 6d Syn. 2s. L.val. nihil.
9 E.2.   Will'mus de Rosse et Petronilla de Narford D'ni 9 E.2.')

Witnesham g Sf 5   Witlesha'

Domsd.   D'n's Edmundus Bacon est patronus illius. Aest. 28 marc. Proc. 7.6d Syn. 2s.

L.val.   Rect. val. 18.13.4. Dec. 37.4. Subs. 32s.

9 Ed.2   Edmundus Bacon D'n's 9 Ed.2.

264

Wiverston k Sd 7

Domsd.   Rect. val. 9.17.11½ Dec. 18.10. Subs. 16s.

    Pr. _____(blank) Syn.

9 Ed.2   Hugo Hovell d'n's 9 Ed 2.

Upon a gravestone (sic)

Woodbridge h Sf 10

A market towne kept on the wednesdaye.

Domsd.   Prior de eadem h't eccl'iam in p'p'ios usus. Aest. 5 marc. Proc. 7 6d Syn. 2s. L.val. nihil.

9 Ed.2   D'n's Comes Norff. D'n's 9 Ed.2.

The p'sonage is merely impropriat without vicarie endowed it belonged to Woodbridge priorie. Now Mr.Thomas Seckford son of Charles Seckford as heire to Mr.Thomas Seckford Mr. of the Requests as being his elder brother his sonne hath it. [109] It is lette for farm for 40 li p' annu'. The Curate is hired by the s'd Mr.Seckford. They pay tithe corne & herbage: also wood & broome if it be sold els not.

There are in this towne these Mannours following.

1. Woodbridge Priorye. Mr.Seckford Lord from his father he from the Mr. of Requests & he of Queene Elisabeth as fallen to hir by the death of Mr.Anthony Wingefelde & his wife without heires of their bodye to whome it was given in that sort at their mariage by K:Henry 8 to whome it fell by the suppression of Rel. houses. It holdeth Court Baron only.

2. Thorphall. Lord S'r Anthony Wingfield from his father S'r Robert who had it as heire to his elder brother Mr.Anthony Wingfeld. Keepeth court baron only.

3. Woodbridge Ufford. L: Mr.Michaell Hare of Brusyard from his father who bought it of the L:Willoughby of Parham. Keepeth court Baron no leete. Vide page 309 4.Hason Hall.

265

Worlingham b Sf 2

There were 2 of them the great cald Alsaints Worlingha' & the lesser cald St.Peters Worlingha'.

Wordwell q Sd 6

Tallow Wrattinge x Sd 8

....

S'ti Nicholai   Wrentham c Sf 3

Lib. 9   1425 fuit patronus et D'n's ville Thomas de Dacre filius

Instit.   primogenitus D'ni de Dacre et de Gisleland.

....

(268)	Wurtham k Sd 7
269	Wulpet t Sd 4

A market towne
Domsd. nihil.

Lib. val.	Rect. val. 6.18.9. Dec. 13 10½ Subs. 12s.
9 Ed.2	Abbas S'ti Ed'i D'n's 9 Ed.2.

270	Wylbye l Sf 9
Domsd.	D'n's Thomas de Hyndringham est p'ronus eiusd. Pr.7.6. Sy. 2s.
L.val.	Rect. val. 26.6.10½ Dec. 52 8¼ Subs. 46s.
9 Ed.2	W'm's de Bovill D n's 9 Ed.2.

	Wyston u Sd 5
Domsd.	Appropriat'r Pr. et Convent. de Horkeslee. Carnag. 6d.
L.val.	Vicar. val. 4.19.4½. Dec. 9.11½. Patrona D'na Regina.
9 Ed.2	D'na Aegidia de Horkesley D'na 9 Ed.2.

271	Yaxley k Sd 7

Yoxford c Sf 3   S'ti Petri
Joh'es Norwich de Yoxford sepelit'r ib'm cond' test' 30 mart. 1428
p'b' 22 Sept. ead' an'o.

(page 272 is blank)[110]

71

In the north side of the churche lay buryed Richard de la Pole sonne of Michael de la Pole Earle of Suff. with this inscription

Hic jacet Richardus de la Pole filius D'ni Michaelis de la Pole nuper Comitis Suffolcie' qui obijt 18 die Decembr' a'o D'ni 1403 cujus a'i'e p'piciet'r Deus.

He layeth in complet armour under his feete a lyon couchant, on his gravestone fower tymes the armes of De la Pole with a flowerdelis on the fesse.

Hard by him layeth also his brother John de la Pole with this Inscription

Hic iacet Mr.Johannes de la Pole filius D'ni Michaelis de la Pole quonda' Comitis Suffolcie bacalaurius utriusq' juris. Canonicus in eccl'ia Cathedrali Ebor' ac in eccl'ia Collegiata de Beverley qui obijt 4. die Februarij a'o D'ni 1415 cuius a'i'e p'piet'r Deus.

On his gravestone 1. De la Pole & Wingfeld Quartered. 2. De la Pole with a crescant 3. De la Pole w'th a mullet 4. De la Pole with an annulet.

On the North side of the Chauncell lay buryed by himselfe John De la Pole duke of Suff. according to the common opinion of the Inhabitaunts in the towne.

On the same side layeth buryed an Earle with his Countesse crowned (*crown of five points drawn*) (which I rather take to be John De la Pole Duke of Suff. & his Duchesse then any other) he layeth in complet armor, under his head a Saracens head with the necke armed coupe gules supported with a wreath ermine & gules, at his feete a lyon couchant or. Under his head a pillowe under hir feete a lion argent. It is holden of the Inhabitants to be the tombe of Michael de la Pole & his Countesse, but the coates about the tombe argue the contrarye (for the brasse with the inscription is reaved of) which are these fower

1. p' pale 1. Quarterly De la Pole & argent a Chief gules over all a lyon ramp. or. then p' pale agayne, 1. France & England Quarterly

a labell of (*page changes*) 3 points argent & Quarterly Mortymer & Ulster.

2. Quarterly De la Pole Arg. a chiefe gul. over all a lyon ramp or.

3. Quarterly France and England a labell of 3 points argent.

4. p' pale Fraunce and Englande Quarterlye a labell of 3 points. & Mortymer & Ulster Quarterlye.

It should by these armes appeare somwhat that he that here layeth interred matched with one of the bloud Royall of Englande & one whose predecessours matched with the heires of Mortymer Earle of Marche and Burgh Earl of Ulster, but to my remembrance the house of Clarence matched with the forenamed heires of Ulster whose heire was matched to Mortymer and his to the house of Yorke, in which right King Edward the 4th before he attayned unto the Crowne was intitled Earle of Marche, whose sister John de la Pole Duke of Suff. marryed & before him none of the De la Poles matched in to the Royall bloud of England.

On the south side of the chancell lay buryed one of the daughters of Edmond de la Pole Earle of Suff. & w'th this inscription on the stone

Hic jacet D'na Margareta filia secunda Edmundi Comitis Suffolcie que obijt vicessimo secundo Januarij a'o D'ni 1498.

On the stone these armes Quarterly 1 and 4 de la Pole and arg. a chiefe gules a lyon ramp. or empaled, 2 & 3 Wingfelde.

On the same side also lay buryed an Earle & his countesse, they say it is Edmond de la Pole Earle of Suff. & his countesse, & the former Epitaph somwhat confirmeth their sayinge, under his head layeth the Saracens head gules coupe, under his feete the lyon couchant about the tombe are these names, Katherina, Margareta, Thomas, Milo, Thomas, Philippa, Elisabeth, Isabella, Johannes. Willielmus, Michaell.

275   In the south side of the Chauncell lay buryed Margerie Almot with this inscription.

Orate pro anima Margerie Almott que obijt 3 Octobris 1511.

The Armes on the same stone are − p' pale on a crosse engrayled betwene 4 eschalops, five roundels whole, & p'ti p' fesse on the higher a goate ramp' on the lower a pale fusilee.[111]

Speckshall resp. pag. 214

In the north side of the chancell lay buryed William Banyard with this Inscription.

     Octobris denoq' die mensis duodeno

     M quadringeno primo quoq' septuageno

     Anno sub Christi tumulo moriens fuit isti

     Curem inuet arca Dei Banyard data globa Wilelmi.

On the tombe are (*sic*) this Coate

Quarterly Banyard & sable a chevron betwene 3 lionceaux ramp. argent.

On the south side of the chauncell upon one Stone the pourtrayture of a man and a woman under them this epitaphe & these armes Arg't on a bend sable 3 eaglets of the first beaked & membred gules,

Hic jacet Joha'es Browne generosus.[112]

276   Halesworth respice pag.117

In the Chauncell there layeth under a marble stone buryed S'r William Argentein over his head this superscription in brasse

Hic jacet Gulielmus Argentein miles D'nus de Halesworth qui obijt 15 die mensis februar' a'o D'ni 1418 cuius a'i'e p'pit. Deus. He layeth pictured in brasse in complet Armour treading upon a lyon about his necke a coller of SS.

73

On it were 2 escotcheons on eyther side of him but are both taken awaye.

In a chappell called Claxtons chappell on a fayre stone is the pourtrayture of a man in a gowne & under him this subscription.

Of your charitie pray for the soule of Willia' Claxton gentlema' which deceased the 17. October in the yeere of our Lord God 1539 on whose soul and all Christen Jesu have mercye.

Over his head on eyther side & at his feete graven in brasse Mercye is my desire.

On ech corner a fayre escotcheon, 1. Quarterly 1. Claxton gul. a chevron entre 3 porcupines argent and azur on a canton gules 3 martletes or. 2. Arg. a fesse quartered azur and gules betwene 3 mascles voyded sable. 3. Quarterly 1 and 4 az. 3 pipes in pale broken or a canton ermine 2 & 3 gules a bende nebule azur & argent betwene 4 cotises or. 4. Claxton ut prius.

2. P' pale all these as they are q'rtered & gul. on a chevron or 3 gemeaux sable. Throckmorton.

3. as the seconde

4th as 1st.

In the first escotcheo' Claxton, Crickman, Stafford, Gardiner, Claxton.[113]

277

Theberton resp. pag.230

On a grave stone in the south isle of the church is this epitaph

Hic jacet Guilielmus Jennye miles unus Justiciarius D'ni Regis de Banco et Elisabeth uxor eius quonda' qui quidem Guilielmus obijt 23 die mensis Decembris a'o D'ni 1483.

On the stone these coates following (*sic*)[114]

Mendlesham resp. pag.166

In the uppermost p't of the south isle is a gravestone having the picture of one in complet armour under his head a dragons head this epitaphe subscribed

Hic jacet Joha'es Knyvet armiger D'ni istius Ville qui obiit 4'o die Decembris a'o D'ni 1418 cuius &c.

At his head on his right hand Knyvet 2. P' pale Knyvet & bendye of 6 or & azur a canton argent. Fitzotes. 3. P' pale Knyvet & the bordure besantie. 4. P' pale this with tbe bordure azur besantie & or a fesse gul. charged with 3 plates. Basset & Huntingfield.[115]

Thorndon resp: pag.233

In the chancell on a stone is the portrayture of a woman in her windingsheete about whose head are these armes p' pale France and England quarterly a labell of 3 points ermine and azur a chevron (*ermine drawn*) charged with 3 bores heades coupe. About the armes these wordes.

These be the armes of Dame Catharine Sewynford sometyme Duchesse of Lancaster that by S'r William Sewynford had sonne & heyre S'r Thomas Sewynford knight father to Dame Catherine wife to S'r Will'm Drury knight the w'h S'r Willia' & Dame Catherine

74

among other had Marie the wife of Edward Grymstone esquier that God hath endued with great vertue and beautye and here is interred (who dyed the 6th of March a'o D'ni 1469.

On the stone these 4 coates more

1. _____on a fess 3 mullets perced.

2. Argent on a chevron 3 boares heades coupe arg.

3. P' pale _____ on a fesse 3 mulletts p'ced & arg. on a chiefe vert 2 mulletts or. Written under this coate Marie Grymstone.

4. p' pale Drury & arg. on a chevron (*ermine drawn*) 3 bores (*page changes*) heades arg. under written Dame Catherine Drurie.

Just by this stone layeth another to the North side whereon have bene the portraiture of a woman & coates but all reaved up.

On the same side is a fayre tombe against the wall of a yard & halfe high on it the portraiture of a man in complet armour. About the tombe this circumscription

Hic iacet Edwardus Grymstone armiger quonda' de Rysha'gles lodge qui obiit die Mercurij v'c't 23 die mensis septembris a'o D'ni 1478.

On the stone these armes 1 (*blank*) on a fesse 3 mulletes p'ced 2. p' pale (*blank*) on a fesse (*blank*)3 mulletes p'ced & (*blank*) 3 gemeaux (*blank*) 3. (*blank*) 4. p' pale on a fesse (*blank*) 3 mulletes p'ced (*blank*) & (*blank*) a saultier engrayled (*blank*).[116]

Gislingham resp. pag.110

On a grave stone in the chauncell this Epitaph

Hic modo quiescunt de Stokys ossa Johannis

Gislingha' Rectoris Christe cui propituis sis

On another these verses

Qui situs his Thomas Nuttallus natus in agro

Lancastri Buriae hac Rector in aede fuit

Qui generosa patris gens et domus ambo voca't'r

Nomine Nuttalli Mater Orella cui

Obiit 23 die Maii a'o D'ni 1571.[117]

Westhorp resp. p.253

On a little stone in the chauncell these v'ses

Sulyard Andreas jacet hic filius qui Joha'is

In Wetherden Natus, fuit iste puer deo datus.

In the North isle of the churche on a grave stone this sup'scription Orate p' a'i'a Elisabeth Wyngfeld uxoris Henrici Wyngfeld militis.

In the Upper part of the churche nere the middle alley a fayre grave stone having on it this escotcheon supported by two angells having it (*sic*) three trefoyles in triangle & under it written

Hic iacet D'n's Mattheus Borgue miles de Francia Natus de Ducatu Bituricensi Hostagiu' in isto regno Angliae pro illustrissimo Principe D'no Duce Aurelianensi qui obiit 15 Julij a'o d'ni 1431.

Nere him another stone on which is written

Pray for the soules of Robert Westchington esquier & Amy his wife who dyed the 15th of August 1517.

The coates in brass reaved.

75

In the middle allye on a grave stone this inscriptio'

Hic iacet corpus Roberti Singleton filii Richardi Singleton nup' servientis Johannis D'no Duci Suffolciensi qui obijt 7 Julij a'o d'ni 1473.[118]

Bacton resp. pag. 17

Under the communion table in the middest of the chancell the portraiture of a priest in his vestiments & underwritten

Hic jacet Thomas Backton Archidiaconus London et Canonicus Lyncoln qui obiit 7'o Februarij a'o D'ni 1396.

In the chappell of the south side of the church a grave stone under which layeth Anne the wife of Will'm Prettyman who deceased 1591. On the stone these armes 1. the goldsmyths armes p'ti per chevron gules & azur in the highest 2 salts covered & chaynes pendant or.[119]

Cotton resp. p.70

In Cotton church in a south chappell called Hemenhalls chappell is a fayre raysed tombe of marble wherin lay buryed some of the Hemynhales. In the window of the same chappell over against this tombe are the p'traytures of 2 knightes armed in male the one holding an escotcheon, on it Or on a fesse entre 2 Chevrons gules 3 eschalops argent. At his feete written Sire Rauff de Hemynhall. The other holdeth in his hand a speare having pendant on his arme the former armes. Under him Sir John de Hemynhall.

Against the North Wall of the Chauncell was a monument of a knight armed buryed but now altogether defaced only remayneth the forme of the Man in wood or stone. They say it was the tombe of S'r W'm Wingfeld alias Wolfe, but I rather iudge it to be the monument of some of the Aspalls as appeareth by the armes azure 3 chevrons or. For S'r W'm Wingfeld Kn't & W'm Wingfeld Esq'r his sonne were both buryed in Dynington churche.[120]

280

Glemham parva. resp. pag.112

On a square stone in the chauncell set against the wall this epitaphe

This silly grave the happy cynder hydes
Of Thomas Glemham son to Christopher
True feare of god and vertues all besides
In this good wight alone assembled were
Ne did there want to well disposed mynde
A body fyne & active therewithall
A lively sprite a courage not behynde
The best resolv'd though stature were but small
Of all good men entirely well beloved
Belov'd of god (great blessings did declare)
In tender years by right of bloud he proved
The noble Duke of Suffolcks one coheire
Whereby his house remayneth well increast
A wife he had that Amy Parker hight

In modest life that mought be to the rest
A myrrour clere & lampe of shyning light
Rare was the love wherein this couple lyved
Full fifteene yeares, & parted then at once
Ruefull the day such iewells that bereaved
Whose want with teares their kynne and contry mournes
But god hath wrought in mercy for the best
From long disease to call them unto rest.

The sayd Thomas dyed in September a'o 1571 and Amy his wife dyed in the month followinge. They had yssue Henry, Thomas and Elisabeth.

On an escocheon in the stone in the toppe therof p' pale first 6 coats 1. Glemham 2. Brandon 3. Bakon of Bakonsthorp 4. sable a bend arg. 5. Banyard 6. Glemha'
then the second pale 1. Parker 2. Morley 3. Lovell 4. azur a lion Ra'p. inter fleur de lis arg. 5. azur a fesse dancye entre 12 billets or 6. Delapole 7. Wingfeld 8. gules a bend fusilee or 9. azur a lyon ramp. or.

On another stone in the same chauncell this epitaph
Here graved is of Glemhams ancient race
John Glemham knight a worthy auncestour
Among these few though first he stand in place
Yet long before that name hath lasted here
In good account though tyme and small regarde
Their due records those elders hath debarred
Of Bakonsthorp a Bakon was his feere
And of that house coheire by just descent
Within this grave intombed also here
In sweet accord they lived most content
In heaven their soules enioyes that lasting blisse
Wherwith the god of mercy meedeth his.

The said S'r John Glemham dyed in the yeere 1535. They had yssue Christopher Edward and Frauncis, daughters Elisabeth and Dorothye

On the escotcheon p' pale first quarterly Glemha' & Brandon & Quarterly 1 & 4 Bakon of Bakonsthorp 2. sable a bend arg. 3. Banyarde.

On a third Stone in the chauncell this epit.
John Glemhams sonne good Christopher
    engraved resteth here
Whome cruell death hath hastened hence
    in prime of all his yeeres
Valiaunt he was, franck, forward, wise,
    and active every waye
And to his frend a faythfull shield
    to serve at each assaye.
His wife Lord Wentworths sister was
    a vertuous aged wight
Whose worthy prayse (though fayne I would)

I spare as now to wright
Because she lasteth yet alive
  but so my willing penne
Will needes I give this little glaunce
  and blase hir thus to men
A woman rare for most respects
  as ever lived here
Doth good to all doth harme to none
  and held of all most deere.
And here shall rest hir bones at lenght
  hir babes and frends amonge
Where to the good of thousand folk
  she lived hath so longe.

282   The sayd Christopher dyed in the yeere 1549 & they had yssue sonnes Arthur Thomas and Charles daughters Elisabeth Anne Marie Catherine & Margarett Maria.

On the stone p' pale first the 6 coates of Glemha' as in the first epitaph and in the second pale the L:Wentworth his eight coates 1. Wentworth 2. Spenser 4. (*sic*) barrye of 6 or & azur a canton ermine. 5. Quarterly p' fesse endent. arg. & gul. 6. azur 3 lucyes heriant arg. & as many croscroslets fitchy or. 7. arg. a saultier engr. gules 8. argent a fesse betwene 2 gemeaux gules 3. Or 3 chevro's gules.

In the church hard by the roodloft on a fayre stone 3 portraytures in brasse a man in his winding sheete on eyther side a woman under them this epitaphe

Orate pro a'i'abus Joh'is Glemham armigeri et Anne ac Alienore uxoru' eius, qui quidem Joh'es obijt (*blank*) die mensis (*blank*) a'o millessimo CCCC (*blank*) et predicta Anna obiit 5 die mensis martij a'o D'ni 1466, et dicta Alienora obijt 30 die Junij A'o D'ni 1480 quoru' a'i'abus p'pitiet'r Deus amen.

Under the portrayture of the dexter woman are the figures of three sonnes & as many daughters, under that of the second 5 sonnes and as many daughters. On the stone above the mans head Glemhams single coate & Quarterly or & gules a bordure engrayled. Over the dexter womans head p' pale Glemham his single coate & quarterly or & gules a bordure engrayled. Over the other p' pale Glemha' & Brandon. Under the epitaph p' pale 1. the 1 wives coate 2. Glemha' 3. 2 wives coate.

On another stone one in complet armour under him this epitaph

Here under layeth the bodye of Christopher Colbe gentleman the fourth son of John Colbe esquier who deceased the 20 day of June 1579

Earth goeth upon earth as mould upon mould
Earth goeth upon earth all glistering in gould
As though earth to earth never turne should
Yet must earth to earth sooner then he would.

On the stone five coates
1. Azur a Fesse betwene 3 eschalops a bordure engrayled or
2. p' pale the former & arg't 3 torteaux in bend betwene to (*sic*) cotises gules

3. over his head Quarterly 1. and 4. the first 2. the second 3. Brewes.
The creast an arme holding a broken sword arg.

4. p' pale Quarterly 1 and 4 the first 2 and 3 the second & Brewes.

5. Brewes alone.

283   On another Stone this epitaph

Here lyeth buryed the bodye of Alice Colbe the daughter of John
Colbe esquier being of the age of 66 years unmaryed deceased the
20th of November a'o 1585.

    If you on earth that live did know

      What rest the dead possesse

    Would not then wish to wander here

      In vale of wretchednesse

On a grave Stone on the north side of the church this epitaph
circumscribed

Orate pro a'i'abus Joh'is Glemham et Rosae uxoris eius et pro
quibus tenentur quor' corpora iacent hic tumulata.[121]

Dynnyngton resp. pag.84

In the Chauncell hard by the roodloft the pourtrayture of one in
complet armour & his wife by him on a stone and this epitaph
subscribed

Orate pro a'i'abus Reginaldi Rous filij et heredis Roberti Rous et
Elisabeth Denston consortis sue qui quidem Reginaldus obijt (*blank*)
die anno 1464, quor' a'i'abus propitiet'r Deus Amen.

The 4 coates that were on the stone are reaved on hir gowne are 2
lyons couchant.

In the chauncell on a fayre stone is a goodly pourtrayture of a
knight armed & fayre arches of brasse on the stone, at his feete a
lyon, under it this epitaph subscribed

Hic jacet tumulatus D'n's Will'm's Wingfeld miles D'n's istius ville
et patronus istius eccl'ie qui obijt primo die Junij a'o D'ni 1398
cuius a'i'e p'pitiet'r Deus. amen.

The two coates reaved.

Hard by this is another fayre stone but worne much by reason of
age, on it the pourtrayture of one in armour & a woman by him
somwhat broken & defaced & once fayrely arched, the two armes
reaved & the epitaph taken of but reserved at the sextens house
contayning these words

Hic jacet Will'm's Wingfeld armiger et Catherina uxor eius D'n's et
patronus istius ville quor' a'i'abus p'pitiet'r Deus amen.[122]

284   In a south chappell lay buryed Thomas Rous esquier and Anne his
wife over them a stone on it no superscriptio' he was father to
Mr.Rous of Hennha' now living and sonne of S'r Anthony the sonne
of S'r Willia' Rous knight.

In the same chappell on a litle raysed stone a child in coates on it
this subscription

Hic iacet Henricus de Bello monte filius et heres Johannis
Vicecomitis Beaumont et Elisabeth uxoris eius filie et heredis Will'mi
Phelip D'ni de Bardolff ac hereditarie terrarum de Erpyngham qui

obijt 6 die novembris a'o D'ni 1442 cuius a'i'e propitiet'r Deus Amen.

On it were 4 coates 1 3 & 4 reaved the second azur 3 cinquefoiles pearced or.

In the same chappell is a fayre raysed tombe on it the massye formes of a Ladye of alabaster under hir head a pillowe at hir feete a dragon, & of a knight armed also of alabaster, under his head an helmet on it a wreath azur supporting a bunch of feathers arg. the circumscription in golden letters altogether worne out the Armes in the window which are Quarterly 1 & 4 Quarterly gules and argent on the first an eagle of 2 & 3 azur 3 cinquefoyles p'ced or, shewe that it is the tombe of Will'm Phelip knight his wife Joane the daughter & heire of Thomas Bardolff L.Bardolff in whose right this Will'm Phelip was Lord Bardolff. He dyed before hir & she dyed about the latter end of the yeere 1446 as appeareth by her last will which was made 7 Sept. 1446 & proved 3 Aprill 1447, wherein she bequeathed h'r body to be buryed in St.Margrets chappell in Dynington.

In this same chappell agaynst the south wyndowe of the same is a tombe somwhat raysed covered with a fayre stone having on it the pourtraytures of a knight in armour & his wife by him & the marks where 4 escotcheons were and this circumscription

Hic jacent Will'm's Phelip armiger qui obijt in die S'c'i Ypoliti a'o D'ni 1407 et Juliana uxor eius que obijt 25 die mensis Maij a'o D'ni 1414 cuius a'i'e propitietur Deus.Amen.

In the window above this tombe p' pale Phelip & gul. a bend betwene 6 eschalops or. 2. Phelip alone 3. p' pale Phelip and vert an escocheon and an urle of martletes argent.

On the east windowe of that chappell toward the lower end of the same about the picture of a knight one v'se & the other about that of a Ladye

Destruat or' nefas mee mentis celsa potestas

Me deitas patris mundet de sordibus atris.[123]

Fresingfeld resp. 105

In the chauncell on a stone the pourtrayture of a man in complet armour & a woman by his side under them this epitaph

Orate pro a'i'abus Will'mi Brewes armigeri filij et heredis Thome Brewes militis, et Isabelle uxoris eiusd' Will'mi, qui quidem Will'm's obijt 28 die Octobris a'o D'ni 1489, quor' a'i'abus propitiet'r Deus amen.

On it 3 coates p' pale Brewes & Quarterly Ermi'e a bend gul. cotised or. & sable a chevrone betwene 3 (*buckle drawn*) arg. Jermy. 2. Brewes alone.
3. (*blank*) a chevron (*blank*) a labell of three points.

On another stone these armes gules a chevron ermine charged with 3 martlets sable & this epit.

Of your Charitie pray for the soule of Symon Topysfeld sometyme of the Eschequer of our Soveraigne Lord the Kinge w'h Symon deceased the 12 day of August in the yeere of our Lord god

1538 & for the soule of Margaret late the wife of the sayd Symon w'h Margaret deceased the 14 day of februarie a'o D'ni 1536 on whose soules Jesu have mercy.

In it are many other grave (*sic*) but the armes & epitaphes are all take awaye.[124]

Westall resp. pag. 251

In this church was buryed Thomas Croftes of Westall esquier in the yeere 1474 in Aprill as appeareth by his will wherin he bequeathed his bodye to be buryed in the Chappell of the blessed Virgin Marie within the parish church of St.Andrew in Westall, as also by the armes on the window in the same chappell which are these p'ti p' pale gules on a Chevron argent 3 hurts azur & arg. 3 mullets sable betwene 2 bendlets engrayled gules, in another window eyther of these by it selfe & empaled as before & underneath

Orate p' a'i'abus Thome Croffts et Johanne uxoris eius.

In a place of the chauncell is a raysed tombe against the south wall, made by Mr. (*blank*) Bawin of the same towne wherin he meaneth to laye himself.[125]

286

Brampton resp. pag.41

In the upperend of the chauncell on a stone

Orate pro a'i'a Thomae Duke armigeri qui obijt 21 die Septembris A'o D'ni 1503 —

Under it these coates. Quarterly Azur a chevro' betwene 3 foules arg. beaked and membr. gules, Duke, & sable a fess betwene 2 chevrons or, 2 annulets (*annulets conjoined drawn*) of the first Banyarde, & Quarterly Duke & azur a faulcon desplayed argent.

On another stone.

Hic jacet Agnes Duke que fuit filia Edmundi Wydewille armigeri que obijt a'o D'ni 1585 cui' a'i'e propitiet'r Deus. Amen.[126]

Schadenfeild resp. pag.

In the chauncell lay buryed Elisabeth Duke & Anne Duke.

Against the south wall of the church on a peece of brasse this epitaph.

Here under lyeth the bodye of Mary Cuddon, the first wife of Willia' Cuddon of Schadenfeld in the Countye of Suff. gent. & one of the daughters & heires of George Harvye of Oldton in the sayd Countie esquier who dyed 22 of November a'o D'ni 1586.

Above on the Wall Arg. a Chevro' gules on a chief azur 3 besaunts. The same q'rtered with arg. a fesse wave gules inter 3 eaglets sable. P' pale this last q'rtered coate and Quarterly Barney w'th a (*crescent drawn*) 2. Gules a chevron ingrayled betwene 3 reedshofs arg. 3. gules a chevro' betwene 3 eaglets arg. 4. arg. on a canto' gules a crosse of the field. The 4 first empaled with q'rterlye gules on a bend arg. 3 trefoyles slipp'd vert a fleur de lis of the seconde 2. Sable a boares head coupe arg. 3. arg. 3 griphons heades erased sable 4. as the 1.[127]

Saterly resp. pag.

In the North window of the chauncell p' pale argent on a bend betwene 2 croscroslets gules 3 mullets of the first & sable a chevron arg. betwene 3 cinquefoyles or & on the same window these two former quartered & empaled with sable guttye a catherine wheele argent. Above these

Orate p' a'i'a p' a'i'abus (*sic*) Roberti Bumpsted .... (*sic*) et Ade consortis sue qui obijt 7 die mensis Aprilis A'o D'ni 1479.

In the middest of the chauncell almost iust by the roodloft on a stone the pourtrayture in brasse of a man armed under him this epitaphe

Orate p' a'i'a Roberti (*change of page*) Bumpsted generosi qui obiit 7 die mensis Aprilis a'o D'ni 1479 cujus a'i'e propitiet'r Deus amen.

The armes underneath reaved.

Against the north wall of the chauncell is a raysed tombe covered with marble the circumscription taken awaye wherin seemeth to have bene buryed one of the Platers w'ch is manifested by the armes about it & the windowe directly above it. In the windowe are these armes v'c't p' pale arg. 3 bendes wave azur & p'ti p' fesse arg. a chevron sable betwene 3 mullets gules 2. vert a lion ramp. argent crowned or. And iust by it in the same window Quarterly 1 & 4 ermine a bend gules escotised or. 2. sable a chevron betwene 3 buckles (*round buckles drawn*) arg. 3. vert 3 faulcons or on as many blocks arg. tyed 4. as 1st.

On the tombe also were 6 escotcheons now only remayne 3 2 in the south side of the tombe 1. that which was last in the windowe 2. p'ti p' pale arg. a chevro' sables betwene 3 mullets gules & (*blank*) a faulcon displayed gules.

At the east end of the same this p' pale Platers & arg. a chevron sable betwene 3 mullets gules. They say it is the tombe of Willia' Platers a yonger brother but the armes borne by Platers on this tombe having no difference of minoritie argue the contrarie.

In the upper end of the chauncell iust by the north wall of the same is (*sic*) on a fayre stone is the portraiture of a man armed in brasse and his wyfe by him under them this epitaph

Orate p' a'i'a Thome Platers armigeri nuper huius eccl'ie patroni et Anne uxoris ejus sororis et heredis Rogeri Denays de Tatyngton armigeri qui quidem Thomas obijt 21 die mensis Septembris a'o D'ni 1479 et predicta D'na Anna obijt 10 die mensis Octobris ex tunc proxime sequente quor' a'i'abus p'pitietur Deus.

On the top of the stone 3 escotcheons 1. Platers single coate 2. Quarterlye arg. a chevron sable betwene 3 mullets gules & vert a lyon ramp: arg. crowned or. 3. p' pale Platers & the last quartered coate.

On another stone iust by this the pourtrayture of a man armed, & under him (*page changes*) this epitaphe

Under this stone lyeth buryed the bodye of Thomas Platers of Saterlye esquier patron of this mannour who had yssue by Elizabeth

287

288

82

his wife one of the daughters of S'r Thomas Jerman of Rishbrook in the countye of Suff. knight 6 sonnes & 6 daughters & dyed the 9 of September 1572.

Underneath this escotcheo' p' pale Platers & (*blank*) a crescant betwene 2 mullets in pale.

On another stone this epitaph in brasse.

Under this stone lyeth buryed the bodye of Willia' Platers esquier true patron of this church who had 4 wifes v'c't Thomasine daughter of George Duke of Freunce esquier by whome he had yssue one sonne who dyed without yssue, Elisabeth daughter of Thomas Tymperley of Hintlesham esquier by whome he had yssue 2 daughters & one sonne Thomasine one of the daughters & heires of Edmond Tyrrell of Beches in the countie of Essex esquier by whome he had yssue one daughter, Mary daughter of William Drake of Hardley in the countie of Norff esquier by whome he had yssue one daughter & 2 sonnes & dyed the 6th day of June in the yeere of our Lord God 1584.

Over it an escotcheon these armes, Quarterly 1 & 4 Quarterlye 1 & 4 Platers 2. arg. a chevron sable betwene 3 mullets gules. 3. vert a lion arg. crowned or.

2. & 3 eight coats Quartered

1. (*blank*) a Chevron (*blank*) between 3 catherine wheeles

2. (*blank*) a Chevron b. between 3 (*blank*)

3. Banyard.

4. Arg. on a fesse azur 3 crownes or.

5. azur. a fleur delis arg. betwene 3 cinquefoiles or.

6. ermine on a Chief gules 3 fusills (*blank*) chargd with 3 (*roundels drawn*)

7. arg. on a chevron gules 3 fleur de lis or.

8. as the 1.

On another stone iust by this the pourtrayture of a woma' and her daughter by hir under hir this epitaph

Here lyeth buryed Thomasine late wife unto Willia' Platers of Saterley esquier one of the daughters & coheirs unto Edmond Tyrrell of Betches in the Countie of Essex esquier who had yssue by the sayd William Susanne Platers & dyed the 8 of May a'o D'ni 1578 on whose soule Jesus have mercy being of the age of 34 yeeres.

Over her head on a fayre escotcheo' all the coats of the precedent stone empaled with Quarterly 1. argent 2 chevrons azur a bordure engr. gules 2. paly of 6 arg. and sable. 3. gules on a chevron argent 3 dolphins nayant vert. 4. (*page changes*) argent a crosse betwene 4 eschalops sable in center of all these 4 coates a mullet or.

In the church on a stone

Hic jacet corpus Roberti Edgar generosi sepultu' qui obijt 9 die augusti a'o D'ni 1594

Over it this escotcheon p'ti p' chevron or and azur on the first 2 fleur delis gules on the seconde a fess fusile of 5 fusills of the first charged with as many eschalops of the third.[128]

Ellough vid. pag.91

In the church on a stone this epitaph

Here lyeth buryed Alyce Joyner sometyme wife of Paule Sydnor esquier & after wife of John Berney of Reedham Esq. w'h dyed the first day of May in the yeere of our Lord god 1558, on whose soule Jesu have mercy. Amen.

Under it is this coat p' pale. Quarterly Berney (*crescent drawn*) 2. Reedham gules a chevron engrayled twixt 3 reedsheafs arg.
3. gules a Chevron betw. 3 eaglets displayed arg.
4. arg. on a canton gules a crosse of the first & or on' a cross engrayled azur 5 fleur de lis of the first all in a bordure engrayled of the second Joyner.

Just by this another stone on it this epitaph.

Here lyeth buryed the bodye of Ursule daughter of John Berney of Reedham esquier & wife of William Sydnor of Willingham esquier which had yssue 3 sonnes and 2 daughters & dyed the 4th day of august in the yeere of our Lord God 1568, on whose soule Jesus have mercy Amen.

Under it p' pale Quarterly Sidnor and Joyner & quart'ly Berneys 4 coates as before.

In the chauncell on a stone the pourtrayture of a man armed under it this epitaph

Hic jacet Gilbertus Bacheler Armiger Quondam Clericus Corone in cancellario D'ni Regis Henrici Septimi qui quidem Gilbertus obijt 29 die octobris a'o D'ni 1500 cuius a'i'e p' pitiet'r Deus amen

On the upper end of the stone
2 Escotcheons bearing
A bend (*blank*) betwene 3 single wings.[129]

290   Stoke juxta Neyland resp. pag.

In the upper end of the North ele of the churche on a fayre stone once adorned with a pourtrayture & 4 escotcheons but now all reaved is engraven this circumscription

Vous qe par ici passez pour lalme sire Johan de Paytone priez le cors de qi ici gist l'alme recyve Jesu Christ Amen

Just by the same also another of more antiquitye all reaved the circumscription in the stone worne out only a word or two appeareth (which showeth it to be the monument of a Peytone. Jane de Peytone ... mercy ... l'ame crist.

In a chappell north called Rothings chappell layeth one in complet armour, the epitaph reaved 4 escotcheons contayning one & the self same coat v'c't gules 3 bugles in triangle arg. They say under it layeth S'r .... Rothing Knight.

In the South ele on a fayr stone having the epitaphe reaved, these 4 coates 1 & 4 (*blank*) 3 Escalops – They think Ab's 2 & 3 (*blank*) 3 cocks in triangle.

On a stone in the south chappell called Tendringe chappell

Here lyeth Edward Waldegrave the fourth sonne of S'r William

84

Waldegrave knight who deceased the 21 June 1585 aetat. 10.[130]

Just by are 2 fayre & auncient stones hertofore adorned with brasse pourtraytures, and armes now all reaved. I suppose under them laye some of the Tendrings.

In the same chappell on a stone the pourtrayture of one in complet harness fayrely arched treading on a lyon with this circumscription

Hic jacent tumulati D'n's Will'us Tendring miles et D'na Catharina Clopton uxor eius, qui obierunt anno D'ni 1408 quor' a'i'abus p'pitiet'r Deus. Amen.

The coates are reaved.

On another stone the pourtrayture of one in complet armour & his wife by him fayrely arched w'th this circumscription

Orate p' a'i'abus Joh'is Howard militis qui obijt a'o D'ni 1400 et Alicie uxoris eius que obijt in festo S'to Luce evangeliste a'o D'ni 1426, quor' a'i'abus p'pitiet'r Deus.

On it p' pale Howard & azur a fesse entre 2 chevrons arg. the 3 other reaved.

On another stone a fayre pourtrayture of a woman, on it this epitaph

Hic iacet Catherina Tendryng quonda' uxor Thome Clopton que obijt D'ni (sic) Veneris ante festu' Pentecostes a'o D'ni 1402

On a fayre Stone the portrayture of a woman under hir this epitaphe

Under this stone is here buryed the bodye of the right honourable woma' & Ladye sometyme wife unto the right high and mightie Prince Lorde John Howard Duke of Norff & mother unto the right noble and puissant Prince Lord Thomas Howard Duke also of Norff. w'h departed this life in the yeere of our Lord god 1456. on whose soule &c.

Above hir head 2 escotcheons 1. on the dext' side Brotherton Howard Warre' & Mowbray quartered in the garter. On the sinister p' pale Brotherton, Howard, Warren, Mowbray, Segrave & (blank) a lyon ramp. betwene croscroslets fitche or empaled with or 3 pales wave gules. In the 3d place the first underneth as the second. 4. Howardes 6 Coates.

On a stone the pourtrayture of a child in swathinge clouts under it

Here lyeth John 2 sonne of Henry L: Windesore & Anne his wife one of the daughters & heires of S'r Thomas Ryvet knight who deceased 1588.[131]

In the Chauncell on a stone the pourtrayture of one armed & by him his wife under them this epitaph

Orate p' a'i'abus Edmundi Danyell et Gratie uxoris eius qui quidem Edmundus obijt 24 die Septembris a'o 1498 et predicta Gratia obijt ... die mensis ... anno D'ni 1500.

On it were 4 escotcheons 1 2 & 4 reaved the 3d Quarterly _____ an hounde (blank) & (blank) a pale fusilee (blank) empaled with (blank) 3 cheverons ermine. He treadeth on a greyhounde.

291

In the chauncell on a fayre stone the pourtraytur of a woman under hir

Hic iacet D'na Johanna Redmeld quondam sponsa (*page changes*) Will'mi Redmeld militis ac filie recolende memorie D'ne Margarete Howard Ducisse Norff. hic superius tumulate que obijt 20 die februarij a'o D'ni 1506 cujus a'i'ie &c.

On it were 4 escotcheons 1 & 3 reaved 2 & 4 (*blank*) a chevron betwene three horsheades erased.

Against the north wall in the upper end of the cha'cell is a raysed tombe of marble which had on it the pourtrayture of a woman, at ech corner an escotcheo' & a circumscription & armes on the side & endes of it but are all reaved. I suppose this to be the to'be of Margaret Duchesse of Norff. before mentioned in the epitaph precedent, this being above the former & no other higher nor in the upper end of the chauncell.[132]

In a north chappell on a fayre stone the pourtraytures of an armed man betwene 2 women, under them this epitaph.

Hic iacet Joh'es Mannok armiger et Alienora uxor eius qui quidem Joh'es obijt 12 die mensis Septembris a'o D'ni 1475 et dicta Alienora obijt _____ mensis _____ 1474

On it were 3 escotcheons, but now reaved. They were over eyther of their heades one.

In the same chappell on another stone the pourtraytures of one in a gowne betwene his 2 wives under them this epitaphe.

Hic iacet Franciscus Mannok armiger duas qui habuit uxores. ex priore quidem unu' filiu' et quinq' suscepit filias ex latera vero, unu' filiu', et tres filias. obijt 8 die mensis Novembris a'o D'ni 1590 a'o aetatis 68.

Labitur occulte aetas
Quid dant divitiae Crassi Crassive talenta?
quid juvat immensus tantus et orbis honor?
O'ia vilescunt que mors rapit ore voraci
Virtutis solide vita perennis erit.

Over it 2 escotcheons 1. p' pale sable a crosse potence arg. & (*blank*) a chevron (*blank*) betwene 3 leop'des heades (*blank*) & 2 the same againe.

Upon the east wall of the same chappell on a peece of brasse a woman kneeling on the dexter side of hir p' pale Bedingfelds 12 coates & sable a crosse potence argent. On the sinister Mannok alone. Underneath this epitaphe.

Elisabetha filia Francisci Mannok armigeri maior natu per Anna' uxorem sua' feliciter e vivis excessit a'o salutis 1587.
Elisabetha aetate vivens, pietatis alumna
catholica numen relligione colens
Faelix morte sua est, infaelix morte maritus
ad mortem et morbi taedia fortis erat.

In the South chappell against the south wall is a monument raysed wherin an auncient Ladye kneeleth & her daughter at hir backe, above them p'ti p' pale Waldegrave and Pagett. This epitaph in golden letters.

This is the monument of the Lady Waldegrave second wife of S'r William Waldegrave the elder knight of Smalbridge in the Countye of Suff. and youngest daughter of the Lord William Pagett of Beaudesert in the countie of Stafford. This Ladye was first maryed to S'r Thomas Ryvett knight who had by hir only one daughter who was marryed to Henry L:Windsore of Bradnha' in the County of Buckingha'. This Ladye Waldegrave was liberall & charitably given all hir life toward the poore, who departed this life the 21 of July in the yeere of our Lorde 1600.[133]

Hevenyngha' resp. pag.

In the Church on a stone this epitaph

Orate pro a'i'abus George Page otherhaw called George Baxter et Dame Margerie uxoris sue.

In the north chappell is a fayre marble tombe raysed against the wall, on it a knight armed under his feete an Elcke & his ladye by him, on each corner an escotcheon 1. Quarterly Hevenyngha' & Redsha' 2. p' pale the former quarter'd coate & azur a frett arg. a chief or. 3 as 2. 4. azur a fret arg. a chief or. about it this circumscriptio'

Hic iacent D'n's Joh'es Hevenyngha' miles et D'na Margareta uxor eius qui hanc capellam fieri fecerunt quor' a'i'abus et o'i'u' fideliu' p'pitiet'r Deus. Amen.

On the west end of this tombe Quarterly Heveny'gham & Gyssynge.

On the south side p' pale Heveningham & argent on a bend sable 3 houlets of the first, Savell. 2. p' pale Hevenyngham & quarterly azur a crosse sarcele or, & lozengie ermine & gules

On the East end q'rt'ly Hev. and Redysham.

Against the same wall stand erected in wood the pourtraitures of 2 knights armed & a Ladye.[134]

294

Huntyngfield resp. pag.

On a stone in the chauncell this epitaph

This earthly coulord marble stone behold with weeping eyes
Under whose cold and massy weight John Paston buryed lyes.
A gentleman by birth & deeds the second sonn to one
S'r William Paston worthy knight deceased long agone.
This gentill esquier in Huntingfeild a widow tooke to wife
That hight Anne Arrowsmyth w'th whome he led a loving life.
Eleven yeers space & somwhat more by whome he also had
One only childe a Virgine milde his aged heart to glad.
In youthfull yeeres this gentillman a gallant Courtier was
With rarest vertues well adornd to Courtiers all a glasse.
A Pensioner to Princes fower Henry the eight that Roy
To Edward King to Mary Queene to Elsabeth our ioy
Which fower he served faythfullye, the Court Laments his end
His country neighbours all bewayle the losse of such a frend.

To poore a present remedy, to honest men an ayde
A father to the fatherlesse, the widows plaint he wayde
Against the hungry traveller his dores were never shut
Against the seely needy soule his purse was never knit
When he had lived three score yeeres and fowre death closed
up his eyes
He lived well and dyed and dyed well & buryed here he lyes.
Anno D'ni 1575 Septembris 21.

Over it an escotcheon contayning the 8 coates of Paston with a
crescant in centre.

On a Stone just by

Here lyeth the body of Elisabeth Cooke daughter to Edward
Cooke & Bridget his wife who deceased the 9 of November in the
yeere of our Lord God 1586

In the church on a stone a litle pourtr. of a man, under
Orate p' a'i'a Walteri Blakey cujus &c.[135]

Cookelye resp. p.68

On a stone

Here lyeth buryed the body of Margery Browne the wife of
Willia' Browne who dyed 17 Sept. 1594, he dyed 22 of November
1587 & lyeth buryed at Rendham.[136]

St.Peters in Southelmham 186

In a North chappell on a fayr freestone the portrayture of a
man & a woman cut in the stone on it this circumscription.

Orate pro animabus Joh'is Taseburgh qui obijt die *(blank)*

On it 2 coates arg. a chevro' betwene 3 palmers puches sable
stringed or & 2. p'ti p' fesse arg. & sable 3 pallets
counterchanged.[137]

Groton resp. p.113

In the upperend of the churche under a stone w'thout epitaph
layeth buryed Mr.John Wynthorp father to John Wynthorp L: of the
Mannour of Groton.[138]

Stanton S'tor' resp. p.216

In the midle ele of the churche towardes the chauncell on a
marble stone this epitaphe

Orate pro a'i'a Florencie Aschefyld vidue que obiit 15 die
mensis Novembris a'o D'ni 1506 cuius a'i'e &c.

The escotcheon underneath is reaved, on the wall right against this
stone is this paynted Sable on a fess entre 3 fleur de lis & a bordure
or, a *(crescent drawn)* sab.

Just by this stone is another having on it the pourtraytures of a
man & woman under them this

Pray for the soule of William Rookewood esquier & Alice his
wife which W'm deceased the 17 day of December in the yeere
1537.

On the upperpart of the stone p' pale arg. 6 rooks sable & arg. on
a fesse entre 3 escotcheons gules as many mulletts or p'ced.[139]

Holton in Blith, resp. p.132

In the south side of the church there lay 2 stones of marbell the brasse reaved.[140]

Bliford resp. p.33

In the isle of the church are 2 stones the epitaph & armes on the one reaved, on the other the pourtrayture of a woman the epitaph under hir reaved above hir p' pale (*ermine drawn*) a bend gules cotised or & barrye of (*blank*) a griphon sergreant.

In the chauncell are 2 gravestones w'thout brasse.[141]

resp. page.218   Stoke iuxta Neyland

In Stoke are many mannours v'c't

1. Stoke Hall which belongeth to the Lord Windsore by the right of his wife as that of Tendringhall. Keepeth court & leete.

2. Tendringhall situate in the parke (comonly called Stoke parke but p'perly Tendring parke) belongeth to Henry L:Windsore by the mariage of his wife the d. & coh. of S'r Thomas Ryvett late of Chipenha' in Suff. who bought it of Thomas the last Duke of Norff. a litle before his attayndure & againe of Queene Elisabeth by reason of the insufficiencie of the former sale by the Duke to whome it came by auncient descent in the right line from S'r Robert Howard K't grandfather to John Howard first duke of Norff. of that sirname who had it in right of his wife the d. and coh. of S'r John Tendringe K't in which name it had contynued for many yeeres together. (the fines of both these mannours are arbitrable & this mannour hath charter warrant.

3. Scotland hall the Lord Mr.Rookwood of Euston holdes court baron only.

4. Netherhall belonged once to the Giffords now to the Lord Windsore aforesayd in right of his wife.

5. Giffords hall apertayned to the Giffords 300 years since, fell afterwards to the King (*blank*) who gave it in exchange to Mr.Mannock for land in the forrest to whome it nowe appertayneth.

6. Levinhall the L: S'r W'm Waldegrave of Smalbridge k't.

Sable a crosse engr, on a X or

7. Paytonhall in the hands of S'r John Payton of Islam in which name it hath contynued for hundreds of yeeres as appereth by the monuments of them that lay buryed in the church. The mannour house standeth in 3 parishes. The hall in Boxforde, the parlour in Stoke and the kitchin in Polstead.

8. Rectorie mannour. To the personage house belongeth coppyhold tennauntes & is in the handes of Mr.Mannock aforsayd.[142]

Barrowe resp. pag.148

In the chauncell a gravestone

Here lyeth Edmund Butts esquier w'h deceased the 7 day of May in the yeere 1542

On another stone under w'h layeth buryed John Crosier sometyme parson of the towne who dyed 1569, this epitaph.

Qui cupit exolvi et cu' Christo vivere, mortem

Non metuit, tali voce sed astra ferit
Tristia iam longe pertesus munera vite
Me precor ut iubeant numina summa mori
Eripe terreno Rex eripe carcere tandem
Et tecu' in celis da mihi Christi locu'.

Against the south wall of the chauncell is a fayr erected tombe of marbell, within the concave arche the pourtrayture of a k't armed kneeling, behind him 3 sonnes. On the dexter side of him one wife at her backe 5 daughters, on the sinister side another behinde her 2 daughters.

Betwene him & his dexter wife these armes Quarterly Heigham & gul. a chevron (*ermine drawn*) entre 3 faulcons flying argent empaled w'th Quarterly 1 & 4 Waldegraves 6 coates & 2 & 3 (*ermine drawn*) a fesse sable entre 3 (*?buckles drawn*). Over his head Quarterly Heigham & the faulcons, the crest an horsehead erased arg' the mantle arg. and gul. Betwene him & his sinister wife Waldegraves 6 cotes q'rtered with (*ermine drawn*) a fesse entre 3 (*roundels drawn*). Belowe about the tombe 3 tymes Higha' quartered with the faulcons in centre a martlett & so in all the former. Within the arched concavitye a long epitaph

Bereft of worldly life in hope to rise to endles light
By Christ desert here rest the corse of Clement Higha'
knight
Whom Suffolck soyle did breede bring up & chiefly foster
aye
In Barrowe where his dwelling was untill his dying daye
Which was the 9 of March since god a mortall man became
The thousand & five hundredth yeere w'h seventy to the same.

The substance of the rest is this. He was loyall, wise, wittye, welspoken, charitable, a lawyer Speaker in the parliament house in the tyme of Phillip & Marie & of their privy Counsell & after Lord chief Baron of the Exchequer during Queene Marie hir life.

In the south isle of the churche on a stone
Orate pro a'i'a Alicie Fyrmyn filie W'mi Coggeshall de Hawkeden que obijt 18 die aprilis a'o D'ni 1513.[143]

Kenforde resp. pag.148
On a stone in the midle isle of the churche
Of your Charitie pray for the soule of Raynold Fysson late of Kenforde who departed out of this transitorie world the 16 of June a'o 1558 & doth lye buryed under this marble stone.[144]

298

Livermere magna
Against the north wall of the churche or 2 barres vert 3 eschallops in chief. The pourtrayture of a man & a woman under them
Orate p' a'i'abus Clementis Clercke quondam clerici Corone cancellarie Regis Henrici Septimi et Alicie uxoris eius qui quidem Clemens obijt vicesimo quinto die Octobris a'o D'ni Millesimo quingentesimo.

Against the north all in the upper end of the chauncell is a tombe somwhat raysed with the pourtrayture of a man armed & a woman by him upon it, an escotcheon underneath them reaved. On the dexter side of the pourtraytures somwhat above them Bokenhams coate alone on the sinister sable, a chevron _____ entre 3 swans heades erased arg. On the west & head end of the tombe 3 coates

1. Arg. a Lyon ramp. gules debrused with a bend azur charged with 3 plates.

2. Or 2 barres sable empaled w'th Clopton.

3. arg. a lyon ramp. gules empaled w'th or 2 barres sables.

On the south side of the tombe.

1. Bokenham & sable a fesse engr: entre 3 fleur delis arg. empaled.

2. Bokenha' empaled w'th barry of 6 gul. and azur a griphon sergreant or.

3. Bohenha' empaled w'th sable a chevron entre 3 swannes heads erased argent beaked gul.

4. Barry of 6 gul. & azur a griphon sergreant or empaled w'th arg. a lyon ramp. sable on his Shoulder a (*crescent drawn*) vert.

5. ermine 3 chevernels sable empaled w'th parti p' pale azur & or a chief gules.[145]

299

Ikesworth resp. p.141

In the upper end of the chauncell is a fayr raysed tombe against the north wall covered with a marble stone, on the south side of it are 3 escotcheons 1. gules a crosse or fretted azur borne by the name of Codington.

2. Codington empaled with or on a crosse in a bordure both engrayled azur 5 fleur de lis of the field Jenour.

3. Quarterly 1. Argent a lyon ramp. gules Bokenham. 2. Or 2 barres sable, Thelnetham. 3. gul. 3 plates charged w'th as many (*cross crosslet drawn*) sable.

4. Bokenham & Jenour.

On the wall above the tombe this epitaph

Here lyeth buryed the bodyes of Richard Codington esquier the first temporall Lord of this Mannour of Ixworth after the suppression of the Abbye which he had of our Soveraigne Lord King Henry 8 in exchange for the mannour of Codington now called Nonesuch in the County of Surrey & Elisabeth his wife sometyme the wife of Thomas Bokenham of great Livermere esquier which had yssue by the said Thomas Bokenha' John & Dorothye. The sayd Richard Codington deceased the 27 day of Maye in the yeere of our Lord god 1567 & the sayd Elisabeth deceased the 8 day of September in the yeere of our Lord god 1571.

above this epitaphe on the dexter side a ma' kneeling over his head Codington his armes, subscribed Codington, on the sinister side a woman at hir backe a sonne & a daughter all kneeling, over his head Bokenhams 4 coates empaled with Jenour. In the upperpart betwene both these former recited escotcheons standes Codington empaled with Jenour.

91

On the south wall of the chauncell at the upper end therof is a fayre monument of alabaster contayning in it this epitaph

Cur gressu' sistis celeres cur figis ocellos?
forte quis hac queris sit tumulatus humo.
Ecquid fama tuas generosi numen ad aures
Nortoni tulerit sat scio fama tulit —
Larga manus pietas, prudentia, candor, honestas
Majores dotes quam latitare queant.
Hunc tegit hoc bustum, lachrymas cur fundis ademptu'
tam claru' terris ingemis esse virum
Flere vetat, vivit, nec fata maligna valebunt
Nomen inextinctu' tollere, flere vetat
Vivit adhuc licet ossa iacent tumulata, legitq'
Praemia virtutis splendidiora suae —
Londinu' Luget, luget Colcestria demptum
Cunctaq' lugubri Buria voce replet.
Ipse sibi solus gaudet, gratulatur ovatq'
Summa tenens summi cu' Jove regna poli
Joh'es Norton

obijt 4 die Julij 1597 aetatis suae 44. Richardus Symons amicus suus chariss. ergo posuit.

The letters are in gold upon black.

Above the epitaph azur 3 swordes 2 in saultier the third in pale all crossing in centre arg. pomeled or, on chief gul. a lyon passant gard. entre 2 maunches arg. his crest a demylion ramp. gul. yssant out of an helmet arg. holding an eschalop arg.

On the dexter side of it this coate, on the sinister the same empaled with arg. a chevron sable entre 3 mains sinisters gules.[146]

Woodbridge resp. pag.264

In the north side of the chauncell on a fayre raysed tombe covered with a marble stone is this circumscription

Thomas Seckford libellor' supplicu' per annos 30 magister posuit sibi sueq' familie in mortis memoria' spemq' vite eternae

In the east window of the same place are Seckford his 4 coates with (*crescent drawn*) for difference.

In the upperend of the chauncell on a litle stone the pourtrayture of a boye in a coate over his head these armes azur 5 lionceaux ramp. arg. a canton ermine under the pourtrayture this.

Joh'es Sherlond obijt 1601 aetatis suae 7°

then these v'ses

Heaven & this stone disioyned keepes
One double fayre in mynde & face
Heaven hath his soule his corps here sleeps
Till ioynd both ioye a ioyfull place.
Thus loosed by death to Christ live knitt
Whome men did love for grace & witt
Christus solus mihi salus.

This child was sonne to Thomas Sherlond of Wynston by

300

Debenham esquier and Sergeant Yelverton his daughter.

Thomas Sherlond his father was a Tanner.[147]

Letheringham resp. pag.158

In the chauncell on a marble stone the epitaph reaved p' pale Wingfeld w'th the cotises and (*blank*) a chevron entre 3 trefoiles slipped. On another fayre stone the pourtrayture of 3 man armed under them this epitaph

Here lyeth S'r Thomas Wingfeld k't, Richard Wingfeld & W'm Wingfeld esquiers sonnes of Rob't Wingfeld knight & of Lady Elisabeth his wife sister to the Duke of Norff.

above their heades 3 escotcheons the midlemost reaved, 1 & 3 p' pale Wingfeld & Warren. Under them also 3 escotcheons 3 reaved 1 & 2 p' pale Wingfeld & (*blank*) 2 barres (*blank*) a ca'ton ermine.

On another stone iust by this

Here lyeth W'm Wingfeld esquier somtyme Sewer to our Soveraigne Lord K. Henry 7 the sonne of S'r John Wingfeld kt. & Dame Elisabeth w'h W'm dyed the 4 day of December in the yeere of our Lord god 1491 on whose soule god have mercy.

Underneath Wingfeld empaled with Waldegrave.

301

In the upper division of the chauncell on a fayre stone is the pourtrayture of one in complet armour & his wife by him, at his feete a lyon, on it 4 escotcheons reaved, this epitaph subscribed.

Hic iacet D'n's Robertus Wingfeld miles et Elisabeth uxor eius qui quidem Robertus obijt 3 die mensis Maij a'o D'ni 1409 quor' a'i'abus p'pitiet'r Deus.

On a very fayre stone garnished & arched w'th brasse is the pourtrayture of a k't armed & by him his ladye, at his feete the armes of Wingfeld at hirs the armes of Bovile this epitaph circumscribed.

Vous qui par ici passez .... sa femme priez que lour almes a dieu soyent recommandez.

On another Stone iust by the pourtrayture of a woman

Hic iacet Margareta Wingfeld uxor Joh'is Wingfeld quor' a'i'abus, then the other halfe of the circumscription going the other way meeteth this. Margareta Russell D'ni Joh'is Russell militis de Comitatu Wigornie.

Over the first halfe a chevron entre 3 (*cross fitchy drawn*) sable empaled w'th or a maunch gules. On the 2 side p' pale Wingfeld & or a maunch gul. I take it she was 1. wife to Russell then to Wingfeld.

On another fayre stone by this the pourtrayture of a man armed under him this epitaph

Hic iacet D'n's Joh'es de Wingfeld miles quondam D'n's de Letheringham cuius a'i'e propitiet'r Deus amen.

On it were 4 escotcheons at ech corner one but all reaved save the 2 which is p' pale Wingfeld & Hastings.

On another fayre stone all garnished w'th brasse the pourtrayture of a k't armed at his feete a lyon upon his brest q'rterly or & sable on the 1. a lyon passant gard. gules, on the dexter side above his head Bovile w'th a martlet gul. in the 1 q'rter, this epitaph circumscribed

Sire William de Bovile Seignour de Letheringham patroun de cieus gist ci dieu de sa alme en face verroie mercie et vous qe cest lu honur et pour l'alme de lui par charite priet et qaraunte iours de pardoun averet.

302 On a very fayre & large stone in the upper part of (*page changes*) the chauncell the pourtrayture of a k't armed & his Lady by his side this subscription

Here lyeth S'r Robert Wingfeld k't & Dame Cicily his wife daughter of the Lord Wentworth which sayd S'r Robert Wingfeld dyed the 19 of March 1596 & the sayd Dame Cicily dyed the 22 of August a'o 1573.

above their figures is an escotcheon contayning 46 coates the 1. Wingfeld the last arg. a fesse dauncy &c.

Against the north wall of the chauncell is a fayre raysed tombe of marble fayrely arched w'th freestone & set forth with many escotcheons. Upon the playne of the marble stone are 4 escotcheons 1. Wingfeld & Bovile quartered, 2. Wingfeld & sable a chevron entre 3 trefoyles slipped arg. empaled. 3. Wingfeld alone. 4. the 3 foiles alone. On the south side of the tombe 3 escotcheons 1. Wingfeld & or 2 barres gul. a canton ermine 3. quarterly Montague & Morthermer empaled w'th the trefoyles, this circumscription in brasse on the marble.

.... D'ne Elisabeth Arundell Ducisse Norff. et Joh'is Gausell militis qui quidem Joh'es obijt 11 die mensis Maij a'o D'ni 1481 ac D'na Elisabeth Wingfeld uxor predicti Joh'is filia Anne Montague Ducisse Exon' et ......

above are many very fayre cotes. Wingfeld & Bovile q'rtered w'th many others, above the mantle & helmet a bull passant halfe sable halfe or.

Against the south side of the chauncell is a fayre raysed tombe sutable in forme to the former on it the formes of one armed at his feete a bull at his head an helmet on a wreath a bulls head coupe sable & his Lady by him, above fayrely arched with freestone & escotcheons but no armes set on them.[148]

Petistree resp. pag.

On a stone in the churche, Pray for the soule of Thomas Starke which deceased the 24 day of August in the yeere of our Lord god 1528 on whose &c.

On a stone in the chauncell the pourtrayture of a man in a gowne betwene 2 women, over his head arg. on a fesse entre 3 escotcheons 302 (*blank*) 3 mulletts or. Over his dexter wife (*page changes*) the former empaled with (*blank*) on a chevron (*blank*) entre 3 griphons heades erased (*blank*) a (*crescent drawn: blank*). Over the sinister wifes head Bacons coate and BlenerHasset his 6 coates, under them this epitaph

Here lyeth Francis Bacon third sonne of Edmond Bacon of Hessett esquier deceased which first maryed Elisabeth daughter to

Cotton of Barton in Suff. & having by hir one only daughter Elisabeth maryed to his second wife Marye daughter & heyre to George Blenerhaysset esquier & by hir having no yssue departed this life the 13 of December in the yeare of our Lord God 1580.[149]

In the upper & north end of the chauncell on a fayre to'be of Freestone lay the pourtraytures in stone of 2 dutchesses wifes of Thomas the last Duke of Norff. at the head of the one most northerly & at hir feete lyeth a dragon at the east & west end of the tombe next hir Howards 4 Coates empaled with L:Audley of Walden. On the more southerly p't the other Lady layeth under hir head an horse couchant at hir feete an hart couchant. On the east & west end of the tombe right against hir Howards 4 coates empaled with Quarterly Daubigny Fitzallan, Rivers & quarterly Matravers & parti p' fesse. On the south side Arundells coates. 2. p' pale Howards 4 coates & Audley 3. Howards 4 coates empaled w'th Arundells 4 coates. 4. Audley alone.

Close unto this is another fayre tombe of the same matter & structure but no pourtrayture upon it. On the north side of it are these coates 1. Howards 4 coates. 2. Henry FitzRoys armes with a bend sinister empaled w'th Howards 4 coates. 3. Henry FitzRoy as before in the garter & a Dukes crowne. 4. Howard alone crowned. At the west end p' pale FitzRoy & Howard as before. 2. FitzRoy alone. On the south end 1. p' pale FitzRoy & Howard. At the east end 1. FitzRoy. 2. FitzRoy & Howard empaled.

In the upperend of the same chauncell on the southerly side is also a very fayre tombe of the same matter & workemanship of the former upon it the complet figure (*page turns*) of a Duke & his Duchesse, he in complet armour, at his feete a lyon, at ech of the fower corners of the tombe is a lyon segant holding up an escotcheon contayning in it Howards 4 Coates.[150]

In the church on a stone

Orate p' a'i'a Agnetis quondam uxoris Roberti Colvyle primogeniti Will'mi Colvyle nuper de Perham qui obijt 22 die Marcij a'o D'ni 1503 cuius a'i'e p'pitiet'r Deus.

In the chauncell on a litle square stone the pourtrayture of a woman with this subscription

Hic iacet Emania Hoo cuius a'i'e p'pitiet'r Deus.[151]

In a north chappell of the church the pourtrayture of a man in a gowne with this circumscription.

Hic iacet D'n's Joh'es Dallyng quondam Rector eccl'ie de Eyk qui obijt 29 die octobris a'o D'ni 1411 cujus a'i'e &c.

On another with a pourtrayture this subscription

Hic iacet Mr.Thomas Sabyn quondam rector istius eccl'ie qui obijt 19 die mensis augusti 1473. cuius &c.

304

In a south chappell I take Bavents chantrie, on a fayre stone the pourtrayture of a man in a gowne & a woman by him at ech corner was an escotcheon but all are now reaved, under them this.

Es testis Christe quod non iacet hic lapis iste
Corpus ut ornetur sed spiritus ut memoretur
Quisquis fueris qui transieris sta perlege plora
Sum quod eris fueramq' quod es pro me precor ora

This circumscription on the stone.

Hic ...... Baro Scaccarij Regis Anglie qui obijt 16 die novembris 1426 et Margareta uxor eius quor' a'i'e p' dei misericordia' requiescant.

They say there lay buryed S'r John Staverton Baron of the exchequer.

On another stone the pourtrayture of one in a gowne, this subscr.

Orate p' a'i'a D'ni Richardi Smyth quondam M'ri Cantarie Bavent qui quidem Richardus obijt 20 Jan. 1504.

On another, Hic iacet D'n's Ed'us Leverich capellanus qui obijt 2 die Sept. a'o D'ni 1583 (*sic*) cujus a'i'e &c.152

305

Waldingfeld parva resp. pag. 244

In the midle alley of the church on a stone this epitaph

Orate pro a'i'a Thome Appulton nativi de Waldingfeld magna qui Thomas ab hac luce migravit a'o D'ni 1507 14 die mensis Octobris.

On another stone adioyning to this

Orate pro a'i'a Margarie Appulton que obijt 4. die Nove'bris a'o D'ni 1504 cuius a'i'e &c. Under this epitaph was an escotcheon but is pulled up.

On a stone the pourtrayture of a man & a woman under them this epitaph

Orate pro a'i'abus Roberti Appylton generosi et Mariae uxoris eius qui quidem Robertus obijt 27 die mensis Augusti a'o D'ni 1526 quor' a'i'abus &c.

On it 4 escotcheons 1. arg. a fesse sable entre 3 apples gul. stalked & leaved vert borne by the name Appylton. 2. Appylton quartered with arg. a fesse betwene 3 (*cross crosslets fitchy drawn*) gules, and then empaled with azur a bend betwene 6 martletes or. 3. arg. a fesse betwene 3 (*cross crosslet drawn*) gul. 4. azur a bend entre 6 martletes or borne by the name of Mountney.

In the upper end of the south alley of the church on a stone

Orate p' a'i'abus Joh'is Appulton et Margaretae uxoris eius qui quidem Joh'es obijt 9 die aprilis a'o D'ni 1481 et Margareta obijt 4 die Julij a'o D'ni 1468 quor' &c.153

Melford resp. pag.165

In Mr.Martins chappell

On a stone the pourtrayture of a woman under hir this epitaphe

Orate p' a'i'a Anne Martyn nuper uxoris Richardi Martyn que quidem Anna obijt 6 die mensis Julij a'o D'ni 1528 cuius &c.

On ech corner of the stone an escotcheon 1. (*blank*) 4 bendletes

96

empaled with arg. on a fesse gules betwene 2 chevrons azur charged with 6 escalops of the first 3 garbes or, by the name of Eden. 2. Arg. a chevron entre 3 mascles voyded sable, by the name of Martyn empaled with (blank) a chevron engrayl. (blank) entre 3 mulletes p'ced. 3. (blank) 4 bendes 4. Martyn alone.

On another stone iust by this

Orate pro a'i'a Elisabethe Martyn nuper uxoris Richardi Martyn que quidem Elisabetha obijt 9 die mensis Marcij a'o D'ni 1559. cuius &c.

306

On a raysed tombe of marble the pourtrayture of a man in a gowne betwene 2 wives the circumscription reaved. I take it under lay buryed some of the Martyns, whose coming up was by cloth making.

On another stone .... Garneys ......

On another ...... obijt 1400 .... Richard Martyn ....

On another stone the p't'e of a man & a woma' in their windingsheetes

Orate pro a'i'abus Rogeri Martyn armigeri et Alicie uxoris eius qui quidem Rogerus obijt (blank) die mensis (blank) A'o D'ni 15.. et dicta Alicia obijt 28 die mensis Decembris a'o D'ni 1520 quror' (sic) &c.

Over his head Martyns single coate over hir head (blank) 4 bendletes.[154]

In the upperend of the chauncell on a fayre stone the portrayture of a k't armed & his Ladye by his side, over his head Cloptons single coate, over hir head a fesse betwene 3 womens heades. This circumscription

Orate p' a'i'abus W'mi Clopton militis et Johanne consortis sue qui quidem W'm's obijt 28 die februarij a'o D'ni millesimo (blank) tricesimo quor' a'i'abus &c.

On another stone hard by this former the pourtrayture of a woman, above hir head 2 coates reaved under hir this Epitaph.

Here lyeth dame Thomasin Clopton late the wife of S'r W'm Clopton k't aunt & one of the heyres of Elisabeth Reynsford daughter of Edward Knyvet late of Essex, w'h Dame Thomasin departed this lyfe in the yeere of our Lord god 1500. whose soul god pardon.

In Cloptons chappell under a stone lay buryed Mr.Frauncis Clopton, 1. sonne of S'r William who dyed sans yssue, the epitaph is taken awaye only remayneth upon the stone an escotcheon contayning empaled Cloptons single coate, 2 checquie (blank) a crosse (blank) & Knyvet with (crescent drawn) in bend.

Just by lay also enterred Mr.W'm Clopton esquier 2. sonne of S'r W'm & Mr.Thomas 3d sonne father to the p'sent heire uncovered & without gravestones.[155]

307

On a fayre stone the pourtrayture of a man armed at ech corner an escotcheon 1 & 4 Clopton alone, 2 & 3 Clopton empaled with arg. a fesse betwene 3 (cross crosslets drawn) gules and at his feete these v'ses

Respice quid prodest presentis temporis aevum,
O'e quod est nihil est praeter amare Deum
This circumscription

Hic iacet sepultus Franciscus Clopton armiger filius et heres W'mi Clopton armigeri qui obijt 5 die aprilis a'o D'ni 1578 a'o Regni D'nae n'rae Elisabethe Regine 20.

Against the North windowe is a fayre raysed tombe on it laying an armed k't, at his feete an hound couchant of alablaster over him these coates 1. Clopton 2. or a lyon ramp. sable debruised with a fesse counter compony or and azur. 3. p' pale Clopton & Drury 4. Clopton empaled with gules a saultier entre 4 crosletes or at his feete in brasse these verses:

Dapsilis, et largus, prudens, et in o'ibus Argus
Artibus et gnarus, generoso sanguine clarus
Clauditur hoc tumulo Clopton Wilielmus in atro
Sed nimis exiguo facto virtutis amico
Hic dum vivebat prudentis nomen habebat
Juste nam cunctis dare suevit sensa salutis
Consiliumq' petens fit letior inde recedens
Cui veniens nempe discordes pacis amore
Nectere gaudebat, dape quos propria refovebat
Pauperibus patuit semper sua ianua, abivit
Nullus ab hac vacuus indigna seu peregenus
Quid moror haec fera mors (*blank*) ut rata vult sors
MC quater sexto Christi quater x simul anno
Hinc mundo rapuit qua xp'c' luce quievit
Augusti mense post festum virginis alme
Quarta nempe die Bernardi vigiliaque
Hinc thori socia fuerat Margeria bina
Prima fuit nata Drury Frauncysq' secunda
Junius utriq' fatum tulit heu male prime
Bis decima luce si nonas dempseris inde
Anno Milleno Domini C quaterq' vigeno
Quarto post anno ruit altera die duodeno.

On a stone not farre from this tombe fayrely arched is the pourtrayture of a woman, on her gowne p' pale (*page changes*) Clopton & gul. a saultier betwene 4 crosses or on eche corner of the stone an escotcheon. 1. Clopton 2. Clopton empaled with Fraunceys as before upon hir gowne 3. Fraunceys as alone 4. as the second.
Under the pourtrayture

Hic jacet Margeria Clopton nuper uxor W'mi Clopton ac filia et heres Eliae Fraunceys armigeri que obijt 12 die Junij a'o D'ni 1424 cujus &c.

Just by this another stone fayrely arched on it the pourtrayture of a woman over hir head Clopton empaled with Drurye, this circumscription.

Hic iacet Margeria Clopton filia Rogeri Drury militis que obijt 19 die mensis Junij a'o D'ni 1420, cujus &c.

On another by the former the p'trayture of a woman on ech corner

308

was an escotcheon the 3 last reaved the 1 is Clopton, on hir gowne Clopton empaled with 2 cotes parted p' fesse 1. (*blank*) fesse ermine 2. arg. a chevron sable. Under hir this epitaph

Hic iacet Alicia Harleston nuper uxor Joh'is Harleston armigeri filia W'mi Clopton armigeri que obijt (*blank*) die mensis Junij a'o D'ni 1440 cujus &c.[156]

On another stone the pourt. of a man armed at his feete an hounde couchant at ech corner Clopton, this circumscription –

Hic jacet D'n's W'm's Clopton miles qui obijt die lunae proximo ante festum S'ti Thomae Ap'i a'o D'ni 1416 cujus &c.

On another the pourtraytures of 2 women underneath

Orate pro a'i'abus Margeriae et Anne filiar' Margerie Clopton que obierunt (*blank*) mense Octobri a'o D'ni 1420.

On another the pourt. of a man in a gowne
Hic jacet Will'm's filius W'mi Clopton qui obijt 10 die mensis Marcij a'o D'ni 1420 at ech corner Clopton.

There is a fayre raysed tombe of marble arched, the brasse that was in the middest reaved, only remaineth an escotcheon cont' p' pale Clopton and sable a crescant betwene 2 mulletes in pale argent.

By this is another fayre raysed tombe of marble also on it no epitaph.[157]

Woodbridge resp. 264

4. Mannour of Hason hall, the court is alwayes kept in Woodbridge in an house holden of the Mannour of Hason. The Mannour house is in Hason. It was hertofore called the Mannour of Hansards as belonging unto the Hansards of which Antony Hansard esq. lived 2 Hen.8. It now belongeth to Mr.Baker of Kent in right of his wife the heire therof.

5. Mannour of Kyngstone lord therof the Deane of Elye keepeth court Baron and a leet of 7s fine.

6. Man: of Sogenho. the Lord Willoughbye was Lord therof who sold it to Mr.Barker of Parham keepeth court most commonly at Ufford.

Of all these mannours the service & customes are ordinarie & the fines arbitrable.

The Leete of Woodbridge hertofore belonged to the Duke of Norff. but within these fewe yeeres Mr.Symon Mawe bayliff of the libertie of St.Etheldred hath raysed a Leete for the levying of a leete fine of viis per annu' only of the houses holden of the Mannour of Kingstone within Woodbridge & Belings.[158]

John Stubbs & Avys his wife made halfe the churche of Woodbridge.

Burgate. resp. pag.50

In the midst of the chauncell is a fayre raysed tombe of freestone covered w'th a goodly marble stone fayrely adorned w'th Brasse & a man in complet armour at his feete a lyon at hirs a wolfe, above his head 2 escotcheons 1. paly of 6 arg. & sable 2. this empaled w'th arg. 3 wolves heades arache gules. Over hir head the Wolves heades arache

99

2. as the second over his head, about the tombe this circumscribed epitaph.

Hic iacet D'nus Willielmus de Burgate miles D'nus de Burgate qui obijt in vigilia S'ti Jacobi Apostoli a'o D'ni 1409 Et Alienora uxor eius filia Thome Vyrzsdelou militis que obijt die mensis ..... a'o D'ni millesimo quadringentesimo .... quor' a'i'abus p'pitiet'r Deus.

This W'm Burgate & Elienour his wife made the fonte in this church, about it is both his & her armes, & this circumscript.

Orate p' a'iab. D'ni Will'mi Burgate militis et D'ne Alienore uxoris eius qui ista' fontem fieri fecerunt.

On a stone in the chauncell

Hic sunt sub fossa Rectoris Simonis ossa
Slack sibi nomen erat pro se petit o'is ut oret.[159]

Brundish resp.pag.47

Under one of the north windowes of the church in the wall is a concaved tombe, on a marble stone laying the p'trayture of one in a gowne & this epitaph —

Sire Esmond de Burnedish iadis p'sone del eglise de de (sic) Castre gist icy dieu de sa alme eyt mercy.

On a stone in the church the p'trayture of one in a gowne above his head 2 escotcheons reaved under him this epitaph

Hic iacet Joh'es Jenney nuper magister Cantarie de Brundish qui obijt 11 die mensis marcij a'o D'ni 1503 cuius &c.

On a raysed tombe of bricke a marble stone upon it in brasse the pourtrayture of a man armed & his wife by him under them this epitaph —

Here lyeth buryed the bodyes of John Colby esq. & Alice his wife who had yssue betwene them 4 sonnes & 9 daughters & the sayd John deceased in a'o 1540 & Alice his wife deceased 1560.

Under them the pourtr. of iiij sonnes & ix daughters, over them in the middest q'rterly Colby & arg. betwene 2 bendletes gules 3 torteaux with the Colbyes creast at each corner an escotcheon 1. Colby alone. 2. Colby empaled w'th arg. betwene 2 bendletes gules 3 torteaux. 3. this last q'rtered, Colby & the torteaux & empaled with Brewse. 4. Brews alone.

On a raysed tombe in the upperend of the chauncell against the south wind. the pourtr. of one armed under him this epitaph

Within this grave entombed lyeth a man of noble fame
A souldier to the prince was he John Colby hight his name
He lived fourty yeers & nine in credit with the best
And dyed such as here you see in heaven his soule doth rest
the 29. November in anno D'ni 1559.

Over his head Quarterly 1 & 4 Colby 2. arg. betwene 2 bendletes 3 torteaux gul. 3. Brews with the creast, on a wreath or azur an arme sable armed or holding a broken sword gul., at ech corner of the stone an escotcheon as in the former of John Colby esquier.

In the midst of the upperend of the chauncell on a raysed tombe the pourtrayture of one armed & his wife by him under this epitaph.

Here under lyeth buryed Francis Colby esq. & Margaret his wife the daughter of the Lord Wentworth.

> Behold the place wherin I lye
> For as thou art sometymes was I
> And as I am so shalt thou be
> From life to death to followe me

In the midst over them, Quarterly Colby, the torteauxes Brews & Colby with the creast as before, at each corner an escotcheon 1. Colby 2. Colby & the Torteaux empaled. 3. Colby & the torteaux q'rtered & empaled with Brewes. 4. Quarterly Colby, torteaux q'rtered & empaled with Brewes. 4. Quarterly Colby, torteaux Brews & Colby empaled with the Lord Wentworth his single coate.

On a raysed tombe of marble in the same p't of the chauncell almost against the north wall, the pourtrayture of one in a gowne kneeling, under him this

> If life in god, & like of good
> If love of Christ & eke his word
> If strife with vice as fire with wood
> If death with fayth in th'only lord
> Are tokens sure of endles blisse
> W'h god prepared hath for his
> Then Thomas Glemham here doth lye
> Who rest with Christ in heaven hye.

Above his head in an escotcheon an escotcheon (*sic*) bearing 1. Glemham 2. Bacon 3. Brandon 4. sable a bend arg. Antingham 5. Banyard 6. Glemham on a wreath (*blank*) a faulcon displayed argent. At ech corner an escotcheon. 1. p' pale Glemham & Brandon. 2. Bacon empaled with the L: Wentworth his 8 coates wherof the first is Wentworth the last Baldesmer.

In the north window of the church a knight kneeling & a lady by him about his neck a collar of SS upon his armour sable a starre of six streames or, on hir garmentes sable many mascles voyded or betwene this written

Orate p' a'i'abus (*page changes*) Ph'i Denys che'l' et Marie uxoris sue qui cu' alijs cantaria' de Brundish fundaverunt ut plenius patet in registro Ep'i Norwicen. datu' cuius a'o 1385.[160]

Rendlesha' sup. p.194

2. The mannour of Covells p'perly Colvyles, the Lord wherof in the 9 of K.Ed.2 was John Colvyle, afterwardes it was in the handes of (*blank*) Fastollf who sold it to the D: of Norff. of whome John Lane gent. of Aysch bought it who left it to yong John Lane of Badingha' his sonne. The fine is arbitrable.

3. The Mannour of Bavents belonged hertofore to that name of Bavent, untill by Adam Bavent it was given for the maintenance of a chantry priest in a chantrye founded by him in Eyke the next towne to this, & to this use was it employed untill all chauntry landes by act of Parliament were given to K:Edw.6 of whome S'r Michaell Stanhop & John Bellowe esq. had it, who ioyntly sold it to W'm

L:Willoughby of Parham of whome John Lane bought it & left it to his sonne John Lane the yonger of Badingha' who now is Lord therof. The fine is arbitrable & the coppyhold landes descend to the yonger sonne.

In the chauncell within the north wall is a raysed tombe & arched on it the p'trayture of a man in a gowne, his crowne shaven at his head 2 aungells at his feet a lyon couchant, along the south side therof this epitaph

Syre Sayer Sulyard gist ici dieu de sa alme eyet mercy.

On a fayre worne stone in the chauncell this circumscription the letters being cut into the stone & filled with brasse.

Orate pro anima D'ni Godefride Lu...yn rectoris eccl'ie de Rendlesham &c.[161]

Aysch juxta Campsee

In the churche on a stone arched w'th brasse the p'trayture of one in a gowne with this epitaph —

Of your charitie pray for the soule of S'r Alexander Inglish sometyme parish priest of this church on whose soule J'u h. mer. & this circumscription

Es testis Christe quod non iacet hic lapis iste
Corpus ut ornetur sed spiritus ut memoretur
Quisquis eris qui transieris sta, perlege, plora
Sum quod eris fueramq' quod es pro me precor ora.

Obijt 18 die mensis Sept. a'o D'ni 1520 cujus &c.

313

In the church the p'trayture of one armed over his head 2 escotcheons under him an epitaph all reaved on the window over against it arg. 3 foules w'th close feete sab. 2. p' pale gul. a bend gobony or & azur cotised engr: outwardly only arg. & that w'th the foules.

In the chauncell the p'trayture of a woman under hir this epitaph

Orate pro anima Alicie nuper uxoris Henrici Byrgett que obijt 18 die mens' Maij a'o D'ni 1493 cujus &c.[162]

Kenton s' p.147

In a south chappell of the churche upon the south wall on a plate of brasse are engraven the pourtraytures of a man kneeling & a woman by him, at his backe 4 sonnes at hirs 9 daughters, over hir head arg. a chevron gul. entre 3 pheons (*pheon upright drawn*), under them this epitaph

Here under this tombe lyeth buryed John Garneys esquier & Elisabeth his wife, which John deceased the xith day of June in the yeere of our Lord god 1524 on whose soul Jesu have mercy.

There are besides 2 gravestones in the chauncell wheron were 4 escocheons but all reaved together w'h the epitaphs.[163]

Badyngham s' p.18

Against the north wall of the chauncell is a fayre monument raysed of a Carbonell there buryed as appeareth by the armes on the top or upper part therof, the other in the lower part being worne out.

1. Quarterly or & sable Bovyll empaled with argent a manch azur Creyk.

2. Bovyll empal. w'th or a chevron entre three eschalops gules Dalenson.

3. Bovyll empal. w'th gul. 6 eschalops arg. Scales.

4. Gules a crosse arg. in a bord. engr. or. Carbonell empal. w'th Bovyll.

5. Carbonell emp. w'th gul. a chevron entre 3 eagles arg. Caston.

6. Caston emp. w'th or fleure sable Mortymer of Attleburgh.

7. Caston emp. with gul. a sault. engr. arg. Kerdeston.

8. Caston emp. w'th vert an escotcheon within an urle of martletes arg. Erpingham.

314
The townesmen hold this to be the tombe of some of the Wingfelds which cannot be there being no mention of Wingfeldes armes upon it other same iudge it to be the monument of a Bovill wh'ch can not be because Bovils were all dead before the matche of Carbonell with Caston. Therfore it can not be but the tombe of S'r Robert Carbonell who maryed Margerie the d. of Caston, which S'r Robert was sonne & h. of S'r W'm Carbonell & the d. & h. of S'r John Bovill k't & of Peronell d. of Robert L:Scales. S'r John was sonne of S'r W'm Bovill & Joane d. & h. of S'r Herbert Dalenson. S'r W'm was sonne & h. of Fitz W'm Bovill who mar. the d. of S'r James de Creyk.

In the south side of the chauncell on a stone this epitaph:

> Hic Catharina iacett maesti pars magna mariti
>> Blennerhasseti tertia nata patris
> Mortua ter deno est quartoq' aetatis in anno
>> Annis quae septem non minus uxor erat.
> Uxor Johanni Cornwalleiso sociata
>> Exemplar morum non mediocre fuit
> Inclita syncero revitebat pectore virtus.
>> Mens proba, cor purum, vita modesta fuit.
> Hic sponsa felix, felix fuit illa marito
>> O non perpetuum vita caduca bonum.
> Nam postquam Sponsu' quinta ia' prole beaset
>> Instando sexta parturiendo perit.
>> Obijt 23 Januarij 1584.

On it 3 escocheons 1. Cornwallei w'th (*mullet drawn*) 2. A fox ramp. (*blank*), w'th (*crescent drawn*) (*blank*) 3. (*blank*) On a bend (*blank*) 3 goates heades (*blank*) 4. (*blank*) 2 barres (*blank*) 5. (*blank*) on a crosse (*blank*) 5 garbes (*blank*) 6. Cornwalleis as before all empaled with Hasset single coate.

2. Hassetts 6 coates marshalled in one escotcheon.

3. Cornwalleys 8 coates marshalled together.[164]

315
Mellis resp. p.164.
In the upper end of the church next unto the chauncell is a fayre raysed tombe of marble on it the pourtrayture of a man in a gowne & a woman by him with this circumscribed epitaph

103

Orate pro a'i'a Joh'is Yaxlee alias dicti Joh'is Herberd de Mellis servientis ad legem qui obijt 19 die Julij a'o 1505 anno regni Regis Henrici Septimi post conquestum Anglie vicesimo Ac etiam pro a'i'a Elisabethe Yaxlee filie Richardi Blondell armigeri uxoris predicti Joh'is que obijt (*blank*) die a'o 15.. quor' a'i'abus propitiet'r Deus.

On the north side of this tombe are 2 escotcheons 1. ermine a Chief endent. gules empaled w'th checquie or & sable a fesse argent. 2. ermine a chevron sable entre 3 mullets p'ced gules empaled with azur a bend argent entre 6 martletes or. On the west end quarterly (*ermine drawn*) a chevron sable entre 3 mulletes gules &˙ arg. 3 buglehornes in triangle sable stringed or, empaled with ermine a chief endented gules. On the south side the Quartered coates of Yaxlee & Bloggett empaled with vert a lyon ramp. argent 2. Yaxlee. 3. Quarterly 1. (*ermine drawn*) a Chief endent. gul. 2. gul. 3 lucies entre 9 crosletes or 3. checquie or & sable a fesse argent 4. gules a fesse & a labell of 3 points or.

On a stone in the church in brasse the p'trayture ....

On another fayre stone in the midle of the church the p'trayture of one armed at his feete this epitaph

Orate pro anima Richardi Floyd armigeri qui obijt 16 die mensis Januarij anno D'ni 1525 cuius &c.

at ech corner an escotcheon 1. (*blank*) on a crosse (*blank*) five crescantes (*blank*) 2. The same w'ch is Floyds empaled with Hobart of Hales. 2. as the 3 4. as the 1.

Against the south wall of the church is a fayre tombe with these verses following

Antonij Yaxlee fuerat qui natus et heres
    Richardus Yaxlee conditur hoc tumulo
Margareta cui coniux obvenerat heres
    Stokes Eboracensi que patre nata fuit
Viribus ingenui, legum studiis, pietate
    Stemmate, connubio floruit ille suo:
Natales rapidum cum fatum sustulit ill'
    Bis ter septenos viderat ille dies
Cujus adhuc terris nomen renovare propago
    Tunc bini nati nata relicto pote'
Quorum qui primus Gulielmus condidit ista
    ut patris chari sint monumenta pia
    Aetatis 42, Obitus 9 Marcii 1558.

Underneath these armes following 1. Quarterly Yaxlee & Bloggettes empaled w'th Quarterly 1. argent a fesse checquie or & gules entre 3 eschalops azur 2. argent 3 fusills gules 3. azur a crosse patonce or charged with a (*crescent drawn*) sable 4. as the first.

2. Quarterly Yaxlee & Boggets (*sic*)

3. Contay'eth 6 coates 1. arg. a fesse checquie or & gules entre 3 eschallops azur 2. arg. 3 fusills gules 3. azur a crosse patonce ut supra 4. arg. on a chevron entre 3 lions heades erased gules a (*crescent drawn*) or. 5. azur on a fesse of 5 fusills or as many eschallops gules

6. sable a bend entre 6 eschalops.

Against the north wall of the churche a fayre erected tombe on it this epitaph

Antonius Yaxlee armiger filius et heres Joh'is Yaxlee servientis ad legem duas duxit uxores, prima enim Elisabetha una filiarum Joh'is Garnish de Kenton armigeri 2. Brigitta no'i'e vero Pennyng. De Elisabetha 7 procreavit liberos. 8 etiam de Brigitta. Conditur in hoc tumulo (*page turns*) cum uxore sua Elisabetha sumptibus Brigitta uxoris sue aetatis 75 obitus 28 Octob. 1559.

Underneath Yaxlee & Bloggett quartered & empal: with arg. a chev. engrayled azur entre 3 eschallops sable

The coate w'th the mulletes is Yaxlee

That with the buglehorns Bloggettes

In the south windowe of the chauncell are these armes v't arg. on a bend azur entre 6 roses gules seeded argent a (*mullet drawn*) of the same all within a border of the seconde under it these verses

Signa p' armorum cancelle dat reparamen

Hoc Jacobus Blondell, celum sibi det Deus Amen.[165]

Lavenham vide p.154

Lavenham vide p.154

This whole towne and Lordship did from all antiquitie belonge to the Erles of Oxford untill it was sold to Alderman Skinner of London who after his death left it to his sonne but with such ambiguitie that whiles his brethren doe contende the mannour in yeerly valewe of 700 li or 800 li is divided & dismembred. The markett upon the Tuesdaye very ancient the charter therof first purchased by Robert Vere D: of Ireland with the fayer at Whitsontide for three dayes, but for the fayer on Michaells day they doe forescribe. No epitaphes w'th ar'es but gravestones w'th clothiers marks.[166]

Acton p.7

Upon another gravestone

Beati qui in Domino moriuntur,

& beneathe in another place Edmundus Danyell 1560 (*sic*) et Margareta uxor eius 1589.

Upon another stone Johannes Danyell & no more w'thout any escotcheons for they are gent' & have dwelled in the town some 7 or 8 descentes ever esquiers.[167]

Chellesworth   + p.61

Chellesworth   + p.61

+ with some Ruines or visible foundations yet permanent. Unto which house somtyme did belonge a parke therunto adiacent which the names of enclosures & evidences in those p'ts do make most manifest though antiquitie hath long since dissolved each tract therof. For the house, the moderne tradition affirmeth that the 1 Duke of Norff' of the name of the Howardes tooke it downe & set it up in Stoke Parke. I have not long since observed the Howardes escotcheons in the windowes of the church which I find now gone. There is no monument in the churche save on the north side in the wall a mention of an arched tombe but so ancient as no escotcheon or tract of writinge is extant. In the chauncell are these armes

azur 3 crownes or

gul. 3 crownes or

azur 2 barres entre 11 (*cross crosslet drawn*) or 4.4.2.1. this 5 tymes in the churche & twice w'th a labell of 5 pointes gul.

or a crosse engrayled sable.[168]

319   Wenham Parva

(*Two fragments are difficult to fit into the text as it stands and may represent further pages of text. One is the beginning of church notes for Oulton — see above, p.58 — the other is the following TA transcript:*

'Hensted

In the town of Hensted were the mannors of Blunstons and Savages but are all as parcell of the mannor of Hensted Bounds — Mr.Brewster bought the mannor of Hensted and Pounds (*sic*) of the Lord Norrys who had it in marriage with Margery Fynes daughter of the Lo: Dacres —

The Mannor of Hensted Bounds Mr.Yarmouth bought of Francis Clopton of Belforth (*sic*) and he of S'r Robert Drurye and he of _____ Clere and the Cleres of Bounds and Bounds of Hensted. In this town is a Hamlett called Hulver Street and the Inhabitants come to Hensted Church and pay to it church charges and for the poor but for all other charges to the hundred of Waynford wherein it is')

NOTES TO THE INTRODUCTION

1   Publ. Norwich, 1938. I am indebted to Dr.John Blatchly for drawing my attention to Mrs.Hood's edition, for the discovery of the College of Arms original of the Suffolk text and for suggesting the whereabouts of the Ipswich and Elveden fragments. See discussion of authorship, p.10.

2   Bodley MS Gough Norfolk 26, front flyleaf.

3   *Catalogue of Sir Thomas Browne's MSS, MS Rawlinson 390 No.11* pr. in Browne, *Works*, ed. Simon Wilkin, 4 vols, London (1836), IV p.468f. For the possible significance of Browne's ownership of the Chorographies, see p.15.

4   *Ib.* p.22. For accounts of Le Neve's life see Francis Rye, *Calendar of Correspondence and Documents relating to the Family of Oliver Le Neve*, Norwich, (1895), and P.Le Neve-Foster, *The Le Neves of Norfolk*, pr.pr. (1969).

5   Hen.3 f.72.

6   Cf.e.g. *ib.* 2 f.37; *ib.* 12 f.25. I have not retained any of Le Neve's additions to the main text unless there is a possibility that they were copied from the original Chorography text. The Anstis copy of the *Breviary* which he used, probably the latest and best version of the Ryece text, is now in Ipswich Central Library. The Register of Butley Priory was edited for publication by A.G.Dickens, Winchester (1951).

7   Hearne, *Collections*, X p.208 qu.Hood p.3n. Mr.West was James West, then of Balliol, 'politician, antiquary and collector of MSS, books, prints, coins, etc., died 1772' (Hood, p.10n.); he was a friend and former tutorial pupil of Hearne's (ex inf. Prof.G.R.Elton, Clare College, Cambridge).

8   The identification of Allen as Le Neve's amanuensis is made by Tom Martin in his transcript of Allen's transcript of the Westhorpe entry in the Chorography Appendix, WSRO E2/41/8b f.322r.

9   Cf. e.g. Hen.6 f.36.

10   Cf. e.g. Allen's copy for Bessingham, marked 'Q Reyces Survey pag.24', Bodley MS Gough Norfolk 34 f.67. Cf. also BL Add.8839-8843 for more of the Le Neve Norfolk collections containing Allen transcripts.

11   Hearne, op.cit. X p.204, qu.Hood p.9.

12   *Notes and Queries* 2d series XI (1861) pp.403-04, prints an account by John Bagford and Thomas Davies, c.1730, of the dispersal of the Le Neve collections. BL Catalogue 270 i 23 (2) is the printed Catalogue of the Le Neve sale by John Wilcox, bookseller, with MS annotations of prices and buyers.

13 Described in a note on the back flyleaf of Martin's Church Notes, now WSRO E2/41/8b, which note was printed by Alfred Suckling, *The History and Antiquities of the County of Suffolk,* London 2 vols. (1846) I p.206.

14 Gough, *British Topography* (1789 edition) II pp.2f, qu.Hood pp.1-3.

15 *Bibliotheca Martiniana*, Booth and Berry's sale catalogue, Norwich (1773), repr. in *Norfolk Antiquarian Miscellany* III (1887) p.395.

16 Now numbered MS Gough Norfolk 26.

17 Sir Thomas Gage refers to the collection as 'MSS Tanner' in his transcript of a Great Barton entry, Hen.79 (iii) f.111; John Gage calls it Bishop Tanner's collection in the MS catalogue of his library, Hen.49 p.124.

18 Gough, *op.cit.* II p.241. John Ives died in 1776. Hood p.22.

19 For the gift to the College of Arms see Hen.49 p.123.

20 See above, p.8; *Bibliotheca Martiniana, loc.cit.* p.395.

21 The Le Neve part of the Collections is labelled Iveagh/Phillipps 1-19. A few more fragments of Le Neve slips from the Suffolk collection are pasted in an interleaved copy of Kirby's *Suffolk Traveller* once owned by Craven Ord, now BL Add.7101-2, but they do not include any fragments of the Chorography.

22 Bodley MS Tanner 135 ff.1-28.

22a On Ryece see C.G.Harlow, 'Robert Ryece of Preston', *PSIA* XXXII (1972) pp.42-70.

23 Hood p.132.

23a Thomas Astle died in 1803; a list of 74 Norfolk and Suffolk MSS belonging to him including 'collections of Peter Le Neve, F.Blomfield' is now item 30740 in the Summary Catalogue of Western MSS in the Bodleian.

24 This is now NNRO MS Accession Mrs.Hood 31.5.73. Shelf P186D. See Hood p.11.

25 I am indebted to Dr.John Blatchly for providing the clue to the identification of Norris's hand. The bulk of Norris's Norfolk collections now form NNRO, Rye MSS 3-6; he owned the *Nomina Villarum* MS discussed, p.10.

26 Gough, *op.cit.* II p.259. qu.Hood p.3.

27 I must acknowledge the kindness of the Manuscript Department of Cambridge U.L. in having certain fragments lifted from their mountings so that I could examine the reverses.

28 Bodley MS Gough MS Gough Suff. 7 f.196.

29 ESRO HD 225/1404; WSRO E2/41/8-9.

30 Hood p.94.

31 *Ib.* p.83

32 Sir Anthony Wingfield's will PCC 7 Strafforde.

33 For Sir Isaac Appleton see below, p.116, n.69.

34   Hood p.153.

35   See p.105.

35a   For Kitson see below, p.114, n.47. For the *Liber Valorum* see *Guide to the Contents of the Public Record Office*, 52 vols. HMSO (1963) I p.88.

36   Cf. e.g. below p.56, Hood pp.123, 125, 147.

37   Hood pp.162-3 on Thetford: '200 or 300 yeere since it had 7 parish churches according to Mr.Cambden, but I finde in the ancient Register belonging to the Deane & Chapter of the church of the holye & indivisible Trinitye in Norwich that [there were] 10 churches ...'

38   Hood p.11. Beckham wrote a couple of polemical pamphlets denouncing Quakerism.

39   Hen.11 f.96.

40   Partly published in *Orford Ness. A selection of Maps mainly by John Norden*, Cambridge (1966), pp.7-17.

41   *Calendar of State Papers Domestic, James I* XII p.43.

42   Cf. e.g. BL Harl.570, a MS copy of the Chorography of Middlesex of 1593, or BL Add.31853, a fair copy of Norden's description of Middlesex, Essex, Surrey, Sussex, Hampshire, the Isle of Wight, and the Channel Islands, 1595; or CUL Mm.3.15 ff.20-22, a complaint of Norden's to the Crown. The last two are signed.

43   Hood p.27.

44   *Ib.* p.139.

45   Cf. the Orford entry, Hen.12 f.103 and, p.58 Le Neve characteristically added at the end of the Orford entry 'Why may not it be a lye rather'.

46   See the Archdeacon of Sudbury's returns to the Articles of 1603, printed in *PSIA* VI (1888) p.361.

47   Hood p.169.

48   *Ib.* p.21.

49   *Ib.* p.113.

50   For Sir Arthur's relations with the gentry of East Anglia see Hassell Smith, *passim*, and particularly pp.229-34 and 253-65 for the Christmas Lane affair. The Chorographer's familiarity with Babergh Hundred may also have arisen from a Heveningham connection – cf. n.75 below, p.117.

51   A Star Chamber case of 1602 (PRO STAC 5 H5/12) gives a detailed if somewhat sensational picture of the Hobarts, their family quarrels and their Catholic sympathies. For the Rous's and the Heveninghams see letters from Reynold Rous of Badingham and Sir Philip Parker to Sir Arthur Heveningham in Aylsham 16.

52   For the Paston connection see below, p.114, n.45. Sir Arthur Heveningham's eldest son married Bridget the daughter of Sir William

Paston in 1601 (Hassell Smith p.159). For John Holdich and the Doylys see *ib*. p.226.

5 3   Hood p.99. Cf. English edition of Camden, 1610, p.482: 'Whome because shee was piously affected, farre from all riotous excesse, and wanton lightnesse, our Ancestours accounted for a Saint.'

5 4   The following 16th and early 17th century antiquaries can be eliminated as authors of the Chorographies simply because of their handwriting; Dr.John Barkham, Nicholas Charles, Dr.John Dee, William Dethick, Sir Symonds D'Ewes, John Doddridge, Sir John Hayward, William Lisle, Sir Henry Savile, John Selden, John Speed and Richard Verstegan (cf. their letters in BL Cotton Julius C.III.); Richard Carew, William Lambarde and Sir Henry Spelman (cf. letters in BL Cotton Julius C.V.).

5 5   Will of Edward Browne, Aylsham 27 — the family papers of the Brownes are scattered through the Aylsham Collection because their heir general married into the Doughty family of Hanworth. On Godsalve see Anthony Harison, *Registrum Vagum*, publ. by Norfolk Records Society, Norwich (1963), p.87.

5 6   Aylsham 347, receipt of George Kempe for Sir Roger, 1581; letter William Payne to John Browne, 1589; on Sir Roger, see Hassell Smith p.222. He died 1588. Aylsham 16, Sir Arthur Heveningham to John Browne, 1612.

5 7   Aylsham 15, Thomas Browne to Robert Redman, 1594; for the *Registrum Vagum*, see above, n.55.

5 8   Browne's patent of office, Aylsham 153 — replaced by 1588 (*Registrum Vagum*, p.88). Aylsham 15, Adam Scambler to Thomas Browne, 1604 and 1600. On Browne's suicide, Aylsham 16, Edward Coke to John Browne, 1612.

5 9   For instance, Aylsham 15, Thoms Browne to Thomas Dey, 1603, or his precedent book for Bishop Scambler, Aylsham 366.

6 0   Aylsham 10, note on the value of the Poringland benefices. On Doyly, Francis Blomefield, *History of Norfolk*, London, 1806 edn. V p.447; Aylsham 16, Doyly to John Browne, 1612.

6 1   *Bibliotheca Martiniana, loc.cit.* p.395.

6 2   See Rye's discussion in *Norfolk Antiquarian Miscellany*, 2nd ser. I pp.83-85. On Edward Browne, Aylsham 16, Edward Browne to Thomas Browne, 31 August s.a. and Aylsham 27, will of John Browne.

6 3   See the detailed discussion of Blomefield's use of the Chorography of Norfolk, Hood pp.6-9.

6 4   Publ. 1838, p.26 — the quotation is of the Barrow church notes (cf. pp.89-90 above).

6 5   On Ryece see above, n.22a.

NOTES TO MAIN TEXT

1*   I am most grateful to Mr.Victor Morgan of the University of East Anglia for alerting me to the existence of these first eight pages of the Chorography.

2*   *Sudfolc* and *Eastangleryc* are in Saxon characters; these three paragraphs are largely culled from Camden's *Britannia* (cf. Appendix III).

3*   This is made up from Camden's material.

4*   Unlike the corresponding section of the Norfolk Introduction, which is made up mainly of Camden's material (particularly from p.418 of the 1600 edition), this paragraph appears to be largely original, suggesting that the Chorographer was more familiar with Suffolk than with Norfolk when he started his project.

5*   The basic information and some of the river-names in this description come from Saxton's map rather than from personal knowledge. Ryece clearly used Saxton's map in much the same way as the Chorographer for his own description of the county's rivers (cf. Ryece, pp.7-13).

6*   An error for 'Wheltham' i.e. Whelnetham.

7*   The Norfolk Introduction also speaks of 'four Lieutenants' for the county (Hood, p.71). However, from 1595 to 1603 the Lieutenancy was in Commission in both counties, and by 1602 the Commissioners numbered twelve in Norfolk and five in Suffolk.

8*   In Norfolk, Saxton's map already provided a letter-code for the hundreds of the county; in Suffolk it did not, and the scheme is the Chorographer's own. It is noticeable that where Saxton's map did not make the boundaries of the Suffolk hundreds clear because they followed a river, as between Mutford and Lothingland or Hoxne and Thredling, the Chorographer gave the hundreds the same letter. Cf. also p.144.

9*   Catholic recusant (*Registrum Vagum*, p.181); impropriator despite an attempt in 1596 by the widow of his elder brother John to prove that she was jointly seized with him and had a right to present (PRO, C2 ELIZ E5/56).

1   Altered to 'Barronet' in a later 17th century hand. Bacon, of Redgrave and Culford, s. and h. of Sir Nicholas Bacon Lord Keeper to Elizabeth I; kted. 1578, Sheriff of Suffolk 1581-2 and Norfolk 1597-8, JP 1572-1624, MP Suffolk 1572, Premier Baronet of England 1611, monument Redgrave 1624. One of the leading county politicians. For shrievalties see PRO *Lists and Indexes* no.IX.

2   This is the altar tomb surviving on the north side of the chancel, with indent of cross and marginal inscription – cf. Nicholas Charles' description of it, c.1600, BL Lansd.874 f.172.

3   See Appendix III.

4   Francis Sone of Grays Inn and Wantisden, JP 1559-62, MP for Orford 1545, 1558, 1559, d.1575 (PCC 41 Pyckering). Details of Suffolk JP's are derived from the sources listed by T.G.Barnes and A.Hassell Smith, *Bulletin of Historical Research* XXXII (1958) pp.232f. and from BL Eger.3788. Details of MP's come from the *Return of Members of Parliament*, 1878, and from PRO E371/402 (i).

5   Hare, son of Sir Nicholas Hare, Master of the Rolls to Queen Mary; JP 1559-69 and thereafter one of Suffolk's leading Catholic recusants, much imprisoned and heavily fined until his death in 1611 — brass at Bruisyard. He sold Friston Hall to James Bacon (BL Add.15520 f.125r) and was brother-in-law to James Hobart of Hales (PCC 38 Wood); James Bacon, Alderman of London, was kted. 1604. For dubbings of knights see W.A.Shaw, *Knights of England,* (1906) 2 vols. Sone sold Alderton Naunton to Bacon in 1589 (Copinger VII p.232).

6   See Appendix III.

7   See Appendix III.

8   Reginald Rous of Badingham, head of a cadet branch of the Dennington family and a cousin of Sir Arthur Heveningham (Aylsham 16, letter Rous to Heveningham). Arthur or Anthony Penning, s. and h. of Arthur Penning of Kettleburgh d. 1593 (brass, Kettleburgh), Michael Hare's Steward; the younger Penning Sheriff of Suffolk 1606-07, JP from 1601. John Cornwallis of Badingham, head of a cadet branch of the Brome family, and involved in the service of the Howard family (CUL MS Buxton 96 Dix bundle no.23).

9   Of Barrow, s. and h. of Sir Clement Higham, Chief Baron of the Exchequer under Queen Mary; kted. 1578, Sheriff of Suffolk 1576-77, MP Suffolk 1586, 1603, Sudbury 1563, Ipswich 1584, JP 1571-83, 1587, 1591-1634. One of the leading county politicians and radical Protestants.

10   29 November 1586 (PRO C66/1325 m.42).

11   John Clench, a protegé of the Crane family of Creeting and Chilton (BL Add.15520 f.26v), Justice of Queen's Bench 1584 (PRO C66/1315 m.23), JP 1583-1607, monument Holbrooke 1607. Thomas Seckford of Bealings, son of Charles. 'The elder house' recalls the efforts of an elder Thomas Seckford (see below, n.109), one of the Masters of Requests to Elizabeth I and a younger son of this family in reviving the fortunes of the Seckfords (PCC 4 Rutland). He d.1587.

12   Henry Reynolds senior, a moneylender (*APC* XVII p.383), in fact married Goldingham's widow (PRO C3/77/27). See also *PSIA* XXIX (1963) pp.198f.

13   It is doubtful whether Henry Bedingfield, son of Thomas of Denham, was knighted; this may be an error of Allen's transcription (Copinger IV p.17). John Rivett of Rishangles, son of Thomas d.1596 (NNRO CCN 56 Skyppon), marr. Elizabeth Brooke of Aspall (1612 Visitation).

14   Sir Henry Doyle of Pond Hall, Hadleigh, kted. 1547, Sheriff of Norfolk and Suffolk 1557-58, JP 1538-61.

15 John Rivett of Bildeston d.1624 (PCC 68 Byrde); sold 'after 1599' (Copinger III p.137). Essex was executed 1601.

16 Hieronymus Henninges, *Theatrum Genealogicum, ostentans omnes aetatum familias*, Magdeburg (1598) 4 vols., IV p.81.

17 William and Robert Goldes paid for £6 and £4 in goods respectively in the 1568 Subsidy for Blaxhall (Suffolk Green Books XII, 1909, p.203), and Henry Cooke paid for £7 in wages.

18 Of Little Glemham, s. of Thomas; kted. 1591, marr. Anne Sackville, da. of 1st Earl of Dorset, 1601; JP 1601-32, MP Lewes 1593, Suffolk 1601, Ipswich 1604 Aldeburgh 1614, 1621, d.1632 (BL Add.19172 f.57v).

19 Younger brother of Thomas the Master of Requests; Groom of the Privy Chamber to Elizabeth I (PCC 4 Rutland); kted. 1603.

20 Sidnor's brass Blundeston 1613; marr. Bridget da. of John Jernegan of Belton, a crypto-Catholic (PRO SP12/171/63). Humphrey Yarmouth was described as of Frostenden, gent. in 1578 (Hatfield MS 139 f.218).

21 Henry Jerningham of Costessey Park, Norfolk, son of Sir Henry one of Mary I's Privy Councillors; a Catholic recusant. His power in Lothingland was criticised by a commission of Protestant Suffolk gentlemen in 1584 (PRO SP 12/171/63).

22 Edward Bacon of Shrubland Hall, Barham, 3d son of Lord Keeper Bacon. Sheriff of Suffolk 1600-01, JP 1592-1618, MP Suffolk 1593, Eye 1588, d.1618.

23 See Appendix III.

24 S. and h. of Thomas, of Playford, Sheriff of Suffolk 1599-1600, kted. 1603, JP 1597-1614, d.1614 (PCC 38 Lawe). His duel with his relative Edmund Withipoll in 1598 caused a considerable stir and the affair reached the Earl Marshal's court (*APC* XXVIII pp.391, 406).

25 Sir Anthony Wingfield of Letheringham, s. and h. of Sir Robert; Sheriff of Suffolk 1597-98, kted. 1597, JP 1584-1606, MP Suffolk, 1588, Orford 1571, 1572. Much military experience (Ryece p.144). Will 1606 (PCC 7 Strafford). Sir Robert Drury of Hawstead, s. and h. of Sir William d.1589; kted. by the Earl of Essex 1591, MP Suffolk 1603, 1614, JP temp. James I. Patron of Bishop Joseph Hall, friend of John Donne (*PSIA* II, 1852, p.11; R.C.Bald. *John Donne and the Drurys*, Cambridge, 1959; Rev.Sir John Cullum, *History of Hawstead and Hardwick*, 2d edn. (1813) pp.170-172.

26 See Appendix III.

27 Of Burgh Castle, Town Clerk of Yarmouth (*Inner Temple Admissions Register* p.5), JP 1589-91; d.1591 (PCC Administrations 1581-95 f.195). He in fact bought the manor in 1560 (PRO E401/1794 f.102v.).

28 Either Robert Forth of Butley Esq. Sheriff of Suffolk 1593-94, JP 1572-1601, and a leading Puritan, d. Feb. 1601 (Muskett I p.112), or his 2d s. and h. Sir William Forth d.1621 (ib.p.120), kted. 1604.

29 Of Denham next Bury s. and h. of Edward Lewkenor of Kingston Bovey, Sussex; kted. 1603, JP 1593-1605, MP for New Shoreham, Newport and Maldon between 1572 and 1593; monument Denham 1605. A leading radical Protestant.

30   Of Claxton, Norfolk, s. of Thomas; kted. 1603, JP 1592-1621, MP Norfolk 1597, 1600, will 1621 (PCC 25 Dale).

31   Michael Stanhope of Sudbourne, s. of Michael; Groom of Privy Chamber 1594 (BL Add.15520 f.120v), kted. 1603, JP 1593-1622, MP Castle Rising 1584, Ipswich 1597, 1601, Orford 1604. In his will, 1622 (PCC 10 Saville) he left £5 to John Sone 'sometimes owner of my Mannor of Wantisden in Suff. yf he be living.' Cf. the version of the Sone descent with another version *sub* Alderton.

32   John Haughfen, brass 1618 Tunstall. Thomas Manning, last Prior of Butley (1528-39) was on the surrender of his house created Suffragan Bishop of Ipswich by Henry VIII (*PSIA* IV, 1874, p.413).

33   See Appendix III.

34   On Coke, Attorney General to Elizabeth I and James I. see *DNB* IV p.685. Coke had estates at Huntingfield through his marriage with Bridget, da. of John Paston of Huntingfield.

35   On Sir Arthur Heveningham see Introduction above, p.13-15, kted. 1578, Sheriff of Norfolk 1581-82 and 1602-03; JP 1578-1622.

36   John Pettus of Norwich bought Cookley Grange from John Smyth 1599 (Copinger II p.40).

37   There is now no trace of either of the tombs and only fragments of the glass described here and in the Appendix, p.76, the tomb in the south aisle may be concealed by the organ. William, son of Peter Pretyman, d.1617 (Muskett II p.306) and bought the manor from Tyrrell in 1593 (Copinger III p.247).

38   'S'ti Edmundi de Gypwico' is an error for Domesday's original 'S'ci Petri de Gypwico'. John Rivett, son of Andrew, marr. Ann da. of James Bacon. Alderman of London (cf. Alderton) and d.1616 (1612 Visitation; Copinger IV p.224).

39   William Bull of Dallinghoo provided one light horse for the national defence effort in 1580 (SP 12/143/10).

40   See Appendix III.

41   See Appendix III.

42   See Appendix III.

43   Thomas Playters of Sotterley, s. and h. of William, a Catholic recusant (Hatfield MS 139 f.215) but himself conformist; Sheriff of Suffolk, 1604-05, JP 1595, 1596-1638; brass Sotterley 1638.

44   The porch is dated 1578.

45   The Marlingford entry in the Norfolk Chorography, Hood p.127, includes a note on the descent of that manor from the Waxhams with the comment 'vide Ellowe in Suff.'.

46   See Appendix III.

47   Elizabeth Cornwallis of Brome mar. Thomas Kitson of Hengrave, kted. 1578, JP 1564-69, bur. Hengrave 1603 and a leading Catholic sympathiser. She was bur. there 1628 (Howard II, p.102).

48   See Appendix III.

49   Edward Page senior of Framlingham bought the Middleton cum Fordley manor in 1590 from Edward Honings of Eye, Receiver of Crown Revenues for Suffolk 1590-1609 (PRO E401/1846-1865) JP 1596-1609, MP Dunwich 1588, Eye 1593, 1597, 1601; PCC Administrations 1609, 69. Honings bought it in 1574 from Philip Tilney of Shelley, Sheriff of Suffolk 1588-89, JP 1574-95, 1597-1602, PCC Administrations 1602, 127, a Catholic sympathiser (PRO STAC 5 T14/35, 10/19). Tilney had sold it in 1569 to Robert Bedingfield of Ditchingham and repurchased it in 1571 (Copinger II p.124). Copinger p.128 calls the other manor Brents Fen and says that Robert Brooke bought it from Sir Owen Hopton's s. and h. Arthur in 1602. Brooke, Alderman of London, made extensive land purchases from the Hoptons at Blythburgh in 1592 (PRO MS Index to Patent Rolls s.v. C66/1383); he was kted. 1609 and Sheriff of Suffolk 1613-14. Sir Owen Hopton of Yoxford and Westwood, Lieutenant of the Tower of London 1570-90, kted. 1561, Sheriff of Norfolk and Suffolk 1564-65, MP Suffolk 1559, 1571, Middlesex 1572, JP 1544-95; PCC Administrations 1595, 83.

50   Arthur Jenney or Jermy of Knodishall and Metfield, s. and h. of Francis; JP 1593-96, will 1605 (PCC 34 Hayes).

51   See Appendix III.

52   See Appendix III.

53   Salters' Company (Papworth p.677). Probably for one of the Awall family, who built the south aisle in the early 16th century.

54   See Appendix III.

55   See Appendix III.

56   Sir Giles Allington of Horseheath Cambs. JP 1559, d.1586 at an advanced age (PCC 49 Windsor; Copinger II p.76).

57   See Appendix III.

58   Humphrey Brewster of Wrentham sold the main Henstead manor to Sidnor in 1585 (Copinger II p.87). Brass Wrentham 1593.

59   There is now no trace of a south chapel.

60   Robert Ashfield of Stowlangtoft, Sheriff of Suffolk 1575-76, JP 1560-1585, 1586-1613, left property to his sons Sir Robert and John 1613 (PCC 78 Capell).

61   See Appendix III.

62   See Appendix III.

63   See Appendix III.

64   See description of Richard Codington's monument p.91. The emphasis on the bequest to Mrs.Elizabeth Codington may be an echo of the chancery suits centring on Nicholas Lusher of Ewell's unsuccessful attempts to contest Richard's will as right heir in 1568-69 (PRO C3/45/7 and C3/113/8).

65.   See Introduction, p.13.

66   Davy MSS. qu. by Copinger I p.40, say Thorpe bought the manor of Sir John Shelton. Robert Thorpe of Grays Inn and Bury St.Edmunds, later of Brent Eleigh (*CPR Eliz*.I p.158, PRO STAC 5 W78/7) made large sales to Sir Ambrose Jermyn in 1569, perhaps forced to because of his connection with the Duke of Norfolk and his disgrace (PRO E401/1813 s.v.21 May; Hen.91, bond as Steward of the Liberty of Bury to the Duke). Sir Ambrose Jermyn of Rushbrooke, kted. 1553, Sheriff of Norfolk and Suffolk 1558-59, 1572-73, JP 1554-77; will 1577 (PCC 15 Daughtry). Sir Robert, his s. and h. kted. 1578, Sheriff of Suffolk 1578-79, JP 1577-84, 1592-1614, Custos Rotulorum 1593-1614, MP Suffolk 1584, 1586, E.Looe 1588. Leading county politician and radical Protestant.

67   Marginal note by PLN: 'q're Archbishop of Canterbury', which corrects the Chorographer's error.

68   See Introduction, p.13.

69   William Appleton of Kettlebaston, 2d. s. of Roger Appleton of Dartford, Kent, and Agnes da. and h. of Walter Clerk of Hadleigh — William was living at the time of the 1612 Visitation. Edward Clerk, Agnes's brother, JP 1555-58; took Uniformity Oath 1569 (SP 12/60/62).

70   Cf. Fuller's story, qu. by Copinger I p.120, of the vicar, Henry Copinger, and his efforts to maintain his rights against successive Earls of Oxford. Copinger, one of the Buxhall gentry family, was vicar 1578-1622 (*PSIA* XXII, 1936, p.300) and Fuller claimed that he had spent £1600 on the law-suit.

71   Robert Lee, who was knighted in 1608, purchased the manor in 1598 of the conservative Bury lawyer Robert Golding and others (Copinger, I p.128), probably as feoffees for Rookwood. Both Rookwood and Drury were noted Catholic recusants (*APC* X pp.310-311) and Rookwood probably regarded his purchase partly as an act of piety since the proceeds from Drury's sale went to aid imprisoned Roman priests (Trappes-Lomax MS collections, unpaginated s.v.Lawshall, Jesuit Library, Farm St. London). Copinger says that the sale by Drury was to Thomas Lovell in 1588; Lovell, of East Harling, Norfolk, was another leading religious conservative (Hassell Smith p.64).

72   Cressey? Cf. Papworth p.264.

73   Devereux inherited from his grandmother, Margaret, widow of Walter, Viscount Hereford (Copinger, IV p.311, and *CPR Eliz*. V, 2290).

74   Cordell, of Long Melford, Master of the Rolls 1555-81, kted. 1555, JP 1554-81, MP Steyning 1553, Suffolk 1558, Middlesex 1563, a discreet conservative in religion; monument Melford 1581. It is unclear whether the Chorographer is referring the date 1573 to the building of the Cordell almshouse as referred to by Camden (see Appendix III) or to the building of Melford Hall. Although Sir Nikolaus Pevsner (*Buildings of England: Suffolk*, 1961, p.322) dates the Hall to the 1550s, its dating is uncertain and it could easily be of 1573 — it is also most unlikely that the Chorographer would refer to almshouses in the terms that he uses of the 'house'. The almshouses were endowed by Cordell in his will of 1581. If the reference is to the Hall, Norman Scarfe suggests that its ruin could be accounted for by its long being untenanted from the time of Dame Mary Cordell's death in 1584 — for Edward Cordell and Lady Abigail lived in London and Mrs.Allington probably lived at Horseheath (cf. n.75 below).

75   Jane marr. Richard Allington of Horseheath (Copinger I p.137) and d. 1602; Edward Cordell, one of the Six Clerks in Chancery, JP 1583-91, marr. Lady Abigail Digby, sister to Sir Arthur Heveningham (Cordell's will 1591, PCC 4 Saintberbe).

76   Thomas Clopton, s. of William, JP 1590-98, brass Long Melford 1598; William, s. of Thomas, kted. 1614, JP 1598-1619; will 1619 (PCC 35 Parker).

77   Edward Bacon junior was s. and h. of Sir Nicholas Bacon the younger (adm. Caius College Cambridge 1581, *EANQ NS* I p.241). Sir Nicholas was not made a baronet until 1611, and Le Neve has clearly misread the Chorographer's 'k't' as 'b't', an understandable error when transcribing the Chorographer's hand.

78   Feltham, formerly of Halesworth, d.1631 (*Inner Temple Admissions* p.83) bought the manor of Milden in 1599 (Copinger I p.160). Copinger p.159 says that Henry s. and h. of Richard Forsett, sold Wells Hall to William Webbe in 1588 and he to Thomas Shorland in 1592, confirming the annotation in the text.

79   Sir Isaac Appleton of Little Waldingfield kted. 1603, will proved 1609 (Muskett I p.329).

80   Robert Cutler junior, s. of Robert senior; merchant of Ipswich, and later of Sproughton (BL Add.15520 f.39v), Bailiff of Ipswich 1591, 1597, 1602 (Bacon, *Annalls* pp.364, 386, 410); Sir William Spring of Pakenham, kted. 1578, Sheriff of Suffolk 1577-78, 1595-96, JP 1571-1600, PCC Administration 1600, 120.

81   Sir Clement Higham of Barrow, Speaker of the Commons 1554, kted. 1555, Chief Baron of the Exchequer to Mary I, retired from public life on Elizabeth I's accession because of his religious conservatism; JP 1529-1571, Custos Rotulorum 1558-1571, Monument Barrow 1571. Stephen Gardiner, conservative Bishop of Winchester 1531-55 and arch-villain of John Foxe's *Book of Martyrs*, came from Bury and had probably known Sir Clement when they were both young men.

82   See Appendix III. Thomas 1st Lord Wentworth was ennobled 1529, JP 1531-51; d.1551.

83   John Maplesden, Archdeacon of Suffolk, inducted to Oulton 1582 (*PSIA* XXII, 1936, p.309). James Hobart of Hales in Norfolk, a leading Catholic recusant, involved in the abortive Norfolk rising of 1571 (PRO SP 12/171/63, and see Introduction, p.13).

84   This fragment probably comes from the Appendix, after p.319. It refers to the splendid early 14th century brass of a priest stolen from the church in 1857; the indent remains. Adam de Bacon was inducted to Oulton in 1301, and to Blundeston in 1312 (*PSIA* XXII, 1936, p.35).

85   Of Brome, son of Sir John Cornwallis, Steward of the Household to Prince Edward. Kted. 1547; Comptroller of the Household to Mary I; forced to retire to private life because of his Catholicism on Elizabeth's accession. JP 1547-58; monument Brome 1604. Despite occasional periods of conformity, the leading figure among East Anglian recusants (see *PSIA* XXIV, 1960, pp.226-271).

86   See Appendix III. PLN notes 'See more after amongst additions', suggesting that the Appendix contained further material on Orford now lost.

87   Edward, s. and h. of Edward Lord Abergavenny.

88   See Appendix III.

89   Of Smallbridge, Bures; kted. 1576, Sheriff 1568-69, 1589-90, JP 1566-87, 1588-92, 1601-14, MP Suffolk 1563. D.1614; interruptions in the Commission of the Peace caused by his wife's recusancy and his own conservative tendencies (PRO SP 12/206/85; *Winthrop Papers*, ed. J.Winthrop, Massachusetts Historical Society, 1929, I p.178).

90   Robert Ryece of Preston, son of Robert; the antiquary and author of the *Breviary of Suffolk* (See Introduction p.16), brass Preston 1638. Ryece senior bought the manor in 1580 (Copinger I p.189).

91   Robert Rookwood of Stanningfield, JP 1554-61, will 1601 (Sudbury Archdeaconry Court 21 Copping); a consistent Catholic recusant (e.g. *APC* XXVIII p.588), succeeded by s. and h. Henry, who became a Roman priest (H.Foley, *Records of the English Province of the Society of Jesus*, 8 vols. 1877-83, IV p.788). Robert bought Mortimers of Thomas Poley in 1565 (Copinger I p.188); Poley was Robert Spring's stepfather (PRO C3/132/87).

92   John Jermyn of Depden, JP 1563-1606, bur. Depden 25 November 1606 (Muskett II p.256) Copinger I p.186 says that John granted Swifts to his eldest s. Thomas, and Henry Firmage, in 1596, which would be more in line with the general date of the Chorography than following its own statement that Thomas had *inherited* the property from his father. Thomas Burlz marr. Thomas's sister Anne and d.1625 (Muskett). Copinger makes Thomas Poley sell Swifts to the Jermyns.

93   See Appendix III.

94   James Spencer bought the manor in 1552 and left it in 1567 to Leonard Spencer, who left it in 1600 to his s. and h. Robert, claims Copinger, IV p.319; but Leonard witnessed Sir Anthony Wingfield's will in 1606 (PCC 7 Strafforde). Probably Copinger is in error and the Chorographer is referring to Leonard.

95   See Appendix III.

96   See Appendix III, and Introduction, p.11 above. John Wentworth of Somerleyton rose from relatively humble beginnings – his father was an Ipswich joiner (Muskett III p.16) – through acting as lawyer for various conservative families in north-east Suffolk (Hen.10 (ii) f.96, Beccles Town Muniments A4/82, 85, PRO SP12/171/63, Folger Shakespeare Library MS Ld.616); Lawyer in King's Bench 1600 (*APC* XXX p.29), Sheriff of Suffolk 1607-08, JP 1596-temp. James I. Will 1619 (PCC 51 Parker).

97   John Brown senior, brasses Halesworth 1581 or Spexhall 1591; John junior sold Burghards in 1596 to Paul Banning (Copinger II p.159), who was kted. 1614, and was a JP temp. James I.

98   Son of Roger Martin; pensioner to Mary I (BL Add.37999 f.6r); subsequently a leading Catholic recusant (*APC* X p.311). Brass Long Melford 1615.

99   Kted. at Cadiz 1596; JP 1600-29, will 1629 (PCC 91 Ridley).

100   JP 1594-95, 1598-1618; Brass Thornham Magna 1618; purchased Stoke Ash of John Parker 1596 (Copinger III p.302).

101   Robert Bell, Chief Baron of the Exchequer 1577 (Hassell Smith p.64) sold the Rectory to Francis Mannock 1568 (*CPR Eliz*. IV, 2154); Mannock was a reluctant conformist (PRO SP 12/188/38); brass Stoke 1590. His son William was a Catholic recusant (APC XXIX p.117); brass Stoke 1616.

102   S. of Thomas, who was JP 1561, 1567-70, brass Little Glemham 1571; see n.18 above, p.113.

103   See Appendix III.

104   See Appendix IIII.

105   There is now no trace of the Muryall inscription, John Muryel was inducted to Barningham near Weston 1385 (*PSIA* XXII, 1936, p.66). George Nunn, clerk, left the manor to John Nunn his s. and h. in 1596 (Copinger I p.399).

106   S. of John Lany of Cratfield, lawyer; possibly benefited from patronage from the Bacons (University of Chicago, Redgrave MS 4133); Recorder of Ipswich 1585 (Bacon, *Annalls*, p.341), JP 1583-95, 1596-temp. James I, MP Ipswich 1586.

107   Of Letheringham, s. of Sir Anthony the elder; kted. 1553, Sheriff of Norfolk and Suffolk 1560-61, JP 1558-96, MP Suffolk 1563, 1572 — a leading county politician. Brass formerly at Letheringham 1597 (see p.94 above).

108   See Appendix III.

109   Thomas Seckford senior of Ipswich and Woodbridge, one of the Masters of Requests 1558-87 (*APC* VII p.17), 2d s. of an earlier Thomas, of Bealings; JP 1559-87, MP Ipswich 1559, 1563, 1572, Suffolk 1571, 1581; endowed almshouses at Woodbridge; will 1587 (PCC 4 Rutland). Charles, his nephew, of Great Bealings, JP 1580-87, MP Aldeburgh 1572, will 1592 (PCC 27 Harrington).

110   Note by Allen: 'These church notes are all posted 1722' — Le Neve continues — 'to the respective towns'.

111   The inscription of the brass for Richard de la Pole remains under the tower with indents of figure and shields. The monument for John de la Pole is probably the indent of canopied figure of an ecclesiastic with marginal inscription and four shields in the chancel; there is an indent for an ecclesiastic in the south chapel, but this has only two shields. The three altar tombs described still survive. The indent of a woman under a canopy with four shields and marginal inscription to north of chancel is probably Margaret de la Pole's monument. Margery Almott's monument is either the indent of inscription and shield or that of female effigy, inscription and four corner lozenges, both in the south chapel.

112   The shield only of the Banyard brass remains, now mural, south of chancel; the quartered coat is Hales of Brampton (Corder 150). Beside the shield is the Brown brass — the full inscription is much longer and mentions Brown's

25 years of marriage to Silvester, his six sons and five daughters and his death on 17 August 1591. There is a further brass for Mary Downing d.December 1601, which was presumably not in position when the Chorographer visited Spexhall.

113   The indent of the Argentine brass, with armoured effigy, inscription and two shields, remains in the south chapel, as does the indent of the Claxton brass, with effigy, inscription four shields and four small scrolls.

114   Cf. Weever's version of the inscription, p.758. No trace of the monument remains.

115   The effigy and the fourth shield of this brass survive.

116   There is no trace of the first two monuments. The effigy of the third brass remained when Davy visited the church in 1809 (Hartismere II f.156).

117   Neither monument remains, although Davy (Hartismere I f.272, 1843) records indent of demi-effigy and inscription in the chancel which may have been for Stokes.

118   Only empty indents remain in the church. The Sulyard inscription is possibly one of the two very small inscription indents in the north aisle; it is difficult to identify the Wingfield or the Singleton inscriptions. The indent of the Borgue brass remains in the nave, a most unusual composition with central shield supported by two figures, inscription and four shields, and the Washington brass is probably the indent of armoured figure and woman on inscription, two groups of children and four shields nearby.

119   No indent of the Backton brass survives, but Davy (Hartismere I f.42, 1831) illustrates an indent of ecclesiastic, inscription and four corner quatrefoils in chancel; Martin (Iveagh/Phillipps 67 p.111, c.1750) illustrates another ecclesiastical effigy with scroll and inscription. The Pretyman brass has disappeared, although another of the same period remains.

120   See above, p.114, n.37.

121   The first three brasses described remain, mural, in north chapel The indent of the brass for John Glemham and his two wives remained on Davy's visit in 1831 (Plomesgate II f.29). Darby (Plomesgate f.14, 1825) describes an indent with effigy and four shields which may have been for Christopher Colby and one with effigy and inscription possibly Alice Colby's, both in nave. The inscription for the second John Glemham was an incised slab which remained, 'very much defaced', when Mrs.Ann Mills visited the church c.1820 (MSS penes Miss Joan Corder, III f.192v).

122   No trace remains of the Reginald Rous monument. The indent of Sir William Wingfield's brass remains, with military effigy, inscription and two shields, in chancel; the other Wingfield brass has completely disappeared.

123   Thomas Rous of Henham 'now living', Sheriff of Suffolk 1590-91, JP 1586-1603, was kted. and died 1603 (will NNRO Norwich Consistory Court Norfforthe f.195v), so these notes can be dated to before early 1603 and so can all the Chorographer's visits preceding them. The indent of Henry Beaumont's brass remains in the south chapel, with effigy, inscription and four standards. The Bardolph tomb remains, as does the indent of the Phelip brass, very mutilated but with traces of canopy, marginal inscription and four shields, both

in the south chapel. All remaining brass was 'laid up' in the vestry in 1662 and subsequently lost (*PSIA* VIII, 1894, p.69). The glass was probably among that destroyed in 1643 (*ibid.*).

1 2 4   The Brewes brass remains; the other monument is difficult to identify among the existing indents.

1 2 5   There is now no trace of the stained glass described. The 'raysed tombe' is in fact against the south wall of the south chapel, and now has above it a brass for Nicholas Bohun d.1602 – 'Mr.Bawin' was his father Francis, JP 1590-92, and a highly litigious character (*APC* XIV, p.109; PRO STAC 5 B47/24, B30/18, F20/30; C3/204/41, C2 Eliz. A1/14 etc.).

1 2 6   The indent of Thomas Duke's brass remains in chancel, with inscription and two shields. Agnes Duke's monument may be the indent with effigy and inscription in nave.

1 2 7   The brass inscription for Mary Cuddon remains on the south nave wall; the heraldry described was painted on a board hanging above, which remained in the early 19th century (Ford Collections, Bodley MS Top.Suff. d.7 p.775) but has now disappeared.

1 2 8   The glass described does not survive. The effigy of the Bumpstead brass remains, with shield and inscription lost. The Playters altar tomb was extensively restored in the early 17th century with new brass figures and inscription; the inscription makes William Playters, who d.1512, the son and heir of the family, which meets the Chorographer's objection as to the lack of differencing in the heraldry. The brass of Thomas Playters d.1479 remains but with a mutilated inscription; all the other Playters brasses remain intact. The other early 17th century 'restoration', the brass for Christopher Playters d.1547, is, notably, missing from the Chorographer's description. The shield and inscription of the Edgar brass are now split between nave and chancel.

1 2 9   The indents of the first two brasses remain under the tower with shield and inscription; the shield of the first remained in the church until early this century. The two shields of the Bacheler brass remain, with indents of armoured figure and inscription; however the second shield bears a mullet within a bordure with a bend overall.

1 3 0   The Peyton indents remain in the north aisle; the Roding monument has disappeared, as has the next monument, although it may be represented by one of the indents in the south chapel. The 3 cocks in triangle may be for Cockerell of Hadleigh and Stoke 'temp. Edw.2' (Corder 116). Edward Waldegrave's stone remains in south chapel, an incised slab.

1 3 1   The effigy of Sir William Tendring's brass remains with indents of shields, marginal inscription and canopy. Of the Howard brass only the double canopy remains with indents of effigies, shields and marginal inscription; Weever p.773 illustrates the brass with the effigies already lost. The effigies of Catherine Tendring and Katherine Howard's brasses remain, the inscriptions lost; John Windsor's stone remains, an incised slab.

1 3 2   The Danyell and Redmeld brasses have disappeared, but their effigies remained when Francis Blomfield visited the church in 1723/4 (Iveagh/Phillipps 79 s.v.Stoke). There is no trace of the 'raysed tombe'.

133   The indent of the first Mannock brass remains in the north chapel, with effigy in armour between two wives, inscriptions, groups of children and three shields, much worn. Francis Mannock's brass survives although the effigies have disappeared. The indent of Elizabeth Bedingfield's brass remains on the east wall of the chapel, and Lady Waldegrave's monument remains in the south chapel. It was this Lady Waldegrave whose recusancy was responsible for Sir William Waldegrave's removal from the Commission of the Peace (*EANQ NS* II p.181, and cf. n.89 above).

134   There is no trace of either the Page inscription or the Heveningham altar tomb. The latter remained when Ford visited the church in 1813 (Bodley MS Top.Suff. d.5 p.509), a wooden altar tomb bearing a marble slab with two wooden effigies and indents of the marginal inscription and shields. The effigy of Sir John remains in the south aisle, but the effigy of his wife was broken up for firewood last century. The other three wooden effigies have disappeared and the north chapel is virtually a Victorian rebuild.

135   The first two brasses survive; the Blakey monument may be represented by part of an indent of effigy and inscription now in the north aisle, but Davy (Blything II f.105, 1833) illustrates two such indents, both apparently with demi-effigies.

136   This is an abbreviated version of the brass inscription, which survives now mural in the nave, with effigies and groups of children.

137   The north chapel has been demolished, and a small fragment of the tomb-chest on which this slab was laid is now built into the north chancel wall, inside. Despite the wording of the description the effigies were not incised into the stone but brasses, for the slab with the indents survived on Davy's visit in 1830 (Wangford I f.115v). The shields are Tasburgh (Corder 191) and Neaches (ibid.418).

138   John Winthrop d.1613 was in fact the son of Adam Winthrop d.1562 whose brass remains in the chancel. He sold the manor to his brother Adam (d.1623) and nephew John, the future Governor of Massachusetts, in 1609 (Muskett I p.25). This entry is altogether puzzling; the elder Adam's brass looks contemporary with his date of death and therefore must have been in the church on the Chorographer's visit.

139   No trace remains of these monuments and the only brass indents that Darby found on his visit in 1828 (Blackbourne p.127) were for an ecclesiastic with inscription and shield above inscription.

140   See n.59 above.

141   The indents of the brasses remain under the tower, worn; the woman's shield is Jenny (Corder 77) impaling ?Downing (Corder 405).

142   Sir Thomas Rivett, of Chippenham in Cambs; originally of Stowmarket, and later of London, Merchant Adventurer (*CPR Eliz.* I p.172), kted. 1578, JP 1577-82; will 1582 (PCC 12 Rowe). Lord Windsor was nephew to Sir William Waldegrave through their Rivett marriages, and he was involved in a duel with Sir William's son Sir William junior in 1587 (*Letters of Philip Gawdy*, ed. I.H.Jeayes, Roxburgh Club, 1906, p.14). Edward Rookwood of Euston was a wealthy

Catholic recusant (cf. e.g. *EANQ NS* I p.117, BL Add.15520 f.72v); cf. n.71 above. Sir John Peyton of Isleham; Cambs. kted. 1586, Sheriff of Norfolk 1589-90, JP Norfolk 1578-1603, d.1630 (Hassell Smith p.389).

143 The Butts inscription was noted in the church by Sir Thomas Gage in 1813 (Hen.79 I f.19v) but had disappeared by 1828 (Davy, Thingo f.21). Another two inscriptions of the Crosyer brass remain, but not this one; indents of three scrolls and effigy with inscription across the breast are illustrated by Davy but are now very worn. The Higham brass survives. The Fyrmyn inscription has disappeared.

144 This has disappeared.

145 The indent of the Clerk brass is now on the chancel floor, with two effigies in shrouds, inscription, two scrolls and achievement. The achievement plate remained in the church in 1926 (Mill Stephenson, *List of Monumental Brasses*, London, 1926, p.463). The indent of the top-slab of the altar tomb remains in chancel, much damaged; the rather odd figure brasses that it bore are illustrated in the *Antiquarian Repertory* III (1807) p.341.

146 The Codington monument remains; the Norton monument has disappeared.

147 The Seckford monument remains, much altered, without inscription; the glass does not remain. The Shorland brass survives.

148 On the Letheringham monuments see J.M.Blatchly, *PSIA* XXXIII (1975) pp.168-194 – they were deliberately destroyed and dispersed in the 1780s. What survived are the brass effigies of Sir Thomas Wingfield, Sir John Wingfield, and many indents, some covered up. Those of Sir Thomas Wingfield, Sir William Bovile and Sir Robert Wingfield d.1409 are readily identifiable.

149 The Starke inscription has disappeared; the Bacon inscription remains although the shields have been removed.

150 All these monuments remain. The second two are respectively for Henry Fitzroy, Duke of Richmond d.1536 and Thomas, third Duke of Norfolk d.1554.

151 Neither monument survives, although the first may be the indent of an inscription now in the nave.

152 No trace remains of any of these monuments except for the headless brass effigies of Staverton and his wife, now mural in the chancel. The indent and part of the marginal inscription of the Dalling brass remained on Davy's visit in 1823 (Loes I f.318).

153 Thomas Appleton's inscription has disappeared; the indent of Margery's remains in the north aisle, with shield and inscription. The effigies and four shields of Robert's brass remain in the north aisle, with inscription, Trinity group and two scrolls lost. There is no trace of the last monument.

154 The indent of Anne's brass remains in the south aisle; Elizabeth Martin's monument cannot be identified. The altar tomb remains with all brass reaved. The next two cannot be identified; the indent of Roger Martin's brass remains in the south aisle, with effigies in shrouds, inscriptions, two shields, scroll and corner quatrefoils.

155 Sir William Clopton's indent is now in the north aisle, with one brass shield of Marowe (Papworth p.768) remaining. Thomasine Clopton's monument may be represented by the indent of lady, inscription, two shields and group of children c.1500 to the east of the last. Francis Clopton the elder d.1559 (Muskett I p.144) and his monument may be represented by the indent of shield and inscription in the north aisle. Thomas Clopton was in fact son of William Clopton *esquire* and father to a younger Sir William ('the present heire'); Thomas d.1598 and is now commemorated by a brass inscription.

156 The effigy and two shields remain of Francis Clopton's brass in the north chapel; William Clopton's monument remains with the brass inscription — another inscription of which the indent remains on the monument must have been already lost by then. The effigies and canopies of the first Margery Clopton and the Harleston brass remain, the other is lost.

157 The indent for Sir William d.1416 remains in the Clopton Chantry, much worn, with effigy, four shields and marginal inscription. One of the effigies only of Margery and Ann's brass remains, as does the brass effigy of William Clopton d.1420. The last tomb may be that for John Clopton d.1497 between the Clopton Chantry and the sanctuary — the other has disappeared, but the heraldry Clopton impaling Jermyn indicates that it was for William Clopton d.1562 whose first wife was Margaret daughter of Sir Thomas Jermyn (Muskett I p.143).

158 Robert Barker of Parham, Barrister of the Inner Temple, JP Suffolk 1601-temp. James I, MP Colchester 1597, 1601, 1604-11, 1614. D.1618. Owed much of his advancement, including his promotion to being Sergeant at Law, to his brother-in-law Sir Edward Coke (Constance M.Dwyer, *The Personnel of Parliament, 1597*, Manchester MA thesis, 1927, p.29). Simon Mawe of Rendlesham originated from Lincolnshire and rose through being a servant of Thomas Seckford the Master of Requests (PCC 4 Rutland), who was steward of the Liberty of St.Audrey with him. He d.1610 (monument, Rendlesham).

159 The Burgate monument remains, though the inscription is somewhat mutilated and the shields have disappeared; the font and its inscription survive. The Slack inscription has disappeared.

160 The Brundish monument and brass remains; the indent of the Jenny brass remains in the nave, with effigy, inscription and two shields. Though the altar tombs of the Colby monuments have been removed the brasses survive almost intact except for the brass of Francis Colby of which only the headless effigy of his wife and three corner shields remain. Francis murdered Francis Fastolf of Pettaugh in 1561, but received a pardon presumably through being Lord Wentworth's son-in-law (*CPR Eliz.* II p.127). The Denys glass has not survived, which is a pity in view of its rather unusual inscription.

161 Sayer Sulyard's monument remains, without inscription, to north of chancel. He was inducted to Rendlesham in 1312 (*PSIA* XXII, 1936, p.77) and was a man of considerable property in the 1327 Subsidy (*Suffolk Green Books* IX vol.II, 1906, index). The second brass has entirely gone. Godefrid Lumkin was inducted to Rendlesham in 1332 (*PSIA* XXII, 1936, p.63).

162   The Inglish brass remains without its marginal inscription. The indent of the armoured man remained on Davy's visit in 1819 (Loes I f.71); the shields in glass, now destroyed, were Blaxhall (Corder 77) and ?Coote (Corder 117). The other monument has disappeared.

163   The Garneys brass remains, now loose in vestry. No trace survives of the two indents.

164   The Carbonell monument remains. The inscription of the Cornwallis brass remains, now mural and hidden by the organ, in the chancel. Since the main Badingham entry is dated 1604 the entries before this entry in the Chorography Appendix can be dated 1602-04.

165   The Yaxley alias Herbert monument remains in the nave, with indents of civilian and wife, marginal inscription and shields on the tomb-chest; shields remained on Martin's visit in 1726, as did the shields of the Floyd brass, which has now totally disappeared (WSRO E2/41/8b f.385r). The Yaxley monuments were partly of wood and survived as late as Davy's visit in 1844 (Hartismere I f.285); nothing now remains.

166,   Thomas Skinner, Alderman and sometime Lord Mayor of London, d.1595 and suits ensued between his sons John and Thomas (PRO C2 ELIZ G5/15).

167   Both brasses mentioned survive in the north chapel, although the date of Edmund's death is in fact 1569.

168   The heraldic glass has disappeared.

APPENDICES

APPENDIX I

Sources of the text

'Tanner' stands for Bodley MS Tanner 135 — all foliation is on the recto side. Hen.1-19 are also foliated volumes in which the foliation is all on the recto side. Certain Hengrave volumes contain two Hundreds and are in two halves; Thingo is in three sections and unfoliated, as is the Ipswich volume and part of Thedwastre.

Introduction, Ackolt, Acton, Akenham, Aldham WSRO Accession 449/5/31/29
Acton Tanner transcript, Tanner f.l
Akenham TA transcript, Hen.4 f.2
Aldham TA transcript, Hen.6 f.5
All Saints S.Elmham TA transcript, Hen.18 f.22
Aldeborough Hen.12 (i) f.4
Alderton See Aldeborough; TA transcript, Hen.19 f.5
Aldringham Hen.12 (i) f.4
Allyngton Hen.12 (ii) f.4
Alpeton Hen.14 f.8
Ampten See Allyngton; TA transcript, Hen.16 (i) f.10
Arwerton See Alpeton
Ashbye Hen.10 f.17
Ashe See Ashbye
Ashfelde l Sf 7 Hen.2 f.15
Ashfeild parva TA transcript, Hen.9 (ii) f.6
Asyngton See Ashfelde
Aye ESRO HD 225/1404 (loose papers)
St.Andros ibid.; TA transcript, Hen. 18 f.43; Martin transcript, WSRO E2/41/8b f.321r
Baddingham Hen.12 (ii) f.11
Badley Hen.4 (i) f.26; TA transcript, *ibid.* f.10
Badwellashe See Baddingham; TA transcripts, Hen.9 (ii) f.10, *ibid.* f.6

Baleham See Badley
Barham Hen.4 f.14
Bareowe Hen.17 (i) *s.v.* Barrow
Barnebye See Barham
Barsham See Bareowe
Beckles Hen.18 f.68
Bawdsey Hen.19 f.11
Bedfield See Beckles
Benhall See Bawdsey; TA transcript, Hen.12 (i) f.10
Basforth Hen.4 (i) f.22
Belynge magna Hen.14 f.14; TA transcript, Hen.5 f.7
Belynge parva See Basforth; TA transcripts, Hen.5 ff.6 and 7
Belsted parva See Belynge magna
Bedingfeild TA transcript, Hen.12 (ii) f.16
Benaker Hen.9 (ii) f.25; TA transcript, Hen.3 f.6
Bernyngham See Benaker
Berton magna Hen.9 (ii) f.22; transcript by Sir Thomas Gage, Hen.79 (iii) f.111r
Berton parva See Berton magna
Bilston Martin transcript, Elveden Hall MS Iveagh/Phillipps 6 f.12r
Blakenham magna Hen.3 f.13
Blakenham super montem Hen.4 f.30
Bliborough See Blakenham magna; TA transcript, *ibid.* f.11
Blaxall Hen.12 f.16
Blyford TA transcript, Hen.3 f.26

Boulge See Blaxall; TA transcript, Hen.19 f.19

Boxford Hen.11 f.16; TA transcript, Hen.2 f.20

Boxstede See Boxford

Blunston Ibid.

Bradfelde St Cleres PLN transcript, Hen.16 (i) f.73

Monks Bradfeld Hen.3 f.31

Burnt Bradfelde See Bradfelde St.Cleres

Bramfeld See Monks Bradfeld

Bradley magna See Burnt Bradfelde; TA transcript, Hen.13 f.6

Bramford Hen.6 f.13

Brantham Hen.14 f.24

Brettenham See Bramford

Bredfeild TA transcript, Hen.16 (i) f.72

Briset magna Hen.4 (i) f.38

Briset parva Ibid.

Brockford Ibid.

Brightwell Hen.5 f.14

Brome Ibid.

Bucklesham Hen.18 f.35

Bungaye Ibid.

Burntileye Hen.5 f.22

Burgate Hen.11 f.31

Burghe See Burntileye

Burgh Castell See Burgate; TA transcript, *ibid.* f.32

Burstall TA transcript, Hen.14 f.30

Butley TA transcript, Hen.12 f.25

Buxhall TA transcript, Hen.15 f.3; f.4 has a note by PLN on Chorography paper.

Candish Hen.2 f.42.

Capell n Sf 13 TA transcript, Hen.14 f.35

Capell e Sf 4 See Candish; TA transcript, Hen.14 f.36

Carleton 1 Sf 9 TA transcript, Hen. 12 (ii) f.28

Carleton a Sf 1 Ibid.

Cattywade Ibid.

Cavenham Hen.9 (i) f.10; TA transcript *Ibid.*

Charsfeld Hen.6 f.19; TA transcript, Hen.10 f.24

Chatsham See Charsfeld; TA transcript, Hen.14 f.39

Chelsworth See Charsfeld

Chempton Ibid.

Cheston Hen.12 f.29

Chillesforde Ibid.

Chilton Hen.13 f.12

Clare Ibid. and f.14

Cleydon Hen.2 f.56; TA transcript, Hen.4 (i) f.43

Clopton Hen.18 f.118; TA transcript, Hen.5 f.27

Cockfeld See Cleydon

Conyweston See Clopton

Cookeley Hen.3 f.48

Copdock Hen.14 f.49

Cornerd magna See Cookeley

Cornerd parva See Copdock

Cotton Tanner transcript, Tanner f.9r; Martin transcript, WSRO E2/41/8a f.14r

S.Cove TA transcript, Hen.3 f.138

Covehithe Hen.18 f.81

Combes Ibid.

Cransford Hen.10 f.30

Cretyngham Ibid.

Dalinghoo Hen.10 g.37

Debach Hen.19 f.40; TA transcript, *ibid.*

Dynnyngton Hen.12 (ii) f.36

Drenkeston Ibid; TA transcript, Hen.16 (i) f.83

Dunnynworth TA transcript, Hen.12 (i) f.36

Easton c Sf 3 Hen.3 f.65

Easton h Sf 10 Ibid.

Easton Gosbeck Ibid.

Earle Soham/Earle Stonham Ibid.

Eyke Hen.10 f.54

Edwardstone WSRO E2/41/8a f.174; PLN transcript, Hen.2 f.71

Eldon See Eyke

Ellowe See Edwardstone

South Elmham Hen.18 f.23

Ewston Hen.9 (ii) f.39

Exnynge Hen.15 f.38; *Ibid.* f.40

Fakenham magna Hen.9 (i) f.40

Fakenham parva See Exnynge; PLN transcript, Hen.9 (ii) f.47

Farnham Hen.12 f.42
Felsham Ibid.
Fernham Martyn Hen.18 f.10
Fernham o'i'u' S'toru' Hen.15 f.43
Felixstow See Fernham Martyn
Finboro magna See Fernham o'i'u' S'toru'
Finboro Parva Hen.17 (i) *s.v.* Flempton
Fynnyngham Hen.11 f.42
Flempton See Finboro parva
Flixton a Sf 1 See Fynnyngham
Flixton b Sf 2 Ibid.
Flouton Hen.3 f.68; TA transcript, Hen.4 f.65
Fordham See Flixton b Sf 2
Fordley See Flouton
Framisden Hen.4 (ii) f.9
Fresenfeld Ibid.
Freston TA transcript, Hen.14 f.60
Fritton Elveden Hall MS Iveagh/Phillipps 11 f.75r
Gadgrave PLN transcript, Hen.12 f.46
Glemham magna Hen.12 (i) f.51
Glemham parva Ibid.
Gorleston Ibid.; TA transcript, Elveden Hall MS Iveagh/Phillipps 11 f.79
Groton See Glemham magna
Grundesboro Hen.5 f.44
Hacheston Ibid.; TA transcript, *ibid.*
Herthurste PLN transcript, Hen.2 f.89
Hadley Hen.3 f.73; TA transcript, Hen.6 f.36
Halesworth See Hadley
Hargrave Hen.15 f.53; TA transcript, Hen.17 (ii) *s.v.* Hargrave
Harcksted Hen.13 f.66
Harleston See Hargrave
Hasylwood See Harcksted
Hasketon Hen.5 f.44
Haverill Hen.4 (i) f.76
Hawkeden See Hasketon
Helmyngham See Haverhill
Hawsted Hen.4 (i) f.70
Hemyngton Ibid.

Hemley Hen.4 (i) f.80
Hengrave Hen.3 f.82; TA transcript, Hen.17 (ii) *s.v.* Hengrave
Henly See Hemley
Heveningham See Hengrave
Henham Hen.3 f.78
Hensted Ibid.
Horningsherth PLN transcript, Hen.17 (ii) *s.v.* Horningsheath
Hesset Hen.16 (ii) *s.v.* Hesset
Hintlesham Hen.14 f.76
Hoo See Hesset; TA transcript, Hen.10 f.68.
Honington See Hintlesham
Higham Hen.9 (ii) f.55
Hepworth TA transcript, *Ibid.* f.51
Hinderclay Ibid. f.55
Holton (St.Peter) Tanner transcript, Tanner f.14r
Holton n Sf 13 Elveden Hall MS Iveagh/Phillipps 14 f.107r
Holbroke Hen.14 f.83
Hopton a Sf 1 See Holton n Sf 13; TA transcript, Hen.9 (ii) f.57
Hopton q Sd 6 Ibid.
Horingflete Ibid.
Homersfeld TA transcript, Hen.18 f.17
Horham Hen.12 (ii) f.57; TA transcript, *ibid.* f.49
Hosely See Horham; TA transcript, Hen.19 f.45
Hoxon See Horham
Huntingfeld Hen.9 (i) f.24; Hen.18 f.22; TA transcript, Hen.18 ff.88, 89
Icklingham Hen.9 (i) f.24
Southelmham St.James Hen.18 f.22
Ilketshall St.Johns Hen.9 (ii) f.72; TA transcript, Hen.18 f.41
Iken See St.Johns; TA transcript, Hen.12 (ii) f.56
Ikesworth See Iken
Ikesworth thorp Ibid.
Ikeworth Hen.2 f.37; TA transcript, Hen.9 (ii) f.72
Burnt Ileye See Ikeworth; TA transcript, *ibid.* f.36
Moncks Ileye Ibid. f.37
Ingham Ibid.

Kenton Hen.10 f.82

Kessgrave Hen.6 f.49; TA transcript, Hen.5 f.56

Kesland Hen.3 (ii) f.9

Kettlebaston See Kessgrave

Knatshall See Kesland

Kirtlow Hen.5 f.60

Kirton f Sf 13 See Kirtlow

Kirkton (Shotley) Ibid.

Langham Hen.2 f.100; TA transcript, Hen.9 (ii) f.86

Lanham Hen.2 f.94

Lawshall See Langham

Laxfeld See Lanham; TA transcript, Hen.12 (ii) f.72

Layston Hen.3 f.94

Lemington Ibid. PLN transcript, Hen.5 f.64

Lestofte Hen.16 (ii) *s.v.* Livermere Magna

Letheringham Ibid.; PLN transcript, Hen.10 f.95

Levermere magna See Lestofte

Levermere parva Ibid.

Lound Hen. 10 f.102

Loudham Hen.19 f.51

Marlesford See Lound

St.Margaret of Akers Hen.19 f.57

Mellis Hen.2 f.123

Melton See St.Margaret

Melford See Mellis

Mendham Hen.5 f.68

Mertlesham Ibid.; TA transcript, *ibid.*

Mettyngham PLN transcript, Hen.18 f.22

Metfeld Hen.2 f.136; PLN transcript, Hen.12 (ii) f.76

Mickfeld See Metfeld

Mildinge Ibid.

Mildenhall Ibid.

Muncksyley/Muncksoham Ibid. f.36

Mutforde Hen.3 (ii) f.14

Nacton See Muncksyley; TA transcript, Hen.5 f.73

Naughton See Mutforde

Nedginge Hen.6 f.79

Nedeham Hen.5 f.68

Nettlestead See Nedginge; TA transcript, Hen.4 f.94

Newborn See Nedeham

Neuton (?) Hen.15 f.50

Newmarket Ibid. f.64

Gipping Newton/Newton See Neuton

Newton p Sd 3 See Newmarket

Neylande Hen.2 f.145

St.Nicholas Hen.11 f.88

Nowton q Sd 6 Iveagh/Phillipps 7 f.65r

Olton Hen.11 ff.88, 90

Oclee See Nowton

Onehouse TA transcript, Hen.15 f.65r

Orford Hen.12 (i) f.103

Otley Ibid.; TA transcript, Hen.5 f.85

Ouesden See Orford

Pakefeld Iveagh/Phillipps 11 f.30r.; Martin transcript, WSRO E2/41/9a f.65r

Parham See Pakefeld; TA transcript, Hen.12 (i) f.65

St.Peters Hen.19 f.63

Petaugh Hen.5 f.87

Petistree See St.Peters

Playforde See Petaugh

Polsted Hen.2 f.153; TA transcript, *ibid.*

Poslingford Ibid.

Preston Ibid.

Rammesholt Hen.19 f.69; TA transcript, *ibid.*

Raydon Ibid.

Redsham Hen.18 f.87; PLN transcript, *ibid.*

Redgrave Ibid.

Redlingfield Ibid.

Rendlesham Hen.10 f.116

Rickinghale Parva Ibid.

Ringesfelde Hen.18 f.91

Rougham Ibid.

Roydon Hen.14 f.92

Rumboro Hen.3 f.125

Rusbrock See Roydon; PLN transcript, Hen.16 (ii) *s.v.* Rushbrooke

Rushmere Hen.3 f.125

Saterley Hen.18 f.102

Saxham magna PLN transcript, Hen.17 (iii) *s.v.*Lt.Saxham
Saxham parva See Saterley; PLN transcript, see Saxham magna
Saxtede Hen.12 (ii) f.85
Saxmundham Hen.6 f.86
Seckford See Saxstede
Semer See Saxmundham
Sheepmedo Hen.14 f.99
Shelley Ibid.
Shympling PLN note, Hen.2 f.157
Sisewell Hen,12 (i) f.76; TA transcript, Hen.3 f.132
Smalbridge Hen.11 f.96
Snape See Sisewell
Somerleytowne See Smalbridge
Sotherton Hen.3 f.135
Southolde Ibid. f.136
Sproughton Hen.16 (iii) *s.v.*Stanningfield
Specksall Hen.2 f.165; TA transcript, Hen.3 f.143
Stanfelde See Sproughton
Stansted See Specksall
Stanton Bodley MS Gough Suffolk 7 f.196v
Sternfeld Ibid.
Stoke Ash Ibid. (recto)
Stoke n Sf 6 Ibid.
Stoke u Sd 5 Hen.2 f.171
Earle Stonham Hen.4 (i) f.120; TA transcript, *ibid.* f.117
Stonham Aspall See Stoke u Sd 5; TA transcript, Hen.4 (i) f.112
Stonham parva See Earle Stonham
Stowe Hen.9 (ii) f.104; TA transcripts, Hen.18 f.113, Hen.15 f.88
Stowlangtoft See Stowe
Stradbrooke Hen.14 f.115; TA transcript, Hen.12 (ii) f.93
Stratford d Sf 11 See Stradbrooke
Sudburye Hen.2 f.181
Sutton Ibid.
Tattington (with Brundish) PLN transcript, Hen.12 (ii) f.99
Tattyngstone Hen.10 f.114
Thelnetham Hen.9 f.110
Thirlow parva Ibid.; PLN transcript,

Hen.13 f.81
Thorndon PLN transcript, Hen.7 f.99
Thorp Hen.3 f.157
Thrandeston Ibid.
Thwate Hen.5 f.100; PLN transcript, Hen.7 f.110
Trymleys See Thwate
Troston Hen.5 f.105
Tudenham g Sf 5 Hen.9 (i) f.40
Tudenham r Sd 1 See Troston
Tunstall See Tudenham g Sf 5
Ufford Hen.19 f.80
Uppeston Ibid..
Walton Hen.3 f.160
Walpole Hen.9 (ii) f.118
Walderswick See Walton
Walsham in the Willows See Walpole
Waldingfelde Magna Hen.2 f.190
Waldingfelde parva Ibid. f.192
Waldringfield See Waldingfelde Magna; PLN transcript, Hen.2 f.188
Whatfeld See Waldingfelde parva
Wangford r Sd 1 Hen.12 (i) f.115
Wangford c Sf 3 Hen.2 f.71
Wantisden See Wangford r Sd 1
Warlingworth Hen.12 (ii) f.119
Wattesham Ibid. f.107
Waybred Ibid.
Wenham Parva Hen.3 f.174; TA transcript, Hen.14 f.36
Wesselton See Wenham Parva
Westall Hen.3 f.177
Weston TA transcript, Hen.18 f.118
Weston mercate Hen.18 f.118; TA transcript, *ibid.*
Westley Hen.17 (ii) *s.v.*Westley
Wethersdale Ibid.
Wetherden Hen.16 (ii) *s.v.* Welnetham
Wheltham magna Ibid.
Wheltham parva Ibid.
Whepsted Ibid.
Whersted Hen.19 f.87
Wixsoo Ibid.
Wickham h Sf 4 Ibid.
Wingfield TA transcript, Hen.12 (ii) f.113
Whitton Hen.8 *s.v.* Whitton
Willingham Hen.18 f.121
Winston Hen.5 f.118

Wisset See Willingham; TA transcript. Hen.3 f.180

Witnesham See Winston

Wiverston Hen.18 f.125

Woodbridge Hen.10 f.123

Worlingham See Wiverston

Wordwell See Woodbridge

Tallow Wrattinge Hen.3 f.184

Wrentham Ibid.

Wűrtham Hen.16 (ii) *s.v.*Woolpit

Wulpet Ibid.

Wylbye Hen.12 (ii) f.111

Wyston Hen.4 (ii) f.17

Yaxley See Wylbye

Yoxford See Wyston, TA transcript, Hen.3 f.190

Appendix, Wingfield – Acton College of Arms Suffolk MS 9 (unpag.), RR 38B Shelf E

The following transcripts of the Appendix exist;

Wingfield TA transcript, Hen.12 (ii) f.114; Tanner transcript, Tanner f.27

Speckshall TA transcript, Hen.3 f.143; Tanner transcript, Tanner f.26

Halesworth TA transcript, Hen.3 f.73; Tanner transcript, Tanner f.12

Theberton TA transcript, Hen.3 f.147; Tanner transcript, Tanner f.24

Mendlesham Tanner transcript Tanner f.22

Thorndon TA transcript, Hen.7 f.97; Tanner transcript, Tanner f.24

Gislingham Tanner transcript, Tanner f.12

Westhorp Martin transcript, WSRO E2/41/8b f.322, Tanner transcript, Tanner f.28

Bacton Tanner transcript, Tanner f.2

Cotton Tanner transcript, Tanner f.9

Glemham parva TA transcript, Hen.12 (i) f.49; Tanner transcript, Tanner f.12

Dynnyngton TA transcript, Hen.12 (ii) f.37; Tanner transcript, Tanner f.9

Fressingfeld TA transcript, Hen.12 (ii) f.40; Tanner transcript, Tanner f.11

Westall TA transcript, Hen.3 f.177; Tanner transcript, Tanner f.24

Brampton TA transcript, Hen.3 f.21; Tanner transcript, Tanner f.4

Schadenfeild TA transcript, Hen.18 f.109; Tanner transcript, Tanner f.26

Saterly TA transcript, Hen.18 f.101; Tanner transcript, Tanner f.25

Ellough TA transcript, Hen.18 f.73; Tanner transcript, Tanner f.10

Stoke juxta Neyland TA transcript, Hen.2 f.170; Tanner transcript, Tanner f.23

Hevenyngham TA transcript, Hen.3 f.83; Tanner transcript, Tanner f.14

Huntyngfield TA transcript, Hen.3 f.88; Tanner transcript, Tanner f.14

Cookelye TA transcript, Hen.3 f.48; Tanner transcript, Tanner f.4

St.Peters in Southelmham Tanner transcript, Tanner f.26

Groton Tanner transcript, Tanner f.12

Stanton s'tor' TA transcript, Hen.19 (ii) f.101; Tanner transcript, Tanner f.26

Holton Tanner transcript, Tanner f.14

Bliford TA transcript, Hen.3 f.26; Tanner transcript, Tanner f.4

Stoke iuxta Neyland TA transcript, Hen.2 f.169

Barrowe TA transcript, Hen.19 (i) *s.v.* Barrow; Tanner transcript, Tanner f.2

Kenforde Tanner transcript, Tanner f.17

Livermere magna TA transcript, Hen.16 (ii) *s.v.* Livermere Magna; Tanner transcript, Tanner f.18

Ikesworth TA transcript, Hen.9 (ii) f.74; Tanner transcript, Tanner f.17

Woodbridge TA transcript, Hen.10 f.122; Tanner transcript, Tanner f.28

Letheringham TA transcript, Hen.10 f.91; Tanner transcript, Tanner f.19

Petistree TA transcript, Hen.19 f.63; Tanner transcript, Tanner f.22

Framyngham Tanner transcript,

Tanner f.11
Wyssett TA transcript, Hen.3 f.180;
Tanner transcript, Tanner f.28
Eyke TA transcript, Hen.10 f.54;
Tanner transcript, Tanner f.10
Waldingfeld parva TA transcript,
Hen.2 f.171; Tanner transcript,
Tanner f.28
Melford TA transcript, Hen.2 f.122;
Tanner transcript, Tanner f.20
Woodbridge TA transcript, Hen.10
f.121
Burgate TA transcript, WSRO
E2/41/8a f.10v; Tanner transcript,
Tanner f.4
Brundish TA transcript, Hen.12 (ii)
f.24; Tanner transcript, Tanner f.3
Rendlesham Tanner transcript
(church notes only), Tanner f.22

Aysch juxta Campsee TA
transcript, Hen.10 f.16; Tanner
transcript, Tanner f.2
Kenton TA transcript, Hen.10 f.82;
Tanner transcript, Tanner f.18
Badyngham Hen.10 f.82; Tanner
transcript, Tanner f.1
Mellis Tanner transcript, Tanner f.21
Lavenham TA transcript, Hen.2 f.94
Acton TA transcript, Hen.2 f.8;
Tanner transcript, Tanner f.1
Chelsworth (Original text) Hen.6
f.19
Wenham parva Ibid.
(*Oulton* See main text list above)
Hensted TA transcript, Hen.3 f.78

APPENDIX II

Suggested reconstruction of the complete original

Reconstruction of the complete original text has been aided by the comparative regularity of the structure of the main text, with its two entries for most pages and roughly alphabetical order of place-names; no page seems to have had more than two entries. Comparison with Appendix I will show where parishes are back to back on a fragment of original text, thus fixing their position relative to each other. References to page numbers in the main text given in the Chorography Appendix have also been useful in reconstruction.

Place-names in brackets refer to those entries which exist only in transcript; those in italics no longer exist and their position is sometimes impossible to establish with certainty; the section between pp.125 and 136 is particularly difficult to reconstruct. The original pagination is given in brackets where it no longer exists but can be reconstructed with fair certainty. Spelling of place-names is as given in the text, or for place-names in italics, as on Saxton's map of Suffolk.

30	Berton magna
31	Berton
	(Bilston)
32	Blakenham magna
	Blakenham sup' montem
33	Bliborough ( )
34	Blaxhall
	(Bliford)
35	Boulge
	Boyton
(36)	Boxford
	Boxstede
(37)	Blunston
	(Bradfeld St.Cleres)
38	Monks Bradfeld
	Burnt Bradfeld
39	Bramfeld
	Bradley magna
(40)	*Bradley parva*
	Bradwell
	Braisworthe
	Brampton
	Brandeston
	Brandon
	Bramford
	Brantham
	Brettenham
	(Bredfield)
44	Briset magna
	Briset parva
45	Brockford
	Brockley
	Brightwell
	Brumeswell
(47)	Brome
	Brundishe
	Brusyerd
	Bucklesham
	Buddesdale
	Bungaye
50	Burntileye
	Burgate
51	Burghe
	Burgh Castell
	Buers
	(Burstall)
	Burye

	(Butley)
	(Buxhall)
56	Candish
	(Capell n Sf 13)
57	Capell e Sf 4
	(Carleton l Sf 8)
(58)	Carleton a Sf 1
	Carsey
(59)	Cattywade
	Cavenham
60	Charsfield
	Chatsham
61	Chelsworth
	Chempton
	Chedber
	Cheston
	Chevington
	Chillesford
64	Chilton
	Chilton
(65)	Clare
66	Cleydon
	Clopton
67	Cockfeld
	Conyweston
68	Cookley
	Copdock
69	Cornerd magna
	Cornerd parva
(70)	*Corton*
	(Cotton)
	N.Cove
	(S.Cove)
72	Covehithe
	Cowledge
73	Combes
	Codnham
74	Cransford
	Cratfeld
75	Cretyngham
	Alsaints Creting
(76)	*Sct.Olavi Creting*
	W.Creting
(77)	*St.Croft*
	Crowfield
(78)	*Culfurthe*
	Culpho
(79)	*Dagworth*

	Dalham	(104)	*Foxall*
(80))	Dalinghoo		Framisden
	Darsham	(105)	*Framlingham*
(81)	Debach		Fresenfeld
	Debden		(Freston)
(82)	*Debenham*		*Freckenham*
	Denham St.John		*Friston*
(83)	*Denham St.Mary*		Fritton
	Denston		*Frostenden*
(84)	*Dermisden*		Gadgrave
	Dynnyngton		*Gayesley*
	Downeham		Geddinge
	Drenkeston		*Gislam*
	(Dunnynworth)		*Gislingham*
	Dunwiche	(111)	*Gipping Newton*
88	Easton c Sf 3		*Glemysford*
	Easton h Sf 10	112	Glemham magna
89	Easton Gosbeck		Glemham parva
	Earle Soham — Earle	113	Gorleston
	Stonham		Groton
90	Eyke	114	Grundesboro
	Edwardstone		*Gunton*
91	Eldon	115	Hacheston
	Ellowe		Herthurste
	South Elmham	116	Hadley
	Elmesett	117	Halesworth
	Elmeswell	118	Hargrave
	Esewell		Harcksted
(94)	Ewston	119	Harleston
	Exnynge		Hasylwood
95	Fakenham magna	120	Hasketon
	Fakenham parva		Haverill
(96)	Farnham	(121)	Hawkden
	Falkenham		Helmyngham
97	Felsham	122	Hawsted
	Fernham St.Genofeve		*Hawley*
98	Fernham Martyn	123	Hemyngton
	Fernham O'i'u' S'toru'	124	Hemley
99	Felixstowe		Hengravc
	Finboro magna	(125)	Henlye
(100)	Finboro parva		Hevenyngham
	Fynnyngham		*Heringswell*
101	Flempton		Henham
	Flixton a Sf 1		(Herningsherth)
102	Flixton b Sf 2		Hensted
	Flouton		Hesset
103	Fordham		Hintlesham
	Fordley		Hoo

	Honington		155	Lawshall
130	Higham			Laxfield
	(Hepworth)			*St.Laurence Ilketshall*
131	Hinderclay			Layston
	Hitcham			*Layham*
(132)	(Holton St.Peter)			Lemington
	Holton n Sf 13		158	Lestoft
	(Holbroke)			Letheringham
	Hopton a Sf 1		159	Levermere magna
	Hopton q Sd 6			Levermere parva
	Honedon			*Lidgate*
	Horingflete			*Linsey*
	(Homersfeld)			*Linsted magna*
136	Horham			*Linsted parva*
	Hosely		162	Lound
137	Hoxon			Loudham
	Hunston		163	Marlesford
(138)	Huntingfeld (1)			*St. Mergret South Elmham*
	Huntingfeld (2)		(164)	St.Margarett of Akers
139	Icklingham			Mellis
	Southelmham St.James		165	Melton
140	Ilketshall St.Johns			Melford
	Iken		(166)	Mendham
141	Ikesworth			*Mendlesham*
	Ikesworth Thorp		167	Mertlesham
142	Ikeworth			(Mettyngham)
	Burnt Ileye		168	Metfeld
143	Monks Ileye			Mickfeld
	Ingham		169	Mildinge
	Ilketshall			Mildenhall
	Ingate			*St.Michael S.Elmham*
	Ipswich			*Midleton*
	Kediton			*Monewden*
	Kelsale			*Moulton*
(147)	*Kettleborough*		172	Munckesyley – Muncke-
	Kenton			soham
(148)	*Kenford*			Mutforde
	Kesgrave		173	Nacton
	Kesland			Naughton
	Kettlebaston		(174)	Nedging
	Knatshall q Sd 6			Nedeham
	Knatshall		175	Nettlestead
151	Kirtlow			Newbourn
(152)	Kirton		176	Neuton (?) u Sd 5
	Kushmere			Newmarket
(153)	*Lackford*		(177)	Gipping Newton –
	Lakenheath			Newton
154	Langham			
	Lanham			

139

	Stutton	250	Wenham parva
	(Sudburne, *s.v.*Orford)		*Wenhaston*
226	Sudburye	251	Wesselton
227	Sutton		Westall
	Swefling	(252)	(Weston)
	Swilland		*Coney Weston*
	Sylam	(253)	Weston Market
	(Tattington)		*Westhorpe*
	Tattyngstone	254	Westley
	Theberton		*Westerfeld*
	Thelnetham	255	Wethersdale
	Thirlow magna		*Wetheringsett*
	Thirlow parva	256	Wetherden
	Thorington		Wheltham magna
	(Thorndon)	257	Wheltham parva
	Thornham magna		Whepstead
	Thornham parva	258	Wherstead
	Thorp		Wixsoo
	Thorpe	259	Wickham h Sf 4
	Thrandeston		Wickham (*Skithe*)
	Thurston	(260)	*Wickhambrook*
	Thwate		*Willesham*
	Tostock	(261)	(Wingfeld)
	Trymleys		Whitton
	Tymworth	262	Willingham
238	Troston		Winston
	Tudenham g Sf 5	263	Wisset
(239)	Tudenham r Sd 1		Witnesham
	Tunstall	264	Wiverston
	Ufford		Woodbridge
	Uggeshall	265	Worlingham
	Uppeston		Wordwell
	Washbrock	(266)	Tallow Wrattinge
242	Walton		*Wrattinge parva*
	Walpole	(267)	Wrentham
243	Walderswick		*Wulverstone*
	Walsham-le-Willows	(268)	Wurtham
244	Waldingfelde magna	269	Wulpet
	Waldingfelde parva	270	Wylbye
245	Waldringfield		Wyston
	Whatfeld	271	Yaxley
246	Wangford r Sd 1		Yoxford
	Wangford c Sf 3		
247	Wantisden		
	Warlingworth		
248	Wattesham		
	Wattesfield		
(249)	Waybred		
	Wenham magna		

(pp.272-319 are complete in the main text. The fragments for Oulton and Hensted, together with further text for Orford, probably belong to later pages.)

APPENDIX III

The Chorography and Camden's Britannia

The Chorographer's use of Camden is of importance in dating the Chorographies, so it is dealt with in detail below. The *Britannia* went through eight editions between its first publication in 1586 and the first English edition of 1610, and most of these editions in turn contained new material. By examining the material used by the Chorographer from Camden it becomes possible to say with reasonable certainty that he used the edition of 1600, and that therefore the original layout of the Chorographies can be no earlier than that year.

Britannia went through the following editions between 1586 and 1610;

(1) *Britannia, sive Florentissimorum Regnorum ... Chorographica descriptio,* publ. by Ralph Newbery, London, 1586.

(2) *...Nunc denuo recognita ...,* publ. by Newbery, 1587.

(3) *...Nunc tertio recognita ...,* publ. by George Bishop, Eliots Court Press, 1590.

(4) *...nunc tertio recognita & magna accessione adaucta primumq' in Germania in lucem edita Francofurdi ...,* 1590.

(5) *...nunc quarto recognita & magna accessione post Germanicam aeditionem adaucta ...,* publ. by Bishop, 1594.

(6) *...nunc postremo recognita, & magna accessione post Germanicam aeditionem adaucta ...,* publ. by Bishop, 1600.

(7) *...nunc postremo recognita, plurimis locis magna accessione adaucta, & Chartis Chorographicis ...,* publ. by Bishop and John Norton, 1607.

(8) *Britain, or, a Chorographicall Description of the most flourishing Kingdomes, England, Scotland and Ireland ... Written first in Latine by W.Camden ... translated newly into English by Philemon Holland ... Finally revised, amended, and enlarged with sundry additions, etc.,* publ. by Bishop and Norton, 1610.

As far as Suffolk and Norfolk are concerned the 1587 edition contained no new material, and the content of the two 1590 editions is identical even down to the pagination. The 1587 edition has therefore been excluded from the table below, and the two 1590 editions are given a single column.

The table below lists places in the main text of the Chorographies which have translations of material culled from Camden; the columns then give the page references of that material in the successive editions of Camden. See footnotes 1* to 8* to the main text (p.111 above) for a summary of the Chorographer's use of Camden in the Chorography Introductions.

NORFOLK CHOROGRAPHY	1586	1590	1594	1600	1607	1610
Attleborough	—	371	361	419	347	473
Aylsham[1]	267	376	366[1]	424[1]	349[1]	478[1]
Baconsthorpe	—	377	368	424	349	479
St.Benet Hulme	268	376	368	425	349	479
Blakeney[2]	—	377	368[2]	425[2]	349[2]	479[2]
Brancaster[3]	269	378	368[3]	426[3]	350[3]	480[3]
New Buckenham[4]	262	370	360	419[4]	346[4]	472[4]
Caister St.Edmund	263	370	361	420	347	473
E.Dereham	270	380	369	428	351	482
Diss	—	—	360	419	347	472
Gimingham	—	—	366	425	349	479
Gressenhall	—	—	370	429	351	482
Houghton St.Giles	—	—	370	429	351	482
Kenninghall	262	370	360	419	347	472
Kings Lynn	270	379	368	427	350	480
Castle Rising[5]	270	380	368[5]	428[5]	351[5]	481[5]
Shelton	—	—	360	419	346	472
Scoulton	—	—	361	419	347	473
Thetford[6]	262	369	359[6]	417[6]	346[6]	472[6]
Tilney	—	—	368	427	350	481
Walpole St.Peter	—	—	369	427	350	481
New Walsingham	269	377	366	426	350	479
Wymondham	270	380	370	429	347	473

Notes

1   These contain a reference to the former ownership of the town by the family of Atholl, which does not appear before the 1594 edition.

2   These contain a reference to Bale calling Blakeney 'Nigeria' which does not occur before the 1594 edition.

3   These contain a reference to Roman coins being found at Brancaster which does not occur before the 1594 edition.

4   These contain a reference to the tenure under which Buckenham was held which does not occur before the 1600 edition.

5   These contain a reference to the D'Albini family which does not occur before the 1594 edition.

6   These contain a reference to statistics in Domesday Book which does not occur before the 1594 edition.

SUFFOLK CHOROGRAPHY	1586	1590	1594	1600	1607	1610
Aldeburgh[7]	258[7]	365[7]	354[7]	412[8]	339[9]	466[9]
Brettenham	256	362	352	410	337	463
Burgh Castle	260	367	357	415	340	468
Clare[10]	256	361[10]	351[10]	409[10]	336[10]	462[10]
Dennington	–	–	355	414	339	467
Easton Bavent	259	366	355	413	339	467
Edwardstone	–	–	352	409	336	463
Erwarton	–	–	352	410	337	463
Exning	253	359	348	406	334	459
Eye[11]	259[11]	367[11]	356[11]	414[11]	340[12]	467[12]
Flixton	260	367	356	415	340	467
Glemham	–	–	354	412	338	465
Gorleston	260	367	357	415	340	468
Hadleigh	256	362	352	410	337	463
Halesworth	–	366	356	414	339	467
Hemingstone	–	–	–	410	337	464
Huntingfield	–	366	355	414	339	467
Hoxne	259	366	356	414	340	467
Ixworth	–	–	350	408	335	461
Long Melford	256	362	351	409	336	462
Nettlestead	–	–	352	410	337	463
Orford	258	364	354	412	338	465
Parham	–	–	354	412	338	465
Rendlesham	258	364	354	412	338	465
Rushbrooke	–	–	–	408	335	461
Somerleyton	–	–	–	408	340	468
Sudbury	256	362	351	409	336	462
Ufford	258	364	354	412	338	465
Wingfield	–	366	354	414	339	467

Notes

7   These have an explanation of the name Aldeburgh as 'the old town'.

8   This edition has an explanation of the name as 'town on the river Alde'.

9   These have both explanations of the name.

10   These have a reference to the burial of Joan D'Acres at Clare.

11   These, correctly, give the name of the 'Norman baron' as *William* de Malet.

12   These incorrectly give Malet's Christian name as Robert.

From the table it will be seen that although the bulk of the new material was introduced into the 1594 edition of *Britannia*, the Chorographer uses material which only occurs in editions including and subsequent to 1600 (New Buckenham in Norfolk; Hemingstone, Rushbrooke and Somerleyton in Suffolk). However, the Chorographer is unlikely to have used editions later than that of 1600, since he correctly refers to *William* de Malet when dealing with Eye, and both the 1607 and 1610 editions incorrectly speak of Robert de Malet. This leaves the 1600 edition as the most likely candidate for his use.

One slight complication to this hypothesis is that the Chorographer follows all editions previous to that of 1600 for the etymology of the name Aldeburgh; however, in this he may have been following local opinion. Alternatively, he may have possessed or used an earlier edition of the *Britannia* in conjunction with that of 1600, which nevertheless was his main source.

In conclusion it should be noted that the notation for the Hundreds given in the maps of the 1607 *Britannia* is entirely different from the Chorographer's own scheme.

APPENDIX IV

The Chorographer's first-hand visits and their dates

This list can only be approximate. Places are listed by Hundred. Where possible an indication of date is given — reasons are to be found in the footnotes to the main text. All entries after the Halesworth entry in the Chorography Appendix must be post 1602, all those after the Dennington entry 1603 and after, and all those previous to Badingham must be of 1604 or earlier.

Babergh

Acton	1604 or after
Brent Eleigh	
Monks Eleigh	
Groton	1602-04
Lavenham	1604 or after
Lawshall	1598-1608
Long Melford	1598-1602
Milden	After 1599 — annotations 1603-08
Nayland	1603-08
Preston	
Stansted	1603 or after
Stoke by Nayland	1602-04
Waldingfield Parva	1602-04

Blackbourn

Barningham	
Hopton	1603 or after
Ixworth	1602-04
Stanton	1602-04
Thelnetham	
Walsham-le-Willows	
Market Weston	1603 or after

Blything

Blyford	1602-04
Bramfield	
Brampton	1602-04
Cookley	1602-04
Fordley	1602-03
Halesworth	1602

Henstead	1602
Heveningham	1603 or earlier
Holton	1602-04
Huntingfield	1602-04
Spexhall	1596-1602
Theberton	1603 or earlier
Wissett	1602-04

Carlford

Bealings magna	1607 or earlier
Bealings parva	
Grundisburgh?	
Otley	

Colneis

Levington?	

Cosford

Bildeston	1601 or after
Brettenham	1603 or after
Chelsworth	1604 or after
Kettlebaston	1603 or after
Nedging	
Semer	

Hartismere

Bacton	1602-03
Burgate	1602-04
Cotton	1602-03
Gislingham	1602-03
Mellis	1604 or after
Mendlesham	1603 or earlier
Oakley	

Stoke Ash	1596 or after	Chillesford	
Thorndon	1603 or earlier	Glemham parva	1603 or earlier
Thwaite		Parham	
Westhorpe	1603 or earlier	Stratford St.Andrew	1603 or after
Wyverston			

Risbridge
Kentford	1602-04

Hoxne
Badingham	1604
Bedingfield	

Samford
Belstead parva	
Freston	

Brundish	1602-04
Dennington	1603 or earlier
Fressingfield	
Metfield	

Thedwastre
Great Barton	
Livermere magna	1603 or after

Wingfield	1602 or earlier

Lackford
Cavenham	

Thingo
Barrow	1602-04
Flempton	1603 or after

Loes
Campsey Ash	1602-04
Charsfield	

Wangford
Ellough	1602-04
Ilketshall St.Andrew	
Mettingham	
Redisham magna	
Shadingfield	1602-04
Sotterley	1602-04
S.Elmham St.Peter	1602-04
Weston	
Willingham	

Cretingham	1603 or after
Dallinghoo	
Debach	
Easton	
Eyke	
Framlingham	1602-04
Hoo	1606 or earlier
Kenton	
Letheringham	1602-04
Marlesford	
Rendlesham	1602-04
Woodbridge	1602-04

Wilford
Alderton	1603-04
Boulge	
Bredfield	
Capel St.Andrew	
Hollesley	1603 or after
Loudham	
Melton	
Pettistree	1603-04
Ramsholt	
Wickham Market	1603-06

Lothingland
Blundeston	1603 or earlier
Burgh Castle	
Oulton	

Plomesgate
Blaxhall	1603 or after
Butley	1604 or earlier

The Hundreds of Bosmere and Claydon, Mutford, Stow and Thredling have no surviving entries which suggest first-hand information.

INDEX

NB Appendix I has not been indexed and items in Appendix II only indexed when they do not occur in the main body of the Chorography text. All place-names are Suffolk unless otherwise stated. Page-references are given in italic for places when they are described in the Chorography text and for persons when they are given a substantial entry in the notes. Women are indexed under their maiden name where identifiable, otherwise under their husband's name. A separate Index for identifiable heraldry has been provided.

——, ——, of Oxborough (Nf.) 36
Beighton, Rev.Laurence 45
Bell, Robert, lawyer 64, *119*
——, Roger, of Haughley 63
Bellowe, John 101
Belstead, Little *29,* 146
Belton 135
Benacre *29,* 31
Benhall 28, 38
Bergh Apton (Nf.) 8
Bessingham (Nf.) 108
Beverley Minster (Yorks.) 72
Beyton 135
Bigod, Hugh, Earl of Suffolk 19
Bildeston 7, *30,* 145
Bing, Bynge, Pettistree, manor 59
Bishop, George, publisher 8
Blackbourne, Deanery of 22, 23
——, Hundred of 9, 22, 23, 145
Blakenham (Nf.) 142
——, Great *30*
——, Little *30*
Blakey, Walter 88, 122
Blatchly, Dr.John 107, 108
Blaxhall *30,* 147
—— Hall, manor 31, 36
Blennerhasset, George 95
——, Katherine, d.1584 103, 125
——, Mary 95
——, Samuel 59
Blomefield, Francis, antiquary 3, 4,
    7, 16, 108, 110
Blundell, Blondell, Elizabeth 104
——, James 105
——, Richard 104
Blundeston *31,* 113, 117, 146
Blundeston, family 32
Blundestons, Blunstons, Henstead,
    manor 106
Blunt, Gilbert, Baron of Ixworth 49
Blyford *31, 89,* 122, 145
Blyth, river 21
Blythburgh 10, 22, 24, *30,* 115
——, Priory 30-32
Blything, Hundred of 22, 23, 38, 145
Bohun, Bowen, Francis, of Westhall
    81, *121*
——, Nicholas, d.1602 121

Booth and Berry, Messrs. booksellers
    3, 4, 108
Borgue, Mathieu, d.1431 75, 120
Borret, John, antiquary 7
Bosmere, Deanery of 22, 23
—— and Claydon, Hundred of 22, 23, 146
Botesdale 23, 136
Boulge *31,* 39, 146
Boulogne, Stephen, Earl of 26
Boun, Bound, family 106
——, John 42
Bourchier Earls of Essex 30, 47
Boutetort, Joan 32
——, John 32
Boutruileyn, Margery 28
——, William 28
Boville, family 27, 103
——, Fitzwilliam 103
——, Sir John 103
——, Sir William 40, 71, 93, 94, 103
Bowers, Milden, manor 56
Boxford *31,* 89
Boxted *31,* 43
Boyton 34, 136
de ——, William 47
Brabant, Duke of 27
Bradbury, William, of Ashill (Nf.) 29
Bradfield Combust 20, 32
——, St.Clare 32
——, St.George 32
Bradley, Great 20, *32*
——, Little 136
Bradwell 136
de Braham, William 32
Braiseworth 136
Bramfield *32,* 145
Bramford 21, 32
Brampton *81,* 121, 136, 145
Brancaster (Nf.) 142
Brandeston 136
Brandon 23, 136
Brandon, Charles, Duke of Suffolk
    48, 57, 76
——, Eleanor 78
Brantham *32*
Bredfield *33,* 146
——Campsea, Dallinghoo, manor 39
——cum Winderviles, manor 33

Buxhall *35*
Bydgood, Joan 81
Byrgett, Alice, d.1493 102, 125
——, Henry 102
Cadwellhall, Hollesley, manor 48
Caistor next Norwich (Nf.) 14, 142
Calthorpe, family 26
Cambridge, Gonville and Caius 29
——, King's Hall 46
——, University Library 4, 6, 7, 108
Camden, William, antiquary 12, 21, 109
——, ——, *Britannia* 5, 8, 10, 11, 110, 111, 141f.
Campsea Ash *102*, 125, 146
—— ——, Priory 31, 33, 54, 59, 69
Candler, Matthias, antiquary 6, 16
Canterbury, Archbishop of 50, 116
Archbishop of Canterbury: Simon Theobald alias Sudbury 65
Canterbury, Dean and Chapter of 50
——, Priory 50, 51
Capel St.Andrew 34, 35, 146
—— St.Mary *35*
Carbonell, Sir John d.1423 27
——, Sir Robert 103
Carbonell, Sir William 27, 103, 125
Carew, Richard, antiquary 110
Carey, Carew, Henry, Lord Hunsdon 48
Carlford, Deanery of 22
——, Hundred of 22, 23, 145
Carlton next Kelsale 21, *35*
Carlton Rode *35*
Caryll, Sir John, of Sussex 49, 54
Castle Rising (Nf.). M.P. 114
Caston, Margery 103
Cattiwade 21, *35*
Cavendish 24, *35*
Cavenham 35, 146
Cawston (Nf.) 8
Charles, Edward 40
——, John 40
——, Nicholas, antiquary 110, 111
Charsfield *35*, 146
Chattisham 36
Chedburgh 136
Chediston 36
Chelmondiston 36

Chelsworth 7, 8, 21, *36, 105*, 125, 145
Chester, Earldom of 61
Chevington 24, 136
Chill, river 21
Chillesford 21, 31, *36*, 146
Chilton-by-Clare 136
Chilton-by-Sudbury 37
Chipley Priory 59
Christmas Lane, Metfield 13, 56, 109
Church notes 9, 12, 24, 38, 40, 43, 46, 47, 53, 57, 58, 62-64, 66, 68, 70, 72-106, 119
Clare 20, 23, *37*, 143
Clare, Deanery of 22, 23
——, stream 20
de ——, Countess of Gloucester 28
—— ——, Earl of Gloucester 33, 35
—— ——, Gilbert I 37
—— ——, —— II Earl of Gloucester 37
Clarence, Lionel, Duke of 37
de Clavering, John 30
Claxton, Hamond, of Norwich 54
——, John, of Gt.Livermere 53, 54
——, William, d.1539 73, 120
Claydon *37*
Claydon, Deanery of 22, 23
——, Cleydon, William 31, 36
Clench, John, lawyer 29, *112*
Clere family 106
Clerk, Clerke, Agnes 116
——, Alice 90
——, Clement, d.1515 54, 90, 116
——, Edward, of Layham 51, *116*
——, Walter of Hadleigh 116
de Clinton, Clynton, John 35
Clopton *37*
—— family 55
——, Anne, d.1420 99, 124
——, Francis, d.1559 97, 106, 124
——, Francis, d.1578 98, 124
——, John, d.1497 124
——, Katherine, d.1408 85
——, Margery, d.1420 99, 124
——, Thomas I 85
——, —— II 55, 97, *117*, 124
——, Sir William d.1416 99, 124

151

Edwardstone *40*, 143
Eleigh, Brent 13, 33, *50*, 116, 145
——, ——, St.James Chapel 50
——, Monks 13, *50*, 56, 145
Elizabeth I 8, 22, 56, 59, 65, 69, 70, 89
Ellough 14, *40*, 69, *84*, 114, 121, 146
Elmham, S. 34, 41
——, ——, All Saints *25*, 41, 49
——, ——, St.Cross 41, 136
——, ——, St.James 24, 41, 49
——, ——, St.Margaret 41, 49, 138
——, ——, St.Michael 41, 49, 138
——, ——, St.Nicholas 41, 49, 57
——, ——, St.Peter 41, 49, 59, 88, 122, 146
Elmsett 137
Elmswell 137
Elveden 20, 40
Ely (Cambs.) 20
—— Priory 28, 54, 64
——, Bishop of 56, 69
——, —— ——, Hervey 41
——, Dean and Chapter of 99
Eriswell 137
Erpingham family 79
Erwarton *26*, 143
Euston *41*
Essex, Earls of, see Bourchier, Devereux
Exeter, Duchess of, see Montague
Exning 41
Eye 7, 20, 23, *26*, 143
——, M.P.'s 113, 115
——, Priory 27, 59
Eyke 19, 40, *95*, 101, 123, 146
Fairfax, Dr.Nathaniel, antiquary 6, 16
Fakenham, Great 41
——, Little *41*
Falkenham 2, 137
Farnham 21, *41*
——, Stephen 36
Farting 45
Fastolf, family 58, 68
——, ... 101
——, Francis, d.1561 124
Felixstowe *42*

Felsham 41
Feltham, Thomas, of Milden 56, *117*
Felton, Sir Anthony, d.1614 33, *113*
Fenn, Sir John, antiquary 3, 4
de Fenton, John, priest 28
Ferre, Guy 49
Fiennes, Henry, Lord Dacre 106
——, Margery 106
Fifteens and tenths 9, 25, 29, 54
Finborough, Great 42
——, Little *42*
Finningham 42
Fires 28, 56, 62
Firmage, Henry 118
FitzOsbert, family 62
——, Katherine 47
——, Roger 51
Fitzralph, le Fitz Raulf, Herman 61
——, Robert 61
——, William 35
Fitzroy, Henry, Duke of Richmond 95, 123
Fleming, Adam 29
Flemings Hall, Bedingfield, manor 29
Flempton 20, 42, 146
Flixton by Bungay *42*, 143
—— —— Oulton *42*
Flowerdew, Edward, lawyer 13
Flowton *42*
Floyd, Richard, d.1525 104, 125
Ford, river 21
Fordham 42
——, Deanery of 22, 23
Fordhall, Melford, manor 55
Fordley 21, *42*, 145
Fornham 20
—— All Saints 41
—— St.Genevieve 137
—— St.Martin 41
Forth, Alice, d.1520 97
——, Robert, of Butley *113*
——, William, d.1621 34, *113*
Forsett, Fosset, Henry, of Milden 56, 117
——, Richard 117
Foxhall 21, 137

Groton 43, *88*, 122, 145
Grundisburgh *43*, 145
Gunton 137
Gunviles, Blundeston, manor 32
Guthrum (Athelstane) 43, 44
Hacheston *43*
Hadleigh 21, 23, 30, *43*, 143
de Hadley, Thomas, priest 28
Hales Hall, Loddon (Nf.) 13
Halesworth 8, 9, 21-23, *44*, 56, *73*,
  118, 120, 143, 145
Hall, Joseph, see Bishops of Norwich
Hansard, Anthony 99
Harbert, John, of Hollesley 48
Hardrichshull, Sir Ralph 27, 40
——, Sir Wakelin 27
Hare, Ann 79
——, Michael, of Bruisyard 25, 26,
  112
——, Sir Nicholas, Master of the Rolls
  70, 112
Hargrave *44*
Harison, Anthony, secretary 14
Harkstead *44*
Harleston (Nf.) 9. 20, 56
—— (Sf.) 44
——, John 99
Harolds, Cretingham, manor 39
Harpole, Horpoul, Wickham Market,
  manor 59, 69
Hartest *43*
Hartismere, Deanery of 22, 23
——, Hundred of 4, 7, 9, 22, 23, 142
Harwich (Ess.) 21
Hasketon 44, 99
——, Hason Hall, Woodbridge, manor
  99
Haslewood 44
Hassell Smith, Dr.A. 14, 15, 112
Hastings, John 58
——, Margaret 93
Hatfield Peverel Priory (Ess.) 24, 26
Haughley 137
Hawghfen, John, of Tunstall 37, *114*
Haverhill 20, 23, *44*
Hawes, Hawys, George, priest 28
——, John, antiquary 6
Hawkedon 45
Hawstead 45

Hayward, Sir John, historian 110
Hearne, Thomas, antiquary 1, 2, 107
Helmingham 45
Hemenhall family 38, 76
de Hemenhall, Sir John 76
—— ——, Sir Ralph 76
Hemingstone *45*, 143, 144
Hemley 45
Hengrave 20, *45*, 114
—— Hall 3, 4
Henham 13, 24, 45
Henley 45
Henninges, Hieronymus, historian
  10, 30, 113
Henningfields Hall, Lawshall, manor
  53
Henry I 58
—— VII 51, 84, 93
—— VIII 31, 41, 50, 53, 55, 57, 59,
  60, 62-64, 69, 70, 91, 114
Henstead 8, 22, *45*, *106*, 145
—— Bounds, manor 46, 106, 115
—— Parpoundes, manor 45
——, family 106
Heptarchy 19
Hepworth *46*
Herberd, John, see Yaxley
Hereford, Viscount, see Devereux
de Hereford, Thomas 34
Herringfleet 9, *47*
Herringswell 137
Hervey, George, of Oulton 81
——, Mary, d.1586 81, 121
——, William 50
Hessett *46*
Hethersett (Nf.) 13
——, Sir Edmund 35
——, Isabella 35
Heveningham 13, 24, *45*, *87*, 122,
  145
—— family 14, 38
——, Abigail 117
——, Sir Arthur 13-15, 38, 109, 110,
  114, 117
——, Sir John I 87, 122
——, —— —— II 38, 109
——, Margaret 87, 122
High Suffolk 19
Higham St.Mary 46

KING ALFRED'S COLLEGE
LIBRARY